Catastrophe
at Custer Creek

Catastrophe at Custer Creek

Montana's Deadliest Train Wreck

IAN CAMPBELL WILSON

MONTANA HISTORICAL SOCIETY PRESS

Helena

Front cover photograph: *Olympian* crash site, Sunday, June 19, 1938. Warren B. Jones, photographer. Courtesy of the Jones family

Cover and book design by Diane Gleba Hall.

Printed in the United States.

Distributed by Farcountry Press, 2750 Broadwater Avenue, Helena, MT 59602, (800) 821-3874

ISBN 978-0-917298-78-3 (paperback; alkaline paper)
ISBN 978-0-917298-88-2 (ebook)

Library of Congress Cataloging-in-Publication data available on request.

For Alison

The only truth I know is you.

This book was made possible in part by a gift from the Wilson-Banks Family and by other generous supporters of the Montana Historical Society Press.

Immortal

Four thousand years lame Vulcan's anvil has been still;
Four thousand years, winged Mercury
Had slumbered on a cloud;
Four thousand years Apollo's chariot of the sun
Had hidden been. No God in aeons
Had spoken once, aloud.

And the—the anvil waked! It wrought anew, with steel.
Swift Mercury aroused, new speeds
Proclaiming to the world.
Apollo's car rose once again on high
To light the way. In western skies
The pomp of Zeus unfurled!

And for one day all gods revived;
Held carnival where new Olympics
Guard the western main!
They wrought—a traveler's paradise
Then christened it.—And penned below
Ye find its name—

The *Olympian*—Fit for the Gods

Contents

Acknowledgments

Prior to doing research for this book, I knew very little about eastern Montana or railroads. Researching and writing this book about the 1938 Custer Creek accident changed all that.

On my first visit to the crash site in Saugus in the summer of 2018, I stopped in Terry to walk the streets. I found my way to the Prairie County Museum, located in a dusty old retail store just off Main Street. To my great fortune, staffing the museum that day was Susan Waples, daughter of Dan Jr. and Mary Haughian. The *Olympian* accident happened near the Haughian ranch on land that the family still owns. This chance encounter opened the door to other family members, including Susan's sister Donna Faber. Both provided stories and invaluable information about their parents and grandparents. They also provided me with unpublished material about the accident.

Plenty has been written about the Custer Creek crash over the years, mostly newspaper articles. An exception is Ralph S. Podas's comprehensive 1992 account "A Point in Time on the Milwaukee Road: The Custer Creek Olympian Tragedy, June 19, 1938." Podas's article, published in a relatively obscure railroad history journal, focused on Frank Merrifield and Hausmer McCoy, the locomotive engineer and fireman, respectively, involved in the crash. Podas also told the story of how the Gehrig family, on their way from Minneapolis to California for a vacation, survived the wreck. The newspaper articles and Podas's work were teasers for me, breadcrumbs marking a trail that required exploring. I set out to learn more specifics about the *Olympian* and to find more survivor accounts. As could be expected, the stories I found provided new details and even included bizarre twists and turns that helped contextualize that dark, soggy night in eastern Montana.

Even though the Custer Creek accident happened over eighty years ago, several survivors are still with us today. Through relatives, I was able to contact and interview George Lallas of Bellingham, Washington, who was seven years old in June 1938. I am thankful to Tommy Rakus, George's nephew, for leading me to George. Finding a website Tommy built called the "Greeks of Washington," I sent him an email and he quickly responded to my inquiry, excited to help with my research in any way he could. George, Tommy, and other members of the Lallas family provided firsthand details on the series of events that landed them on an *Olympian* tourist coach car headed back home to Bellingham. George later survived another near-death experience while fighting as a U.S. marine in the Korean War. Sadly, George died in September 2022 at age ninety-two.

I was also able to track down and interview Paul Gehrig's youngest son, Louis, the family historian. Though he had not yet been born when the accident happened, Louis provided a trove of information about the experience that his parents and his brothers and sisters had aboard the *Olympian* en route to a California vacation.

If there is a heroine in this book, it would be Florence Hand Maguire, who was traveling from Milwaukee to Miles City to attend the wedding of her younger sister, Irene. In my research, I learned that Irene was living in Helena, Montana. Irene's eldest daughter, Mary Ann Baumgartner, kindly arranged a meeting and interview with her mother. I spent three hours with Irene, who recalled in detail the events of more than eighty years past. Irene died on July 13, 2021, at age 104. Her positive energy and zest for life was truly an inspiration for me.

In the summer of 2021, I received a surprise phone call from Candi Wolfe, Frank Merrifield's granddaughter. Somehow, she had learned of my research, and wanted to reach out to learn more about her grandfather and the circumstances of his death. Candi and her sister Lori—the daughters of Frank and Marie Merrifield's youngest child, Phyllis Ann—flew to Bozeman to visit and share information about their family, and see the crash site in Saugus. Phyllis was only two months old when her father died at Custer Creek. I am deeply grateful to Quinn Haughian, the son of

Dan Jr., for taking the time to escort the Merrifield ladies to Custer Creek. It was a trip they will never forget.

I am also grateful to the dedicated staff at Dartmouth College's Rauner Special Collections Library for help and guidance in researching the Hanscom twins. A special thanks to Julia Logan, assistant archivist, for her patience with my inquiries, and for allowing me to dig through the Dartmouth files. My appreciation also goes to Helene Rassias, a high school classmate of mine, for leading me to Julia and the Rauner Library.

In my efforts to research selected *Olympian* families, I was surprised at how valuable the Ancestry.com website was as both an informational resource and a venue for reaching out to family members. Using Ancestry, I was able to make initial contact with relatives of many families in the story, including the Hands, Gehrigs, Merrifields, Lallases, and Clancys.

The friendly staff at the Miles City Public Library, especially Jean Nielsen (now retired), were always willing to help and to lend a hand with my research. The Montana Historical Society (MTHS) staff, especially publications manager Diana Di Stefano and photograph archivist Heather Hultman, were enormously supportive of my research. They provided access to processed and unprocessed collections as I searched for images of the accident and the construction of the Milwaukee Road's Puget Sound Extension through eastern Montana in the early 1900s. The MTHS and its dedicated staff is a gem for anyone who is interested in the fascinating history of the Treasure State.

Thank you to the folks at the Milwaukee Road Historical Association (MRHA), particularly Bo Storozuk, who referred me to experts and materials as needed for my research. The organization connected me with Ted Douglas of the MRHA, with whom I established an email relationship. Ted is very knowledgeable about the Milwaukee Road and its trains, locomotives, personnel, logistics, and operational details. He was extraordinarily patient with me while answering many of my questions.

I read as many books as I could find about the Milwaukee Road and its *Olympian* passenger trains to better understand the history of the legendary railroad. I am especially grateful for August Derleth's wonderful and very detailed history of the Milwaukee Road's first hundred years, written in 1948; Stan Johnson's book, *Olympian: A Ride to Remember,* an account of his 1941 ride on the train from Chicago to Tacoma; and a series of magazine-style books written by Bill Wilkerson, a veteran steam locomotive engineer who operated out of Miles City. Stan Johnson's three-day journey to the Pacific became my ride almost eighty years later, as his book became a roadmap of sorts for telling my story. I delighted in reading the details about the train and its operations, along with seeing photos and memorabilia of a time gone by.

I came across Bill Wilkerson's books while combing the internet for stories about the Milwaukee Road. They are hard to find in libraries, unless you want to purchase them on eBay, so I was pleased to find many of the dozen or so books he wrote in the 1980s and 1990s at the Montana Historical Society. I would have loved to spend a day with Wilkerson, who died in 2002, kicking around the railyards of Miles City and listening to his stories about the golden days of trains and steam locomotives. His deep knowledge of the day-to-day operations of the Milwaukee Road, the history of the *Olympian*, and the colorful locomotives that steamed out of Miles City were pure gold for a novice like me.

Other notable books that informed my writing include *The Milwaukee Road West* by Charles and Dorothy Wood; *Milwaukee Road Remembered* by Jim Scribbins; *Appetite for America*, Stephen Fried's magnificent book about Fred Harvey; Dale Martin's 2018 book *Ties, Rails, and Telegraph Wires: Railroads and Communities in Montana and the West*; George H. Drury's *Guide to North American Steam Locomotives*; and *Montana: High, Wide, and Handsome*, Joseph Kinsey Howard's wonderful state history.

The books written and compiled by Mary Haughian on the history of Prairie County and the small rail towns such as Mildred and Ismay where she spent her childhood were wonderful resources and fun to read. A favorite was her book *Wheels Across Montana's Prairie*, a compilation of family stories of life during the homesteading years of the early twentieth century. While Haughian's books tell the area's family stories, Evelyn Cameron's photographs preserve its imagery. I obtained several books about Cameron and her photography on my first trip to the Prairie County Museum. While I had not heard of Cameron before, she is a legendary figure in Terry and eastern Montana who took thousands of black-and-white photos in the early twentieth century, capturing the hardscrabble life of the area's homesteaders, ranchers, and sodbusters. Together, Haughian and Cameron's works are essential resources for gaining insight into life on the eastern stretches of the Yellowstone River from the turn of the twentieth century through the Depression years.

Apart from the chapters on the history of the line, I refer to the Chicago, Milwaukee, St. Paul and Pacific Railroad as the Milwaukee Road—a trademark adopted in 1928—throughout the book. From its roots in the late 1840s, the company name went through many iterations, which I have listed in the appendices. Apologies to any who may find fault with this approach.

As the author of *Catastrophe at Custer Creek*, I take full responsibility for the facts and information presented in the book. Sorting through over one hundred newspaper articles and the numerous well-intentioned but conflicting accounts of the accident and its aftermath required patience and relentless attention to detail. There will be readers who may differ with my interpretation of the facts, but to be clear, I have not embellished the story of the demise of westbound *Olympian* No. 15.

Profound gratitude goes to my editors, Cody Ewert of the MTHS and Audrey Spillane. I credit Audrey with helping me early on to transform a jumble of facts and information into an exciting story about a major historical event, the worst train accident in the state's history. My good friend Steve Roberts served as my mentor and life coach throughout the research and writing process.

Last, but certainly not least, I am deeply thankful to my family for standing by my side as I retreated to my small office, went back in history, and toiled in railroad research. Heartfelt thanks goes to my loving wife and partner, Alison Banks, who never stopped encouraging me to find the facts and to write the story.

I will never look at train tracks stretching to the horizon in the same way.

—Ian Campbell Wilson

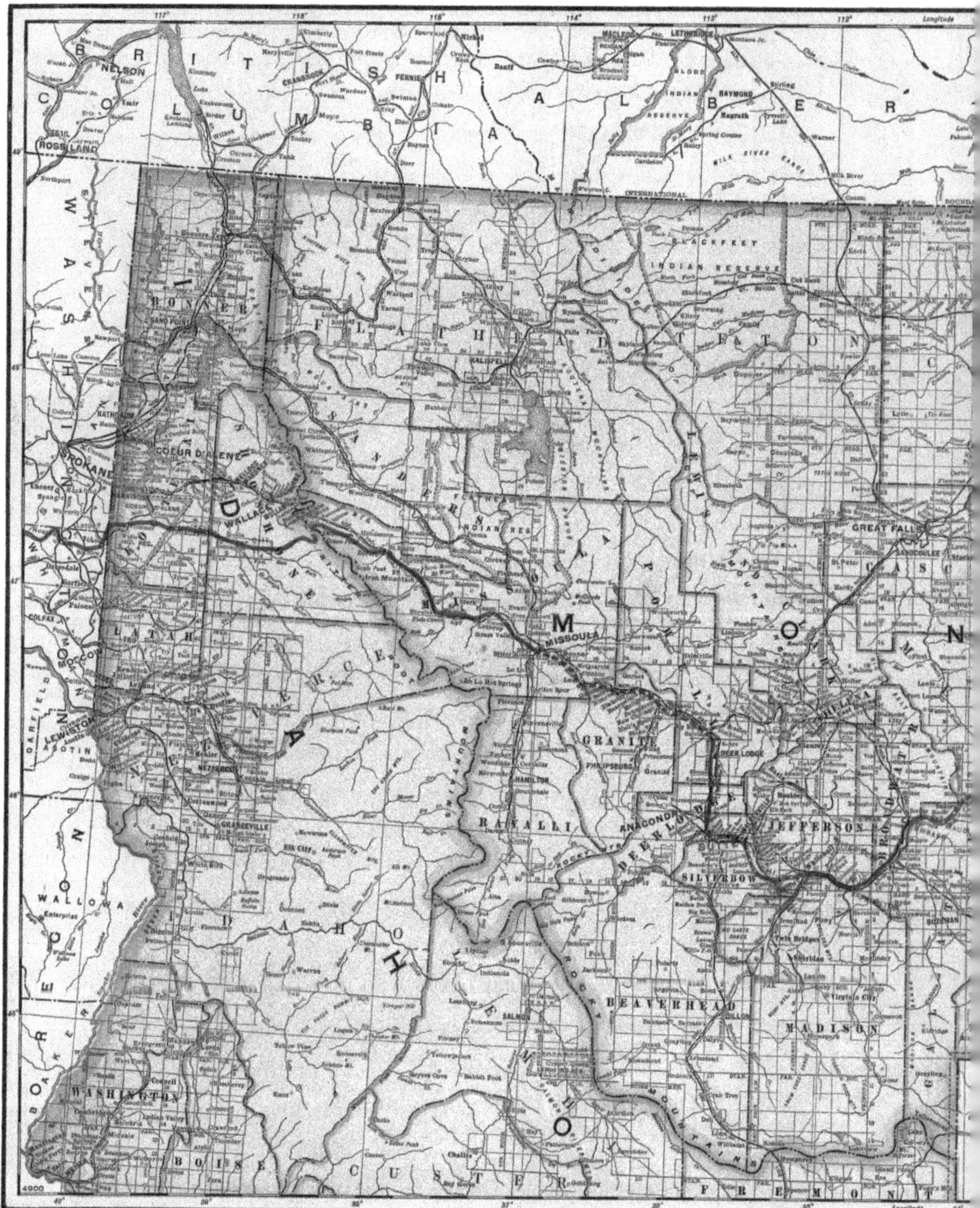

NELSON
ROSSLAND
CRANBROOK
FERNIE
MACLEOD
LETHBRIDGE
RAYMOND
INTERNATIONAL
BLACKFEET
INDIAN RESERVE
BONNER
SPOKANE
COEUR D'ALENE
WALLACE
KALISPELL
GREAT FALLS
MISSOULA
LATAH
COLFAX
LEWISTON
ASOTIN
GARFIELD
GRANITE
PHILIPSBURG
HELENA
DEER LODGE
RAVALLI
HAMILTON
GRANGEVILLE
ANACONDA
JEFFERSON
SILVERBOW
WALLOWA
BEAVERHEAD
SALMON
DILLON
MADISON
BOZEMAN
WASHINGTON
BOISE
CUSTER
FREMONT
4900
Longitude

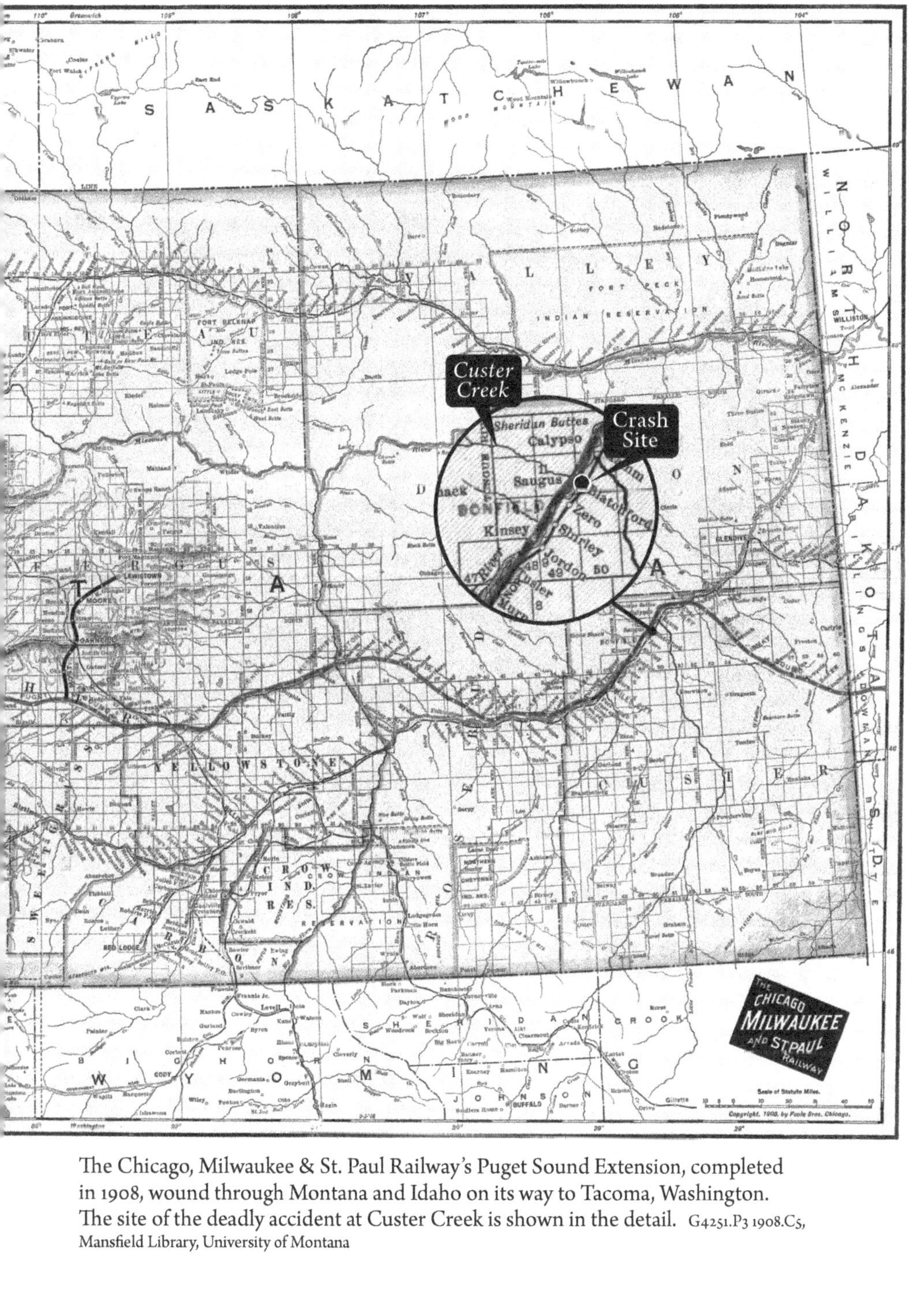

The Chicago, Milwaukee & St. Paul Railway's Puget Sound Extension, completed in 1908, wound through Montana and Idaho on its way to Tacoma, Washington. The site of the deadly accident at Custer Creek is shown in the detail. G4251.P3 1908.C5, Mansfield Library, University of Montana

Introduction

On Sunday, June 19, 1938, families across the United States celebrated Father's Day. There was nothing to celebrate that day in Miles City, Montana, where daybreak brought news of a horrific train wreck twenty-five miles north of this remote cow town. It wasn't just any train, however; it was the *Olympian*, an elite passenger train owned and operated by the legendary Milwaukee Road. The *Olympian* was one of the finest and fastest long-distance express trains of its time, a self-proclaimed "traveler's paradise." With about 190 passengers and crew aboard, the train derailed violently in the middle of the night while crossing a bridge over a small creek named after George Armstrong Custer.

Catastrophe at Custer Creek follows the final journey of westbound *Olympian* No. 15, from its midnight Chicago departure to its tragic plunge a day later in the roaring, frigid waters of Custer Creek. News of the crash went viral by 1938 standards, and the normally sleepy Miles City, known mostly as a rodeo town and railroad stop, played the beleaguered host to a crush of news reporters from all corners of America. It was the train wreck heard 'round the world.

The sudden demise of the *Olympian* shocked a nation that was just beginning to see brighter days, having survived the worst of the Great Depression. Summer travel season had begun, and bookings for coach seats and sleeping berths on the *Olympian* were in high demand. Despite the popularity of automobiles, trains remained the primary method of travel for most Americans, offering safe and reliable service. In fact, the passenger safety record for the Milwaukee Road and for the *Olympian*, specifically, was stellar. Company brochures touted the *Olympian*, with its steel-armored cars, as "an imperishable train."

The Tacoma-bound *Olympian* that departed from Chicago's magnificent Union Station on June 18 carried both the thrill of summer adventures and homecomings and the clockwork routine of railroad life. Kate, Nell, and Margie Clancy of Bloomington, Illinois, had set off to visit family in California. Nineteen-year-old twins Dean and Donald Hanscom, fresh from their sophomore year at Dartmouth College, were headed to their summer jobs in Seattle. For Thomas and Esther Lallas and their three children, on their way home to Bellingham, Washington, the *Olympian* represented the homestretch of an international journey. A vacation in Yosemite National Park awaited eight members of the Gehrig family from Minneapolis. Nurse Florence Hand Maguire was traveling to a landmark event, the wedding of her younger sister. Henry Shipley, an off-duty locomotive fireman, was simply hitching a ride back to his base in Miles City.

At the throttle of the locomotive stood fifty-nine-year-old engineer Frank Merrifield. His trusted mate, fireman Hausmer McCoy, was at his side. The pair had been running steam-powered locomotives out of Miles City for the Milwaukee Road for a quarter century. Merrifield, as experienced as one could be in handling the intricacies of a massive four-hundred-ton steam engine, had covered this same section of track hundreds of times. He had no reason to expect that this run would be remarkable, never mind the one that would expose his long-held secret. Seven cars behind Merrifield's locomotive, Chicago-based porter Louis Williams was working another hundred-hour week, acting as valet, concierge, servant, janitor—and soon much more—for the twenty-five passengers assigned to his tourist sleeper car.

On the ground in Saugus, Montana, rancher Dan Haughian Jr. worried over his fields of alfalfa and corn. His ranch along the banks of the Yellowstone River stretched to within a mile of Custer Creek, a stone's throw from the mainline track of the Milwaukee Road. Meanwhile, trackwalker Lou Goplen, boss of a ten-mile section of Milwaukee Road track that included Custer Creek, conducted his daily inspection duties between Calypso and Saugus.

Unknown to all, a storm system barreling eastward was on a direct collision course with the *Olympian.* Montana had been sweltering under an unusual June heat wave leading up to Father's Day weekend, with temperatures along the Yellowstone River exceeding ninety degrees for several days. Most afternoons, thunderstorms threatened but ultimately retreated. On June 18, however, a series of violent "cloudbursts," pushed by powerful jet-stream-fueled winds, pummeled communities along its path before stalling over mountain ranges near the Terry Badlands. For hours that evening, epic amounts of rain drenched the headwaters of Custer Creek. The torrent hurtled down clay hills on its way to the Yellowstone River, pulling trees, stumps, fences, livestock, and everything else into its muddy fury.

A small bridge supported the Milwaukee Road's mainline track across Custer Creek. In a tragic twist of fate, the *Olympian* reached the bridge just as the normally dry creek bed transformed into a raging river, twenty feet deep and a mile wide. The flying flagship of the Milwaukee Road never stood a chance. In the minutes and hours that followed, strangers on and off the train converged in a frantic race to save lives and care for the injured. The drenching rainstorm and remote location of the wreck delayed the arrival of rescue crews and medical help, leaving surviving passengers and crew on their own until sunrise.

The wreck killed forty-nine passengers and crew members and injured another seventy-five, making it the worst train accident in Montana history. The disaster was also a serious blow for the Milwaukee Road, then operating under bankruptcy protection for the second time in a decade. The company had not lost a paying passenger to an accident on any of its trains in over twenty years. The *Olympian* accident at Custer Creek would stand as the company's worst accident since it started operations in the 1850s.

In a night remembered for its darkness, innumerable acts of bravery and kindness illuminated a scene of unspeakable tragedy at Custer Creek. *Catastrophe at Custer Creek* tells the story of *Olympian* No. 15 and honors the victims and heroes of its fateful final journey.

CHAPTER 1

Saugus Cowboy

Lights blinked on at about a quarter after four in the morning on Friday, June 17, 1938, in the small but tidy ranch house of Dan Haughian Jr. The morning stars were still bright, streaks of light were just beginning to appear in the eastern Montana sky, and the air carried the first hints of another brutally hot day. Haughian would soon be on his horse to check on his fields. Like every other rancher, sodbuster, and homesteader in Montana, he watched the weather anxiously. Recent trends promised trouble.

The thirty-one-year-old Haughian lived near a speck of a town called Saugus along the west bank of the Yellowstone River between Miles City and Terry. This hardscrabble country—memorably captured in the work of early twentieth-century photographer Evelyn Cameron—is marked by badlands, stretches of desolate prairie broken up by striated mounds of gray, black, and red clay. Ranching in this environment was never easy, but the past few weeks had been more challenging than usual. Daily high temperatures in the high eighties and lower nineties threatened the survival of Haughian's newly planted alfalfa, prairie hay, and corn. On mornings like this, Haughian's body no doubt felt the aches and old injuries of cowboy life. In earlier days, he had competed every July in the Miles City Stampede, a local rodeo. Now, he was content to sit in the bleachers, beer in hand, and watch the young wranglers try to survive eight long seconds on the back of a four-legged tornado. When it came to working on his ranch, however, Haughian still showed the same dogged determination and concentration he'd displayed busting broncs. He was a man in motion from sunrise until long after sunset.

Haughian came to Saugus as a young man in the late 1920s. His family's ranch, nestled about fifteen miles west of town as the crow flies in the foothills of Little Sheep Mountain, felt like an outpost. He had also understandably tired of sharing a small farmhouse with nine brothers and sisters. Now on his own, his small, three-room house must have felt like a grand space. For company, and to help with ranch chores, he invited his friend Francis Motherhead to join him.

A decade on, he remained an unabashed bachelor. As his wife Mary, who he met and married years later, quipped, "The Irish didn't believe in getting married early. They wanted to be able to provide for their family." Haughian was a handsome man, inheriting his father's sparkling eyes, high cheekbones, and angular face. His quiet demeanor belied an intelligence well beyond what one would have expected for a person with only a few years of formal education. Action, not words, set the standard in his world. It was a work ethic his Irish immigrant parents, Dan Sr. and Susan, drilled into him at an early age.[1]

The elder Haughians had arrived in the area just after the turn of the century, when the west side of the Yellowstone was still home mostly to grazing cattle, large herds of sheep, and packs of wild horses. The population centers in the area, Miles City and Terry, were on the opposite side of the Yellowstone, nestled next to the mainline track of the Northern Pacific Railway. At that time, there were no bridges connecting the two sides of the river in this part of Montana. Getting across meant taking what the locals called a tramway, a crude river ferry that carried people, wagons, horses, and livestock from one side to the other using thick ropes and a pulley system. In winter, once the Yellowstone froze, those daring enough could walk across the ice.

All of this changed in 1908, when the Milwaukee Road (then known as the Chicago, Milwaukee & St. Paul Railway) carved its own rail bed on the west side of the river for its new 1,400-mile Puget Sound Extension, running from the Missouri River in South Dakota to Tacoma, Washington. With this audacious initiative, the railroad intended to join its rivals, the Northern Pacific and the Great Northern, in boasting of a transcontinental run to the Pacific. Like those other railroads, the Milwaukee Road would transform lives and landscapes along its route, which upon completion would stretch from Chicago to Puget Sound, creating population centers and prosperity where it decided to lay tracks and dooming the places that it bypassed.

The teams of surveyors dispatched by the Milwaukee Road railroad in 1906 to identify a path for the new rail line to the Pacific did not exactly throw darts at a map to select the new route. Railroads typically followed river corridors due to their generally flat grades. Existing overland trails—often carved by U.S. Army regiments—were also attractive to the surveyors. Large sections of the Puget Sound Extension through the Dakotas and Montana followed overland trails used by wagons of the army to supply its troops during the Indian Wars of the 1870s and 1880s.

Samuel Gordon, a Miles City old timer and businessman, recalled the isolation of the community in the 1880s: "Our mails came intermittently, whenever the stage from Bismarck [North Dakota] could dodge the Indians and make the high-water fords and we didn't feel as if we had anybody to care for but ourselves." It took thirty days for an overland freighter carrying several wagons of furniture and pulled by a team of eight oxen to make a round trip from Ekalaka, just west of where Montana borders both Dakotas, to Miles City. Today, it is less than a two-hour drive, about 115 miles.[2]

The Milwaukee Road's new rail route in eastern Montana required building two 270-foot bridges across the Yellowstone River north of Miles City and a third steel bridge in Forsyth. The first bridge, located about six miles west of Terry, was named for the tiny hamlet of Calypso, situated on the west bank of the river. Its twin was built about thirty miles south, near the community of Kinsey. Between the two, the railroad built a small pile and timber trestle—later upgraded to steel and concrete—spanning Custer Creek, a wash feeding into the Yellowstone that was dry most of the year.

Unpredictable weather and flooding made railroad construction along the river costly and dangerous. In June 1906, a cloudburst filled the headwaters of the creeks above the valleys where grading for the tracks was in progress. Floodwaters "swept down the full width of the valley by night, carrying away food and wood, drowning horses and mules as well as two men, and sweeping away tents, hay, oats and materials." Several other men were killed during an attempt to haul a large steam shovel across the river with cables near Bonfield Bluffs, about midway between Terry and Miles City.[3]

Undeterred, the Milwaukee Road pushed through the badlands of eastern Montana and reached Tacoma in 1909. A series of small stations popped up along the thirty-four miles of mainline tracks on the west side of the river, and the names Calypso, Saugus, Bonfield, and Kinsey soon appeared on Milwaukee Road timetables and train schedules.

The railroad industry, along with government boosterism, helped fuel the homesteading boom that brought the Haughians and so many others to eastern Montana. Unfortunately, the favorable weather and abundant rainfall that welcomed the early settlers quickly turned to years of relentless drought, cruel prairie winters, and biblical swarms of locusts and pests that devoured fields in hours. Many homesteaders suffered from the isolation and unforgiving loneliness of their new environment, and the arrival of World War I and the Great Depression drove many to seek out new opportunities elsewhere. By the early 1930s, 80 percent of the settlers who had arrived bright-eyed and confident two decades earlier were gone, many of them broken and bankrupt.

Small railroad towns like Saugus, Kinsey, Calypso, Fallon, Mildred, Ismay, Baker, and Marmarth, once teeming with new energy and legions of homesteaders, withered and tipped into a painful spiral of decline. At its height, Saugus boasted a post office, grocery store, and a small elementary school. By 1938, they had all been shuttered. Only decrepit wooden buildings remained of the Saugus gone by.

The Haughians, meanwhile, defied the overwhelming odds. As other homesteaders fled, the family shrewdly acquired abandoned land, stitching together multiple smaller parcels into holdings sizable enough to support their herds of sheep, cattle, and horses. Dan Haughian Sr. would often say, "Never sell your land. Fight for it. Without land you're just a drifter." These words came to serve as the family creed.[4]

On that 1938 morning, however, Dan Jr.'s focus was on the irrigation pumps he had recently purchased to channel the cold, clear water of the nearby Yellowstone River into his fields. In the face of Mother Nature's fickle ways, these pumps represented survival. As his horse carried him from pump to pump, Haughian could hear the shallow rapids rippling between the roosters' morning calls. At 5:15 A.M., the Milwaukee Road's elite passenger train, the *Olympian* No. 16, thundered by on its way to Chicago, right on schedule. Its westbound counterpart to Tacoma, the *Olympian* No. 15, would pass by his ranch after midnight, at about 12:35 A.M. The *Olympian* was an express train, so it would not stop in Saugus. His new pumps were working, but Haughian had cause to worry that if the heat wave continued, pumps may not be enough. He needed rain.

WHILE eastern Montana residents like Haughian looked forward to the possibility of rain that weekend in June, the scene the following week made their previous concerns seem trivial. A few days later, on June 24, just outside of Glendive, fifty miles north of Saugus, Duane and Lee Parks walked along the banks of the Yellowstone River at dusk. In normal times, they would have been fishing. Instead, they were searching for bodies.

The two young Miles City men were part of a river posse recruited to find passengers missing after a terrible train crash. Five days earlier, in the early morning hours of Sunday, June 19, the Milwaukee Road *Olympian* No. 15 derailed while crossing a bridge at Custer Creek during a fierce storm. Many of the unsuspecting 190 passengers aboard had been hurled into the creek and swept downstream into the Yellowstone River.

Milwaukee Road officials called on the Parks brothers within hours of the accident to bring a railroad electrician who could restore the telephone and telegraph wires that had been torn down in the crash. Communication was vital to the ongoing rescue effort, and bad road conditions made their boat the fastest option. As they navigated the swift currents in the eerie morning stillness, a column of dark smoke led them to the wreck. "God, how could anyone survive?" Duane Parks thought as the scene came into view.[5]

Duane and Lee joined a makeshift camp of rescuers at Custer Creek and for the next two days pulled bodies from demolished train cars. The grim task was heart wrenching, as when Duane discovered the body of a young girl buried in the piles of twisted metal and debris. Crash survivors had witnessed many of their fellow travelers swept away in the night by the raging creek waters. Word spread that the body of a man believed to be an *Olympian* passenger was found near Sidney, almost one hundred miles downriver from the crash site, near the North Dakota state line.

When the recovery effort moved from the crash scene to the Yellowstone River, the brothers assumed the task of searching a fifty-mile stretch from Terry to Glendive. The Parks brothers would never forget the experience. The severe rainstorms that had been a major factor in the *Olympian* accident had overwhelmed all the creeks and coulees in the area, flooding the Yellowstone with muddy water and wiping out any prairie life unlucky enough to be in the water's path. Duane and Lee found themselves rowing through hordes of field mice bobbing in the current—"millions of them"—along with a bizarre menagerie of rabbits, snakes, horses, cattle, and deer, all disoriented and thrashing for their lives. Carcasses choked the murky waters.[6]

Wielding six-foot wooden poles equipped with hooks on the ends, Duane and Lee poked around stumps and other debris while looking for the missing. The work was slow and tedious. The Yellowstone's meandering bends carve a complicated path across eastern Montana, its relatively shallow course splitting often to create channels around small islands and sandbars. The brothers found several corpses in their first two days. They developed a system: one would stay with the body to keep it from floating farther downstream, while the other would find a nearby home to call the sheriff. Clothing, luggage, hats, shoes—all from *Olympian* passengers—floated around them as they searched, constant reminders of the horror that occurred days before.[7]

The weather slowed them down. Daytime temperatures in Miles City and Terry exceeded ninety degrees for several days in a row that week. Glendive was sweltering at close to one hundred degrees, a possible record. Late every afternoon, rainstorms forced the brothers to take shelter. Yet they still covered about ten river miles a day. On occasion, the county sheriff motored by in his flat-bottomed powerboat to check on their progress. Lights strung across bridges from Terry to Sidney allowed searchers to continue working around the clock. Visible from a great distance, they cast ghostly shadows as the water flowed beneath the bridges.

As night fell on Friday, the appearance of porch lights and ranch houses signaled to the Park brothers that they were approaching the small town of Glendive. Duane and Lee scanned the river edges and sandbars for a safe location to pull in for the night and set up camp. More than once, they had fled sandbars overrun with rattlesnakes. Their clunky rowboat, heaped with dirty camping gear, clothes, jugs of fresh water, and a cooler, required skilled maneuvering in the current of the bloated river.

As they steered their craft in the direction of a small sandbar on the south bank of the river, something caught Duane's attention. Even after the experience of the past few days, what Duane saw in the distance must have shocked him. No longer missing was *Olympian* passenger Nell Clancy, age sixty, of Bloomington, Illinois.[8]

CHAPTER 2

Confluence in Chicago

Union Station, Friday, June 17, 1938

The big day had finally arrived for Kate Clancy. At last, she was setting off for an extended summer vacation to California with her sister, Nell, and their eighteen-year-old niece, Margie. The three women had reservations that evening on the Milwaukee Road *Olympian*, an express transcontinental train that departed from Chicago every night at a quarter after eleven. After months of planning, the Clancys were headed first to Seattle, then down the Pacific coast to visit relatives in the Golden State.

It was the trip of a lifetime for seventy-two-year-old Kate and her younger sibling Nell, who was almost sixty. Kate had lived and worked in Chicago for years, but since her retirement she and Nell had rarely ventured far from their hometown of Bloomington, Illinois. For Margie, the trip was a return to her birthplace. Her parents, Phillip and Ida Clancy, had lived in California, and both Margie and her older brother, Edward, were born in the Fresno area. But Ida died unexpectedly when Margie was only four. Phillip bounced around California with the two children for a few years but never quite found his footing after his wife's death. In 1932, he decided he needed his sisters' support to raise his young family and returned to Bloomington.

Both trained educators who never married, Kate and Nell Clancy happily opened their doors to Phillip and his two children. The Clancy family's Locust Street home, bought by their parents years before, was alive again with the sound of children playing, music lessons, and birthday parties. The Clancy sisters embraced Margie and Edward as their own and took great pride in helping Phillip raise his two children.

Kate, Phillip, and Nell's parents came to America in the 1850s as part of an early wave of Irish immigrants. Their father, Edward Clancy, arrived in Bloomington just before the start of the American Civil War. While many Irish immigrants during that period were illiterate and had little job training, Edward had skills in metalworking, describing himself as a "molder of iron." He found employment in a foundry producing cast-iron fences, urns, benches, and then, during wartime, munitions for the Union Army. Discrimination against the Irish was rampant, and young Edward kept his head down and worked hard at the foundry. With a small but steady salary, Edward took up residence with twenty other immigrants in a boarding house owned by John O'Brien, an Irish-born saloonkeeper.[1]

It was not long after his arrival in Bloomington that the thirty-two-year-old Edward encountered young Johanna Philomena O'Neil, ten years his junior. The O'Neils had also made the treacherous crossing to America from Ireland in the early 1850s. Johanna's mother, Mary, widowed at age thirty-seven with six young children, was determined to give her children a better life than what Shanagarry, Ireland, could offer. She took matters into her own hands and booked seats on the ocean liner *Balmoral* in 1851, sailing for New Orleans from Liverpool, England. With support from relatives and the promise of honest work, Mary O'Neil and her six children found their way to Bloomington.

Amid the Civil War, Edward and Johanna married in January 1862. Their first child, Katherine P. ("Kate") Clancy, was born in the summer of 1863. Five additional children followed, including Phillip in 1874 and Ellen ("Nell") in 1879. The youngest of six, Nell was always considered the baby of the family.

All these years later, the Clancy women boarded the *Alton Limited* in Bloomington at half past seven to get to Chicago. The train made frequent stops, taking almost four hours to travel 136 miles. The *Alton Limited* may have been pokey, but it would deliver the Clancys to a Union Station abuzz over new developments in train travel in the Windy City.

At precisely nine in the morning, an eager crowd waiting at Chicago's LaSalle Street Station felt the trembling of the concrete passenger platform beneath their feet. Through a cloud of steam, a stunning gunmetal gray and blue bullet of a locomotive rumbled up to the bumper post, completing what had become the fastest New York to Chicago passenger train run in history. The New York Central Railroad's redesigned *Twentieth Century Limited* had departed Grand Central Station sixteen hours earlier and had covered the 960-mile distance in record time. Unveiled just two days earlier, the newly futuristic train, which had been making the same run since 1902, captured Chicagoans' imaginations. An all-metal shroud, the brainchild of industrial design genius Henry Dreyfuss, now sheathed the train's locomotive. Its stylized bullet nose and shark-like fin split the air as it roared down the track, pulling opulent cars built by the Pullman-Standard Car Manufacturing Company.

The speed of the *Twentieth Century Limited* matched its dazzling style. On the express run between New York and Chicago, it averaged sixty miles per hour; on level stretches of rail, it could exceed cruising speeds of eighty miles per hour. The sleek new train shaved thirty minutes off the route's previous time. In a full-page newspaper advertisement marking the *Century*'s inaugural run, the Pullman Company declared a "new epoch" for rail travel.[2]

The launch of this captivating vision of the future came at the perfect time for Chicago's mayor, Edward J. Kelly. Like many other major American cities in the 1930s, Chicago was wrestling with ruinous conditions unleashed by the Great Depression: bread lines, unemployment, labor strife, a public school system in tatters, racial tension, and crime. By 1938, with economic recovery moving at a glacial pace, an impatient Mayor Kelly worked furiously to convince Chicagoans that better days lay ahead. It helped that Prohibition was over; the Cubs were on their way to securing the National League pennant; and organized crime had largely been tamed. The city's crime rate, however, continued to soar. In fact, on June 14—Flag Day—the *Chicago Daily Tribune*'s "Crime Clock" announced that 16,504 crimes had been committed in the city since the first of the year, including ninety-five murders. More than two dozen of these crimes had come in recent weeks at the hands of the so-called Dawn

Bandit, who robbed gasoline station attendants and patrons at sunrise, making off with thousands of dollars. The bandit had eluded a citywide police dragnet for weeks, and Chicagoans remained on high alert.[3]

Despite, or perhaps to distract from, the dismal crime update, the mayor had planned two celebrations for that day. He released ten thousand public school students early to gather at Stanton Park for a "show your colors" event where they saluted an enormous American flag. While the children cheered, Mayor Kelly held a media event in his office to commemorate the unveiling of the new *Twentieth Century Limited*. Mugging for the cameras and boasting about the accomplishment, Mayor Kelly shoved a special plaque into the hands of a smiling W. F. Schaff, vice president of the New York Central.[4]

Top brass from the Chicago-based Pullman-Standard Car Manufacturing Company also attended the event, having built the *Century*'s luxurious cars. Pullman called the *Century*'s record speed a new standard for rail travel, insisting it was as important to life in America as the driving of the golden spike in 1869. The Elgin National Watch Company also joined in on celebratory events, taking out large newspaper advertisements touting that the "split second accuracy" of Elgin timeclocks determined the precise moment of the train's departure.[5]

A few hours after Mayor Kelly launched the new epoch in train travel, another era in his city abruptly ended. Acting on a tip from the fugitive's father—a policeman—detectives ambushed twenty-three-year-old Harold Keen as he arrived at a friend's house. The young Keen, who had committed crimes since he was ten, was killed in a hail of gunfire. The Dawn Bandit's reign of terror was over.[6]

AMID the fanfare, nineteen-year-old twins Donald and Dean Hanscom, en route from New York to their summer jobs in Seattle, arrived on the *Twentieth Century Limited* that Friday morning. Once they reached Seattle, they would be staying with their uncle, Zac Hanscom, who owned a house on Hunts Point, a small peninsula outside the city surrounded by beautiful Lake Washington. While Donald and Dean were used to traveling well, being among the first to travel on the brand-new, streamlined version of the *Twentieth Century Limited* was heady even for them.[7]

Since its launch in 1902, the *Century* had catered to the rich and famous. With its crimson welcome mats, an ingenious marketing tool, it literally coined the term "red carpet treatment" for its first-class passengers. It attracted the elite of Chicago and New York, including leading politicians and businessmen such as Teddy Roosevelt and J. P. Morgan.

Its creator, George Daniels, the enthusiastic chief of the New York Central Railroad's passenger service, spared no expense in outfitting the train with just about every creature comfort imaginable. The train included a barbershop, secretarial services, a fully stocked library, and Art Deco murals for its affluent passengers. The food and dining facilities on the train were on par with some of New York's finest restaurants. White linen tablecloths, cutlery made of real silver, and fresh flowers adorned every table. Even the menu and matchbook covers on the train sported a Henry Dreyfuss design. After dinner, the immaculately dressed dining car steward and white-gloved waiters magically transformed the car into a rolling nightclub called the Café Limited.

After a day's work in New York, a businessman could board the train before its daily departure from Grand Central Station at six o'clock, have a wonderful meal, get a good night's sleep, and step off at nine in the morning in Chicago ready for another day of business. The return *Century* to New York departed from LaSalle Street Station at four in the afternoon, arriving in Grand Central Station at nine the following morning.[8]

Donald and Dean could envision themselves someday taking part in this exclusive commute. With means, connections, and education, they were on track to become the type of businessmen they had rubbed elbows with while enjoying an onboard dinner of veal steak and Philadelphia capon. And while they might have still been too young to join them for cocktails in the Café Limited, the twins carried themselves with the easy confidence of young men on the rise with the world at their feet.

Donald and Dean's mother, Ann Hanscom, had seen them off at Grand Central Station the previous evening. Ann had reason to be proud of her two handsome sons and was pleased that they would be visiting relatives in Washington. For the Hanscoms, Seattle was home. The former Ann

Rosalind met and married her husband, Dean Jewell Hanscom, there. All three of the couple's children were born in Seattle as well. After college, Dean landed his first big job, working as a passenger agent for the Pacific Mail Steamship Company, which was then absorbed by the Dollar Steamship Company in 1925. Hanscom thrived working for the Dollar Line and became a favorite of its owner, Captain Robert Dollar, who by 1929 owned the largest fleet of cargo and passenger ships in America. Its passenger ships carried about fifty thousand passengers annually and docked in every major port in the world.[9]

The Great Depression hit the Dollar Line hard, as did the death of its namesake and founder in 1932. Amid this upheaval, Hanscom was promoted into the executive ranks and dispatched to New York City to serve as chief passenger agent for the company. The new job in New York City meant a cross-country move for the family. In 1935, they purchased a home in Bronxville, about fifteen miles north of Manhattan in Westchester County. In the 1930s, Bronxville was developing into one of the most affluent suburbs in the country. The easy train access into New York City made it an ideal location for families of America's rich and famous. Joseph P. Kennedy owned homes and property in Bronxville, as did radio and television host Jack Paar and World War I flying ace Eddie Rickenbacker.

It would never be Seattle, but Bronxville worked well for the relocated Hanscom family. The twins spent their junior and senior years at Bronxville High School, where they played football and worked as cub journalists for the school newspaper. After high school they both joined the class of 1940 at Dartmouth College. Only two years into their studies, Dean and Donald were already seasoned travelers. Thanks to their father's influence, they'd spent the summer before their freshman year circling the globe as cadets on the Dollar Line's SS *President Wilson*, a luxury passenger steamship.[10]

Having toured the major ports of the world, Dean and Donald knew how to spend a free day in a city and had visited Chicago with their parents as children. Now, exiting their Pullman sleeper in suit coats and ties, the boys set off to see everything they could of the city before heading to Union Station for their departure on the westbound Milwaukee Road *Olympian* No. 15. June had been a month of rain and clouds in Chicago, but sunshine, blue skies, and a temperature in the seventies greeted the twins that morning. A perfect start to their summer adventure.

At about the same time the Hanscom twins arrived at Chicago's LaSalle Street Station, the eastbound Milwaukee Road *Olympian* No. 16 eased up to the platform on the north side of Union Station's Grand Concourse, completing its 2,188-mile, fifty-eight-hour run from Tacoma. Like the *Twentieth Century Limited,* the *Olympian* made an impressive arrival. The massive, ninety-five-foot-long, fifteen-foot-high, black F-Class Hudson steam locomotive rumbled into the station, hissing and clanging, its brakes squealing, its six enormous drive wheels enveloped in a plume of hot steam, smoke, and mist. The pungent smell of oil and grease permeated the air.

After the train came to a full stop, passenger car doors opened almost simultaneously and porters jumped out in their dark blue uniforms to set up stepstools for the departing passengers. The porters wiped down the outside brass support columns so passengers would not get their hands dirty. A big smile, a helpful hand, and a pleasant "good morning" and "welcome to Chicago" greeted each departing passenger.

Once on the platform, passengers entered the bright and airy Grand Concourse, a colossal structure of glass, steel, and marble. Erector Set–style beams of exposed, latticed steel arched as they met the glass ceiling that lit up the train platforms by day. Elegant chandeliers decorated with birds, bees, butterflies, and flowers hung on cables from the ceiling. At night, the chandeliers provided light for the constant stream of passengers bustling across the glassy marble tiles of the concourse.

Opened in 1925, Chicago's Union Station sprawled across thirty-five urban acres on the west side of the Chicago River between West Adams Street and West Jackson Boulevard. The third in a series of Union Stations on the site, it was designed in the Beaux-Arts style by Chicago architect Daniel Burnham, who used modern materials such as glass, marble, and iron to create grand spaces within the station. Ten years in the making, the massive complex of locally quarried limestone buildings, train sheds, and track, much of it below street level, cost about $75 million (roughly $1 billion in 2020 dollars). An estimated thirty thousand Chicagoans showed up to tour the massive new train hub at its grand opening.

A consortium of four major railroad companies financed the station's construction, with most of the initial money coming from the Chicago & Alton Railroad and the Pennsylvania Railroad. The name "Union" was deliberate, since the station would eventually be home to at least four independent railroad companies, including the Chicago, Milwaukee & St. Paul Railway.[11]

By 1938, the Milwaukee Road had exclusive rights to ten of the dozen tracks in Union Station's north-end shed but used all twelve at busy times. With twenty-four train platforms continually in service, the Grand Concourse bustled day and night. That year, more than three hundred passenger trains pulled into or departed from Union Station every day, moving fifty thousand passengers and their hundreds of tons of luggage.

AT a quarter after eleven that morning, the *Alton Limited* from Bloomington pulled into Chicago's Union Station. The Clancys were not in a hurry. Arriving early in the day, they had plenty of time for sightseeing, finding a good restaurant, and satisfying their interest in history and culture by visiting a museum or two. Kate Clancy, who had lived and worked there for years, knew Chicago especially well.[12]

After arranging to have their luggage transferred to the Milwaukee Road's *Olympian*, the Clancys exited the Grand Concourse using the graceful staircase with three-inch-thick travertine marble stairs on the west side. There, they would have arrived at the headhouse, comprising a multitude of retail stores and restaurants on the first level and offices on the upper levels. The original design for the structure included twenty-six floors of office space, but only eight were ever completed. Most of the offices were occupied by employees of the Milwaukee Road, including the general passenger agent, the overlord of all aspects of passenger travel for the company. The Pullman Car Company also had employees located in the headhouse offices.

Their first stop, like that of many passengers, might have been the women's lounge. According to a Union Station booklet, the lounge boasted "homelike appointments equal to those of the finest clubs and hotels," offering "a quiet, inviting spot for reading, conversation with friends, or perhaps a short letter to the folks back home."[13] The main waiting room in Union Station, the Great Hall, took up an entire city block. The room featured a barrel-vaulted, 219-foot skylight soaring 110 feet above the polished marble floor. Massive Corinthian columns gave the space a stately elegance, while strategically placed oversized oak benches, which seemed much smaller in such a cavernous space, allowed weary passengers and travelers like the Clancys to sit in awe of the surroundings and watch the throngs of people moving in waves throughout the station.

The Clancy women enjoyed lunch at the Red Lion, a cafeteria-style restaurant located on two levels off the Great Hall. A table on the balcony afforded a view of the main floor but was far enough away from the hustle and bustle to provide a quiet place to discuss plans for the rest of the day. Even though the restaurant was a cut below the Golden Lion, the station's premier restaurant, both establishments—like all the eating options in the station—were operated by Fred Harvey, known widely as "America's Caterer." Elegantly dressed, white-gloved waiters moved with precision and efficiency across the tiled black-and-white checkerboard floor. Below them, on the first level, the famous "Harvey Girls," wearing the company's trademark black-and-white uniforms, served travelers around a large, U-shaped, diner-style counter.

Having settled on their plans, the Clancys were ready to set out. A whole day in Chicago. A California vacation with their favorite niece. A trip on the famed *Olympian*. Nell and Kate Clancy could hardly remember a time when they felt this happy and energized. At the same time the Clancys passed through Union Station, another family bound for the West Coast on the *Olympian* was also regrouping from the first leg of their travel.

THOMAS and Esther Lallas and their three young children—Anna, age ten; John, eight; and George, seven—had no plans for sightseeing in Chicago. After a night struggling to sleep in their coach seats on the overnight train from New York City, finding a comfortable place to bide their time until departure was enough. Anna, suffering from recurring bouts of severe abdominal pain likely caused by an onset of appendicitis, was especially weary.

By that point, even the youngest of the children was conditioned to endure seemingly endless stretches of downtime. They had been traveling for weeks, venturing across the globe from their home in Bellingham, Washington, to their homeland in Greece, and now back to the United States. The Lallas family's odyssey had not been planned as a round-trip. Tom and Esther, as much as they appreciated their adopted community and the opportunities they found in the United States, agonized over raising their Bellingham-born children so far from their roots. Would the children retain their heritage, their devotion to the Greek Orthodox Church, and the core values that brought strength to the tight-knit Greek community? Tom and Esther made a point of speaking to each other in their native language at home and insisted that the children learn both English and Greek. Still, frustrated by the children's growing Americanization, the couple decided the family must return to Greece.[14]

It would be a familiar journey for the two. In the fall of 1910, fourteen-year-old Tom Lallas had braved a month-long voyage across the seas as part of a massive wave of Greeks—mostly men and boys—who emigrated to the United States between 1900 and 1920. While Greece had been slow to industrialize and faced economic stagnation, jobs reportedly abounded in America. Desperate to make a better life for himself, Tom decided to take a chance and leave his homeland. After several years in New York City, Lallas took the logging and timber industry skills that he had learned in the mountains of Greece to the Pacific Northwest. There, he joined a sizable community of Greeks in the small seaside village of Hoquiam, located at the mouth of its namesake river next to Aberdeen, Washington. Tom soon found work as a laborer for the Northwestern Lumber Company, which controlled the major logging and sawmill operations in the area. It was no small irony that the young emigrant found himself living in the shadow of a mountain that bears the same name as a mythical peak in Greece: Mount Olympus.[15]

While working in Hoquiam, Lallas applied to become a naturalized American citizen in 1913. Due to restrictions on citizenship and the nation's involvement in World War I, it took more than a decade for his papers to be processed and approved. During this time, Lallas relocated to Bellingham, Washington, in search of more meaningful work.[16]

In 1925, with citizenship papers finally in hand, Tom returned to Greece to marry his hometown sweetheart, Estara Trambaklos, and bring her back to the United States to start a family. With sculpted waves of short black hair framing a kind face and confident eyes, Esther, as she was known in Bellingham, kept up with American women's fashions in the 1930s and liked to dress glamorously, albeit on a limited budget. She was often seen wearing a colorful dahlia as an adornment on her dresses. The couple's three children arrived between 1928 and 1931.

In Bellingham, Tom partnered with an ambitious local grocer, Art Howard, to open a produce business. The older Howard, a seasoned businessman, saw potential in Tom Lallas. After a fire had gutted Howard's building, the two worked together to rebuild the grocery store in a new downtown location using an entirely new business model. They decided to assemble multiple independently owned food shops under one roof and one banner: the Stop & Shop Marketplace. It was pure genius.[17]

Consumers flocked to the marketplace in the heart of Bellingham to buy meat, fish, fruits, vegetables, bread, and milk. Inside, an establishment called the Stop & Eat Café served breakfast and lunch, and shoppers frequented a popular soda fountain called the Buttercup Dairy. The business had "grown every year in this location," Art Howard beamed in a 1936 interview. In fact, the Stop & Shop had grown by 30 percent annually, and Howard predicted the coming years would even be better. The business became an anchor for growth in Bellingham's grocery district for years to come.[18]

Lallas thrived in Bellingham. Howard was impressed by his work ethic and ideas for growing the business, as well as his uncanny ability to anticipate what customers wanted. "He had vision, which was valued by Howard," recalled George Lallas, Tom's youngest son. In addition to his business acumen, Tom's kind-hearted nature and community spirit were widely recognized. When a friend's truck blew its tires in eastern Washington while loaded with fresh fruit and vegetables, Tom arranged to have new tires delivered immediately to the stranded driver. He was known to bring crates of fresh oranges for teachers and staff when visiting his children in elementary school. His devotion to improving downtown Bellingham inspired talk of him one day running for mayor.[19]

Nevertheless, immersing his children in authentic Greek culture was so important to Tom Lallas that he was willing to sacrifice the life he had built over nearly thirty years in the United States by moving his family back to Gravia, the couple's ancestral village in central Greece. According to Greek mythology, this ruggedly beautiful, mountainous region was the center not only of Greece but of the world. But the Lallas children did not take well to life in Greece, even after having several months to adjust to their new surroundings. Miserable, they missed their friends and began acting out, as only young children can. In light of the children's unhappiness, Tom and Esther abandoned their idea and booked one-way tickets back to America.[20]

Now, after weeks of excruciating travel, Tom and Esther had reason to feel their spirits rise upon reaching Chicago. They just had to make it through the day before one more train ride would finally return them to Bellingham. Whatever disappointment they may have felt over their failed repatriation, Tom and Esther had once and for all settled the question of where home was for the Lallas family. In their hearts they would always be Greek, but it was now time to embrace the future their children would enjoy in Bellingham as Americans.[21]

CHAPTER 3

No Ordinary Train

Chicago, Illinois, Friday, June 17, 1938

Louis Williams walked out of his small, rented flat in south Chicago looking to catch a ride to Union Station. Suitcase in hand, Williams moved briskly down the street, enjoying the sunshine on a cool, crisp June day. He wouldn't see his wife, Ruth, and their young daughter, Constance, again for a week. He had been assigned to work on the Milwaukee Road's flagship passenger train to Tacoma, the *Olympian*. The round-trip journey of 4,376 miles meant at least six long days of work on the rails.

Growing up as a Black teenager in 1920s Chicago, Williams watched his two older brothers, Willis and Cleopas, develop successful careers as porters after training with the Pullman Palace Car Company, a venerable Chicago institution. Louis saw how impressive they looked dressed in the Pullman uniform: a crisp blue suit with brass buttons, white shirt, black tie, and polished black shoes, all topped off by the smart-looking cap with the words "Pullman Porter" emblazoned on a silver plate. He listened to his brothers' stories of traveling the country, meeting interesting people, and having enough money in their pockets to take care of their families and even buy a house. Securing employment as a porter meant status in the Black community. It may have been the lowliest position on the train, but for many it was a coveted job.

After Willis and Cleopas presumably vouched for their younger brother's good character, as would have been required by the Pullman

Company, the door opened for Louis Williams. He started his training in his early twenties, young for porter work by most accounts, and the Milwaukee Road soon hired him to work passenger trains operating out of Union Station.

The twenty-five-year-old Louis lived with Ruth and eighteen-month-old Constance in the segregated township of Bronzeville, just south of downtown Chicago and about an hour's commute from Union Station. A community of three hundred thousand Black Americans living in close quarters in mostly white-owned tenements, Bronzeville arose from the Great Migration. Beginning in 1915, millions of southern Blacks, seeking to escape the poverty and racial violence of Jim Crow, made their way north in hopes of building a better life in urban centers such as Chicago, Detroit, Cleveland, and Pittsburgh. Facing restrictions and barriers to housing throughout the city, many of the new arrivals took up residence on the city's south side, in an area known derisively by white Chicagoans as the "Black Belt." Soon, the nascent community became a renowned center of Black culture and business. By the 1920s, the proudly renamed Bronzeville rivaled New York's Harlem in its importance to Black America.[1]

Louis Williams and his family were part of the Great Migration. The grandson of enslaved people, Louis was born in Alabama in 1913, several years before his parents uprooted their family of four young boys and moved 750 miles north to Chicago in search of a better life. The family settled into a small, rented flat on Bronzeville's East 48th Street, a few blocks north of Washington Park, where their surrounding neighbors were nearly all recent migrants from the South.[2]

Louis's father, Will, found a job as a brick mason, while his mother, Pearl, worked out of the family home as a hairdresser. In the late 1920s, the family suffered a devastating blow when Will died, leaving Pearl as the head of household, which now included a fifth son, Leon, born in 1925. Pearl looked to her three oldest sons, Willis, Cleopas, and Motier, to help support the family. By 1930, Willis and Cleopas were working fulltime as Pullman porters, and Motier was employed in an ice cream factory.[3]

While her older sons helped keep the family afloat, Pearl insisted that Louis finish his schooling. She enrolled him at the Tilden Technical High School in Chicago, which in the 1930s was a public, four-year institution for boys that provided training in professions such as architecture, advertising, welding, and auto repair. Dominated by students with German, Polish, and Irish last names, Tilden reflected the diversity of its neighborhood and enrolled the children of nearby Black families as well. In addition to its technical curriculum, Tilden also boasted an outstanding athletics program. Louis, who was tall with a broad-shouldered, muscular frame, became a standout football player for the powerhouse Yellowjackets.[4]

Upon entering the workforce, Williams encountered, like his brothers, new forms of racial hostility and discrimination. Segregation was technically illegal in the North, but still quietly if not openly practiced and enforced in everyday life. His locker in the basement of Union Station was separated from those of his white colleagues. Being Black required that he use caution in deciding which bathrooms, drinking fountains, and eating areas to use. To avoid uncomfortable situations, Williams likely followed the common practice among Black porters of packing his own sandwiches and fresh fruit to eat while at work.[5]

Thomas Fleming, a Black journalist who spent time as a young man working the rails as a cook, wrote about the painful paradox porters like Williams faced on the job: "The porter reigned supreme on George's [Pullman] sleeper cars. But the very definition of their jobs, of their kingdom, roiled in contradictions." Fleming explained that the porter "was servant as well as host. He had the best job in his community and the worst on the train. He could be trusted with his white passengers' children and their safety, but only for the five days of a cross-country trip. He shared his riders' most private moments but, to most, remained an enigma if not an enemy."[6]

As always, on the morning of June 17 Williams made certain to get to Union Station on time. Being late was an offense that could cost him his job. His usual day began long before any passengers boarded and continued long after everyone had departed. On a transcontinental train like the *Olympian*, a one hundred-hour work week was typical.

After arriving at Union Station, Williams changed into his uniform and caught a ride with fellow porters and other personnel on an empty train returning to the Western Avenue yard, the massive servicing site for all Milwaukee Road passenger trains and locomotives. In the twenty minutes it took to travel the three miles northwest of Union Station, Williams could briefly relax, close his eyes, and enjoy the train's gentle rocking, knowing these would be his last truly restful moments for the next several days. Air thick with smoke and coal dust signaled his arrival at the Western Avenue yard, where the sheer size of the Milwaukee Road's operations was on full display. In 1938, the company had about 1,200 steam locomotives and close to 1,000 passenger cars in its inventory. Hundreds of railroad cars of all types—coaches, sleepers, diners, parlor cars, express cars, and baggage cars—stood in lines that stretched as far as the eye could see, ready to be deep-cleaned, restocked with linens and food supplies, and serviced if repairs were necessary.

The constant parade of locomotives in and out of the immense brick roadhouse for service and repairs kept the yard in a fog of pollution. Both the westbound and eastbound *Olympians* passed the facility daily, taking several minutes to get from one side of the yard to the other. The yard was a city unto itself, with hundreds of skilled employees and laborers working around the clock.

Williams navigated this mass of train cars and equipment to find *Olympian* No. 15 being prepped for its daily departure to Tacoma. The train's conductor would have given him a sleeper car assignment for the trip. Like many other railroads, the Milwaukee Road had its own line of sleeper cars, called tourist sleepers, but also contracted with Pullman to use its line of luxury sleeper cars as well. The tourist sleepers used by the Milwaukee Road in the 1930s were high-end knockoffs of the Pullman sleepers, which for decades had set the standard for railroad comfort and opulence. "You'll feel like royalty" when traveling in tourist sleepers, promised one Milwaukee Road advertisement. "These rooms are the last word in luxury offering everything for your complete privacy. The cost? Surprisingly low." The more expensive Pullman-Standard sleepers were popular among passengers seeking a higher level of comfort and service. The Pacific-bound *Olympian* usually had three tourist sleepers and three Pullman sleepers as part of its train. Depending on the time of year and passenger volume, Williams alternated between tourist sleepers and Pullmans. The pay was about the same, but the tips were much better on the Pullmans as they attracted a wealthier clientele.[7]

Given his lack of seniority, Williams would not have been surprised to learn he was assigned to one of the *Olympian*'s tourist sleepers, number 5725. His car was also known as tourist sleeper C, since it would be the third in the lineup that night, behind sleepers named the Ipswich and the Choteau. When the *Olympian* was fully assembled, Williams's sleeper was positioned in front of the dining car, a good place to be for its passengers, who had easy access to the train's excellent meal service.

In better times, railroad companies assigned two porters and a conductor to each sleeper car. But the lean years of the Great Depression required that a single porter take full responsibility for managing the affairs of the sleeper, which could hold as many as forty-eight passengers. The tourist sleepers had twelve sleeping sections, six on each side of the car, anchored by a ladies' lounge—complete with dressing tables with mirrors, two sinks, a tooth-brushing station with a small sink, plush couches, lounge chairs, and one toilet—and a smaller men's lounge at each end. The sections in the center of the car—away from its wheels and axles—offered the quietest, smoothest ride.[8]

Holding as many as four adults, each sleeping section had upper and lower berths that could be closed off for privacy with heavy maroon velour curtains. Luggage and shoes could be stored under the lower berths, which folded down to become seats. Williams had as many as forty-eight beds to make each night—a chore that he would repeat multiple times on the journey to Tacoma. In the evening, Williams "made down" the beds by popping the upper berth in the ceiling open. The next morning, he "made up" the beds, converting them into comfortable seats for his passengers. Each berth also included reading lamps and quick-access storage for small items under each window in the form of a woven rope hammock. In the early 1930s, the Milwaukee Road installed air conditioning in many of its passenger cars. The railroad's insignia was sewn onto all blankets, and two pillows were provided for each sleeping berth.

Under the ever-watchful eye of the conductor, who ultimately bore responsibility for everything on the train, Williams took charge of the hours-long process of ensuring that the sleeper car was sparkling clean, fully stocked, and in perfect working order for the passengers who would board later in the evening. Armed with vacuums, mops, sponges, and squeegees, Williams and the cleaning crew combed through every square inch of the sleeper, ensuring that its cleanliness met the company's strict standards.

Still learning the ropes of his job, Williams would have kept the so called Pullman Bible handy. A fifty-page rulebook for porters, this pocket-sized reference covered guidance for personal grooming (no mustaches, sideburns, or beards) and explained how the uniform must be worn. It directed porters on how to properly address passengers, fold blankets and bath towels, fluff pillows, shine shoes, call out scheduled stops, and set window shades, among other tasks. The rulebook was more than required reading: porters, waiters, and train attendants were expected to memorize it.[9]

Since the air conditioning only worked when the train was powered and assembled, opening the car doors and the lounge windows was the only way to air out the car and rid it of any smells that could permeate the soft, cushiony seats and headrests. Williams scrutinized each berth, testing every indoor light and call button. He also checked stocks of toilet paper, bathroom towels, bed linens, blankets, and pillows.

Pullman porters wore dark blue wool jackets that could become uncomfortably hot even in otherwise pleasantly mild weather. Fortunately, Louis Williams would not yet have had to wear his as he completed his pre-trip checklist. Passenger boarding was still hours away, and shirtsleeves would do as he and other employees rushed to prepare the *Olympian* for its 2,188-mile journey. He had a full car that night. Just about every sleeper berth had been reserved for the trip to the Pacific. The summer tourist season of 1938 had begun.

CHAPTER 4

Miles City

Friday, June 17, 1938

As Louis Williams prepared the *Olympian* for departure in Chicago, Frank Merrifield, a veteran Milwaukee Road engineer, was at his home in Miles City, Montana. Merrifield could pick almost any schedule or train run he wanted. With over thirty years with the company under his belt, he outranked most other engineers in the Trans-Missouri Division and was considered one of the best at handling a locomotive. He could have worked freight trains and made more money, but Merrifield chose to be in the engineer's seat pulling the *Olympian*. There was prestige associated with piloting the company's flagship passenger train. And Merrifield had earned his status.

Frank Calvin Merrifield was born August 2, 1879, on the family farm in Greenleaf, Wisconsin, a small town named only six years earlier for Emery B. Greenleaf, the president of the Milwaukee & Northern Railroad. Frank was the second of five boys and one girl born to George and Addie Merrifield. The Merrifields' small farm fed the family and produced enough surplus to sell in local markets during the summer months. In the early 1880s, however, the family sold their land in Wisconsin and moved to Dakota Territory, settling as homesteaders onto another quarter section—160 acres—of farmland near the township of Keystone, deep in the Black Hills. Keystone started as a mining boomtown after prospectors discovered gold in the area. There is no evidence that the Merrifield family had any direct involvement in the gold rush, but the many colorful characters seeking their fortune in the hills, along with the attendant proliferation of saloons and brothels, must have provided an exciting contrast to life on the farm. After being struck by lightning while working in the fields, George decided to give up farming and find another source of income to support his growing family. In 1884, with Addie pregnant with twin boys, he moved the family to the Monango, an agricultural community in present-day North Dakota, and secured a new job selling farm equipment. The Merrifields raised their children there until they tired of the lonely prairie and moved to Los Angeles in 1906.[1]

Frank grew into a strapping young man, with a handsome face, a carefully coiffed mane of dark hair, and an impressive handlebar mustache. In 1899, at twenty years old, he left Monango and moved back to Wisconsin after hearing of an opportunity for work in Green Bay, fifteen miles north of Greenleaf. At the time, Green Bay was headquarters for a major operating hub of the Milwaukee Road called the Superior Division. Fascinated by trains and steam locomotives since childhood, Frank worked his way into the cab of a Milwaukee Road locomotive in 1902, shoveling coal as a fireman. It was hot, dirty, and exhausting work, and held little long-term appeal for Merrifield. He dreamed of being an engineer, with a throttle in one hand and waving to children with the other as he passed by, hurtling to a distant location down the track.[2]

Pursuing his career with the railroad, Merrifield followed the Milwaukee Road to Miles City in 1910, just as its new transcontinental line to the Pacific became operational. The Puget Sound Extension required legions of trained men—engineers, firemen, conductors, brakemen, section crews, track laborers, telegraphers, dispatchers, mechanics, and many others—to staff the newly established stations in towns and cities along the line. The Northern Pacific Railway had laid its tracks through Miles City in 1882, and as Miles City businessman Samuel Gordon would describe its arrival in 1918, "It was the incoming of the railroad that called the turn on our primitive life and introduced the manners and customs of the older civilization into our little world." By 1910, however, the Milwaukee Road would lay sole claim to Miles City. Strategically located near the halfway point between Chicago and Tacoma, Miles City was headquarters for the

Milwaukee Road's Trans-Missouri Division, responsible for all company operations from Mobridge, South Dakota, to Harlowton, Montana, a rail distance of about 530 miles. It also had responsibility for an additional three hundred miles of branch lines in Montana and the Dakotas.[3]

Acquiring hundreds of city acres along the Yellowstone River, the company invested millions to build an elegant brick passenger station, a freight depot, warehouses, division offices, boiler shops, and blacksmith and machine shops for servicing and repairing locomotives and the hundreds of passenger and freight cars that operated within the division. A massive brick roundhouse with twenty-four stalls was built for sheltering and servicing a sizable fleet of steam locomotives. Water towers, sand houses, oil houses, coal storage facilities, and a sprawling materials yard fit for a transcontinental railroad were also located within the railyard. To keep the yard powered day and night, the Milwaukee Road built its own coal-fired powerhouse. Its one-hundred-foot-high smokestack could be seen from any part of the city. The coal came from the company-owned Bull Mountain coal strip in Roundup, Montana. At its pinnacle in the 1920s, the Milwaukee Road employed about a thousand residents of Miles City, the most significant employer in town by far.[4]

The Merrifield home, a small, bungalow-style house with a tin roof, was a five-minute walk from the Milwaukee Road railyards, which enveloped Frank's world in a constant din: the hum of the power plant, trains arriving and departing, steam whistles, bells clanging, brakes screeching, the loud bangs of cars being locked together, and the occasional shouts of the railway workers heard over the rest of the noise when the wind was right.

When on duty, Merrifield had to be up early, since the daily eastbound *Olympian* No. 16 pulled into the Miles City station at about five in the morning on its way to Chicago. Merrifield would take the *Olympian* as far as Marmarth, North Dakota, about 128 miles east, and then turn the locomotive over to the next engineer. Merrifield then spent the day in Marmarth before returning home after midnight, piloting westbound *Olympian* No. 15. Merrifield's long days on the rails were hardest on his wife, Marie. Twenty years younger than Frank, she managed the household and the couple's four young children, all under the age of twelve.[5]

Across town from the Merrifield home, George and Rose Hand were in a frenzy of last-minute preparations for a major family celebration. Their youngest daughter, Irene, was getting married in a few days and they would soon have a house full of company, including their eldest daughter, Florence, who lived and worked as a registered nurse in Milwaukee, Wisconsin.

Readying their house for the arrival of guests, Rose was a whirlwind of energy. Fastidious about cleanliness and planning, she always heeded the stern advice that her Swiss mother had given her as a new bride: "When you are having guests for dinner, always have it ready in plenty of time and be rested so when they arrive you won't meet them at the door with a red face and a towel in your hand."[6]

Rose had sent George, a policeman for the Milwaukee Road, scurrying all over Miles City that afternoon with a list of errands and shopping. The Hands were determined to give their youngest daughter a proper send-off. In some ways, Irene's wedding represented the culmination of all that George and Rose had accomplished together in a life that was not without its challenges.

The grandson of Irish immigrants, George grew up in Mobridge, South Dakota, an outpost that transformed into a boomtown when the Milwaukee Road made it the primary staging area for its new Puget Sound Extension rail line in 1907. He went into the meat business with his brother David, and their Hands Butcher Shop found a ready market for its beef and bacon among the army of rail workers. When construction work on the new line wrapped up, however, their fortunes reversed, and the brothers eventually abandoned the business.[7]

George, by now married to Rose and a father to baby Florence, had always dreamed of becoming a farmer. He bought 120 acres of land in McLaughlin, on the west side of the Missouri, but raising crops turned out to be far more difficult than George ever imagined. With better luck, he may have overcome his lack of experience, but bad weather and an unrelenting drought prevented the family from achieving some measure of security. The final blow came when young Irene contracted polio. Driven to bankruptcy, the Hands retreated to family in Mobridge. There, George found work as a nighttime policeman with the Milwaukee Road. It may not have been his dream, but it offered a steady paycheck. He eventually came to appreciate the job, and the Milwaukee Road respected his work ethic and professionalism. The company relocated George to Miles City in the early 1930s.[8]

The Hands bought a large house on East Main Street, a quiet, tree-lined stretch in one of Miles City's older neighborhoods. The five-minute walk downtown included crossing the mainline tracks of the Northern Pacific Railway. To make ends meet, George and Rose converted their home into a boarding house. At any given time, the Hands provided temporary lodging for between six and eight men, most of them railroad workers. Rose cooked for the lodgers and kept the house tidy, charging a fee for meals and a bed.

Located on the west side of town on the banks of the Yellowstone River, the Milwaukee Road railyard was a city within a city, and all of it was George Hand's beat. Unlike the municipal police, he did not wear a uniform or carry a gun. In suit and tie, and always sporting a gray fedora, George patrolled the sprawling railyards by night on foot and in a car. Slim and athletic-looking, the forty-eight-year-old railroad cop cut a dapper figure, looking more like a private detective than a patrolman.

Though money was always tight, the Hands were community-spirited and generous. George often brought home young boys he caught riding freight cars, making sure the stowaways were cleaned up and cared for. He once brought home a twelve-year-old boy, dirty and hungry from riding the cars. As his daughter later recalled, "My father wanted to find his parents, so we took him in, fed him, bathed him, and had him sleep with my twin brothers until his parents could be found—which happened the next day." George Hand was so trusting that he even lent his car to a transient stranger for several days so that the man could fetch his family in Sheridan, Wyoming. Other than George's bitter contempt for bankers and lawyers after his bankruptcy experience, there was "not a mean bone in his body," Irene said of her father.[9]

On Friday, June 17, Irene and her fiancé Byron Roberts had left the Hand home early in the morning for Roundup, Montana, to visit relatives for the weekend. This gave her parents a little more space to get ready for her sister Florence's arrival prior to the wedding, set for the following Wednesday. Florence's new husband, Bernard Maguire, had been unable to get the time off from his job at the Milwaukee Road to attend the wedding, so the oldest Merrifield daughter was traveling by herself. She would be arriving in Miles City on the *Olympian* early Sunday morning, just after midnight.

CHAPTER 5

The *Olympian*

The spring of 1938 marked twenty-seven straight years for the daily *Olympian* run from Chicago to Tacoma, Washington, by far the longest running of any passenger train service on the Milwaukee Road system. The first *Olympian* rolled out with great fanfare on May 28, 1911, heralded by the company as the standard-bearer for long-distance luxury train travel. It was no ordinary train, the company boasted, but rather a ride "Fit for the Gods."[1]

According to company legend, the Milwaukee Road brass had difficulty naming the new transcontinental train. Of the hundreds of names considered, "none seemed to suggest sufficiently the real magnificence of the equipment—its powerful construction, its beauty and its luxury." Then suddenly it came, like a thunderbolt from Zeus himself: *Olympian*. When word spread, the name's adoption was "instantaneous." As the company brochure swooned, "The West never has had a train approaching this one in excellence. The East has none of equal desirability for all classes of travel. There is no other train in East or West approaching this in elegance that does not charge an extra fare."[2]

In 1911, the *Olympian*'s new, all-steel coaches and sleeper cars—built in the company's West Valley Avenue shops—were indeed a big improvement over the creaky wooden cars used by most railroads at the turn of the century. The company's engineers introduced steam heat in all the new train's cars. Gas lamps were out, replaced by electric lights placed in sconces and ceiling fixtures made of real cut glass. Air conditioning was still years away, but the company added electric fans to provide comfort on coaches and in the sleeper berths.

The Milwaukee Road described the sleeper berths as wonderfully comfortable and "homelike." They also touted the spaciousness of the accommodations: "The berths in the sleeping cars—really are higher,—really are wider,—really are longer,—which is tremendously helpful to those passengers who may themselves be a little higher, or a little wider, or a little longer than the average."[3]

Local and long-distance telephone service was another innovation introduced on the 1911 *Olympian*, although connections were only available while the train was stopped at a designated station. Passengers could reserve time to make calls on a telephone located in the lounge-observation car. In an appeal to traveling businessmen, the company offered passengers the option of receiving "Olympiangrams"—short bulletins that included updates on world events, the stock market, and the train schedule—while en route.

In 1911, the company announced that the 2,188-mile trip from Chicago to Tacoma and Seattle would take only seventy-two hours. In the years to come, however, shorter stops, smoother rail, and faster, more reliable locomotives made an even larger dent in that travel time. By 1938, the Milwaukee Road had reduced the duration of the journey to about fifty-eight hours.

In a decidedly unglamorous basement room of Union Station on the morning of June 17, the engineer, fireman, and conductor assigned to take the *Olympian* No. 15 eighty-five miles north to Milwaukee that night huddled together to review weather updates, track conditions, and the latest orders issued by the station's chief dispatcher. After the meeting, they would catch a ride three miles north to the Western Avenue yards to take charge of a class F6 Hudson, a steam locomotive with six driving wheels, that was "getting hot" in the yard's massive roundhouse. It took hours for a bed of coal in a brick-layered firepit of the locomotive to generate enough heat to produce enough steam to move its drive wheels.

Meanwhile, a small, squat locomotive called a "yard goat" had begun to gather, one by one, the scattered individual cars of that evening's

Olympian, coupling them together to form a single, organized train "consist." The arrangement of a train consist—with cars sorted by class, type, and grade—was deliberate and systematic. The locomotive and its tender, laden with fuel and water, was always placed first. Directly behind the locomotive and tender came the U.S. Mail express and baggage cars, called "head-end" cars since they were at the front of the consist. Tourist-class coaches and sleepers followed next. The first-class cars, luxury lounge cars, and Pullman-Standard sleepers were positioned toward the end of the train, as far as possible from the loud, thundering locomotive and the smoke, smells, and dust of its ash plume.

The *Olympian*'s diner car usually sat in the middle of a consist, allowing passengers equal access from the lower-fare tourist coaches and sleepers in the front, and the first-class cars in the rear. The parlor car, also called an observation car, was always at the end. Usually a Pullman-supplied, luxury-style lounge car with large windows, it was reserved for first-class passengers. When the conductor was otherwise occupied, however, coach passengers often snuck through to take in the passing scenery while seated in comfortable swivel chairs.

In 1938, a typical consist for the westbound *Olympian* included eleven cars, not counting the locomotive and tender: one express U.S. Mail car, one baggage car, two tourist coaches (also known as "day cars" or "sitting cars"), three tourist sleeper cars, and the diner car. Two luxury Pullman-Standard sleeper cars and a parlor car brought up the rear. In order to assemble the *Olympian,* the stubby yard goat would have needed to range across the Western Avenue yard that evening to snag the proper cars. Preparing for the westbound departure, the U.S. Mail and the baggage cars were being loaded with thousands of pounds of letters, packages, and passenger luggage for delivery to stations and towns along the route. On a separate track near the yard's commissary, the chief steward of the forty-eight-seat diner car carefully supervised as railroad workers stocked the car with enough food supplies to serve two dinners, three lunches, and three breakfasts for the *Olympian*'s 190 or so passengers and crew. In the Pullman section of the yard, teams cleaned and outfitted the two luxury Pullman-Standard sleepers and the parlor car. The two tourist coach cars and three tourist sleepers owned by the Milwaukee Road underwent the same process on their own sidetrack.

After the yard goat assembled the nine passenger cars of the *Olympian* consist, another yard locomotive took control of the train, slowly pushing the line of cars three miles back to Union Station's north shed. With twilight descending on Chicago, the *Olympian*'s interior car lights were turned on, illuminating the porters and dining car staff while they took care of last-minute details. As the *Olympian* approached the station, a trainman on the back deck of the parlor car used signal flags to help the locomotive engineer, who sat nine cars forward, navigate the remaining distance to the bumper post at the platform. Once the cars were parked at the station, the yard locomotive decoupled from the *Olympian* and chugged back to the service yards.

Next, the conductor made one final review to ensure each car was ready for early boarding. Passengers with sleeper-car reservations could board the *Olympian* at nine in the evening, more than two hours prior to departure. The ceiling lights were dimmed, and the porters hung "Quiet Area" signs at the front and rear end of the cars. Once passengers started boarding, Louis Williams's duties began in earnest, and he had to be "at the ready" during the entire fifty-eight-hour journey. While travelers boarded the sleeper cars, the mail and baggage cars were also pushed back to track nineteen and coupled to the front of the parked *Olympian* passenger cars.

Operating under its own power with its six large drive wheels in reverse, the Hudson steam locomotive and attached tender, filled with twenty tons of coal and fifteen thousand gallons of water—enough for about two hundred miles—was coupled last, at about a quarter to eleven. The westbound *Olympian* No. 15 now stood complete, ready to depart Union Station at precisely fifteen minutes past eleven. With a Hudson at the front, it promised a speedy ride to Milwaukee.

Hudson locomotives were among the strongest, fastest, and most reliable steam locomotives ever used by the Milwaukee Road for its fleet of express passenger trains. The locomotive sped down the rails like a "scared deer," according to Bill Wilkerson, a Miles City–based engineer for the Milwaukee Road and author. "If the Milwaukee class designation 'F' stood for FAST," Wilkerson mused, "they all lived up to their designation." Under the control of a skilled and experienced operator, Wilkerson noted, the "[Hudson] locomotives would really perform."[4]

In fact, on July 20, 1934, a Milwaukee Road–owned Hudson set a world speed record on the eighty-five-mile run from Chicago's Union Station to downtown Milwaukee. Throttle wide open, engineer Bill Dempsey and his Hudson reached speeds of 103 miles per hour and averaged almost 90 miles per hour over long stretches, smashing the previous record by almost 10 miles per hour.[5]

In 1927, the New York Central tested the first prototype, specifically designed to haul longer trains with more passenger cars, on its Albany to Syracuse run along what would become the new engine's namesake river. Impressed by the results, the New York Central ordered a fleet of 195 Hudsons to be built by the American Locomotive Company (ALCO), the most numerous such fleet owned by any railroad company in the nation.[6]

Looking for a more speedy and reliable locomotive, the Milwaukee Road contracted with the Pennsylvania-based Baldwin Locomotive Works for its own Hudsons. By 1938, the Milwaukee Road operated a fleet of twenty-two. First deployed on the Chicago to Minneapolis runs, they were also perfectly suited for the *Olympian*'s 914-mile run between Minneapolis and Harlowton, Montana. It was not unusual for a single Hudson to make the 1,828-mile round-trip run for the *Olympian,* underscoring its durability. In fact, Baldwin boasted that one of its Hudsons completed ten round trips in a month between Minneapolis and Harlowton—more than eighteen thousand track miles—without any days lost for servicing.[7]

The Hudsons were powerful enough to save the Milwaukee Road money by all but eliminating the need to add "helper locomotives" for more pulling power on steeper grades. Helper locomotives were only called to support a Hudson in the event of a severe winter storm, when heavy snow or drifts buried the tracks.

The Hudson was well-suited for pulling up to twelve passenger cars. While the standard daily consist for a westbound *Olympian* was set at eleven, seasonal demand could increase the size of the consist by a few additional cars. Also, during nice weather in summer, the Milwaukee Road added a twelfth car to the rear of an *Olympian,* an open-sided observation car for the spectacular trip over the mountains of Montana and Idaho. When a train had more than twelve passenger cars, the Milwaukee Road would bring in its new, larger, more powerful Northern locomotive, called an S2, which had eight driving wheels compared to the Hudson's six. Given that the June 17, 1938, westbound *Olympian* would not include an observation car in its consist, a Hudson would be making the run.[8]

CHAPTER 6

First Stop: Milwaukee

Friday, June 17, 1938

> Suddenly, the train—slowly from under
> the web of city streets, the ramps, the streaming cars:
> slowly, like a great beast gathering in its black length the thunder
> to hurtle away into the dark countryside under stars
>
> —August Derleth, "The Milwaukee Road"[1]

With reservations on the Choteau, one of the *Olympian*'s tourist sleepers, the Clancy women were among the first of about 150 passengers to board the *Olympian*. For some passengers, especially families with young children and older folks, the 11:00 P.M. departure time might have seemed late. These travelers especially would have found the option to board up to two hours in advance a welcome convenience.

An "indicator board" at the entrance of their gate in Union Station welcomed passengers and listed the train's scheduled stops. Just beyond, a reservations clerk sitting at a small portable stand checked tickets and directed them to their train car. As specified in the Pullman rulebook, Louis Williams and his fellow porters stood next to the fold-down stairs at the entry door of each car, lending a hand to each passenger as they boarded, careful to "avoid a poor appearance, such as leaning on cars, hands in pockets, etc." Union Station redcaps and other porters assisted with carry-on luggage and showed passengers to their seats or sleeping berths.[2]

Serving as something of a combination between a valet, bellhop, janitor, and concierge, Williams spent the next hour guiding passengers to their berths in sleeper C, carrying their luggage, and settling them into their new home for the two-day-plus ride to Tacoma. The Pullman bible specified that all porters "call the passenger's attention to all of the berth ventilation controls and to all facilities in rooms, such as individual ventilation controls, folding beds, toilet facilities, etc., and explain their operation." Williams also would have been expected to "inform the passenger of the club, lounge, observation, or dining facilities available and mention the hours these facilities are available and their location in the train."[3]

A line immediately formed to use the ladies' lounge, as many passengers changed into their pajamas and started getting ready for bed. In the cars, "quiet" signs hung on fasteners at each end of the partition facing the end door or in the hallway. They would remain up until seven in the morning and then would be rehung at nine each night. An hour later, it was Williams's duty to dim the inside ceiling lamps, taking care himself to be especially quiet, as many passengers chose to settle into their berths and go to sleep before the train departed.[4]

Having woken up before dawn and spent a full day in Chicago, Kate, Nell, and Margie Clancy were undoubtedly eager to settle into their berths on the Choteau. Likewise, the Lallas family was relieved to make their final boarding for home, with seats reserved in the designated smoking car to accommodate Tom's cigarette habit. In tourist coach 420, which sat just ahead of the Ipswich, a sleeper car, the family shared four coach seats that faced each other. Before everyone got too comfortable, Esther took Anna, John, and George for a final bathroom visit before bed. With everyone covered in blankets and the coach car lights dimmed, the Lallas family was ready for sleep.[5]

The Hanscom twins were likely among the last passengers to board the *Olympian* that evening. Friday marked the beginning of their summer break from college, and they presumably would have made the most of their day sightseeing around Chicago. Upon arriving at the platform, the Hanscoms were directed to the Choteau, the same tourist sleeper as the Clancys, under the care of porter Robert Nolan.

The *Olympian* was ready to depart. The indicator lights on the platform turned from yellow to green, prompting the conductor to call out "all aboard" and swing his lantern in a wide arc from his knee to his head for the locomotive crew to see. Following two short blasts of the Hudson's steam whistle, the engineer released the brakes and, with a steady hand, eased the throttle open. In a cloud of smoke and steam, with pistons chugging slowly at first, then rhythmically, the six large drive wheels of the Hudson turned and gained speed as it headed north toward Milwaukee.

Given the sprawling Union Station yards and the web of tracks connecting Chicago's multiple train stations with the rest of North America, the Hudson locomotive's full capabilities had to be restrained until the train was about twenty miles north. With the city lights fading in the distance and open track ahead, the engineer could signal the fireman to lay on the steam so that he could open the throttle and accelerate to a cruising speed of about sixty-five miles per hour.

It would be a straight shot to Milwaukee for the *Olympian* that night. Known as the "Velvet Line" by passengers, the eighty-five-mile journey between Chicago and Milwaukee enjoyed a reputation as the smoothest of any railroad. The well-worn track and gentle rocking of the cars as the train sped north created the perfect conditions for the tired passengers to sleep. As many Milwaukee Road employees knew, the *Olympian* would soon bring them past the site of one of the nation's last great train robberies. In the dark of night on June 12, 1924, the notorious Newton Gang robbed a Milwaukee Road–operated train near the town of Rondout at gunpoint and made off with $3 million in cash (about $45.4 million today). The bandits were soon caught and most of the money was retrieved, except for the roughly $100,000 that Jess Newton had buried near San Antonio, Texas. On his way to Mexico, Newton got so drunk in local bars that he forgot where he buried the cash. The money has never been found.[6]

Just after midnight, the train crossed the state line into Wisconsin, closing in fast on the birthplace of the Milwaukee Road railroad company. In the 1830s, tired of the rutted dirt roads that plagued the small community of Milwaukee, and that threatened its future growth, a small group of local businessmen banded together to examine transportation options. At that time, people living in the interior of the country relied on water routes—rivers, lakes, and man-made canals—to transport goods. These businessmen, however, came up with an ambitious plan to spur Milwaukee's expansion and boost its prosperity: they would build a rail line from the shores of Lake Michigan to the Mississippi River, about 185 miles due west. Gaining access to a major water route like the Mississippi River promised to open a host of new business and trade opportunities for the enterprising citizens of Milwaukee. It was a grand idea, albeit one that was a decade or two ahead of its time. In 1830, only twenty-three miles of railroad track had been built in the United States. By 1840, this number would increase to 2,800 miles of rail, then to 9,000 miles by 1850, most of it in the eastern and southern parts of the country. Time, however, was of the essence: Milwaukee was the fastest-growing settlement in Wisconsin Territory, and its community leaders were fiercely competitive with their urban neighbor to the south, Chicago. "If we build the first [rail line] and get to the Mississippi first, Chicago will not dare approach our territory," insisted Byron Kilbourne, an early mayor of Milwaukee and leader in the effort to establish a rail system in the territory. Transportation was in Kilbourne's blood. A well-educated son of an Ohio congressman, he was also the son-in-law of John Fitch, an early inventor of the steamboat.[7]

Kilbourne's vision was finally realized on Wednesday, April 15, 1857. On a fine spring day, hundreds of people gathered in the small western outpost of Prairie du Chien, on the eastern bank of the Mississippi, to watch the first passenger train from Milwaukee arrive in a choking cloud of ash, cinders, and smoke. A local artillery company marked the moment with a two-hundred-gun salute. A *Milwaukee Journal and Sentinel* editorial cheered the occasion: "So opens the first link of the iron chain which is to connect us to the Mississippi. May two years hence see it stretched across the State!"[8]

Appropriately christened the *Prairie du Chien*, the steam-powered locomotive completed its 185-mile journey pulling three passenger cars, a luggage car, and an eight-gallon keg of water from Lake Michigan.[9] To the great enjoyment of the cheering crowd, the celebration that evening included pouring the keg into the Mississippi, symbolically merging the great lake with the mighty river.[10]

Despite this triumph, Kilbourne's leadership proved turbulent for the Milwaukee & Prairie du Chien Railroad, an early predecessor of the Milwaukee Road, with the entire business almost lost in an ugly financial scandal. Shortly after the American Civil War came to an end, a brighter future for the struggling company arrived in the form of Alexander Mitchell. A financier and on-again, off-again member of the railroad's board of directors, Mitchell was selected to replace the erratic Kilbourne as president. For a company seeking stability and growth, the astute and even-keeled Mitchell was just what it needed.

Once at the helm, Mitchell pursued acquisitions and favorable mergers for the fledgling railroad with a focused intensity. After securing ownership of railways leading to the Twin Cities of Minneapolis and St. Paul, Minnesota, the newly renamed Milwaukee & St. Paul Railroad was the Midwest's largest by 1867, controlling about 820 miles of track. Mitchell's efforts to grow the railroad soon became the stuff of legend. In one instance, after learning that a bank in his native Scotland held the controlling shares of a crucial railway, he boarded an ocean liner to Glasgow and shortly thereafter took control of the company. In his first four years as president, Mitchell almost tripled the railroad's size, to 2,300 miles by 1870. The *Chicago Post* sang Mitchell's praises as a businessman and referred to him with the sobriquet "Alexander the Great."[11]

Determined to keep the railroad growing and independently owned, Mitchell pursued a line to Chicago. In early 1873, the company accomplished this goal and soon added to its name, becoming the Chicago, Milwaukee & St. Paul Railway (CMSP). By 1880, CMSP passenger and freight trains ran an astonishing eleven million miles annually on the 3,775 miles of track now controlled by the railroad. By any standard, Mitchell's railroad was now a major player in the industry.

At Mitchell's direction, the company built a Gothic-style station in downtown Milwaukee, a three-story brick fortress with elegant granite facings that was completed in 1886. Locals referred to the building—officially named the Milwaukee Union Depot—as the Everett Street Depot since the main entrance of the station was on West Everett Street. Like many rail stations built in the late nineteenth century, it was in the heart of the city, with the beautiful Fourth Ward Park on its north side. It was a refined space, even for the Milwaukee Road employees, whose offices took up most of the second floor. One observer noted that "never before did train-dispatchers have more comfortable or beautiful quarters."[12]

ON June 18, 1938, the massive oak doors with stained-glass windows at the Milwaukee Union Depot swung open just after midnight, and in walked twenty-four-year-old Florence Maguire. Her husband, Bernard, who had insisted on driving his new wife to the station at this late hour and helping her check her luggage, followed. The tall, dark-haired nurse was on her way to Miles City to attend the wedding of her younger sister, Irene.

Both Florence and Bernard had deep family ties to the railroad industry, and to the Milwaukee Road in particular. Florence traced her roots to McLaughlin and Mobridge, South Dakota, both railroad towns founded by the Milwaukee Road. Long before her father, George, took a job as a policeman with the Milwaukee Road, Florence's grandfather on her mother's side, Charles Haffeman, helped build the company's first bridge across the Missouri in 1907, setting the stage for the Puget Sound Extension.

Bernard grew up in Butte, Montana, the location of the massive Anaconda copper mines. When his father became ill and unable to work, Bernard dropped out of high school to help support his family. He became an apprentice electrician for the Milwaukee Road, a job that would take him to Miles City, where he met Florence.

Florence had been on the path to become a nurse since she was ten years old. Her mother, Rose, had been forced to quit school after the third grade to help support her struggling family in Wisconsin by working in a glove factory. Rose, whose first language was German, was determined that all her children would get a full education and secure respectable employment. Florence's younger sister, Irene, remembered sitting by their coal-burning stove in McLaughlin, South Dakota, when suddenly her mother declared, "You're all going to college!" in her broken English. Rose wanted Florence to be a nurse, naming her after Florence Nightingale, the founder of modern nursing. Rose also chose Florence's middle name—

Gilles, the patron saint of the disabled and needy—purposefully. Irene, meanwhile, was to be a schoolteacher.[13]

After three years of training at Miles City's Holy Rosary Clinic, Florence passed her exams to become a registered nurse in 1934 and was soon a supervisor at the county hospital. Friends in Miles City introduced her to the handsome Bernard Maguire, a tall man with a quick wit and a big smile to match. They fell in love and married in February 1938. It was not uncommon for women in the 1930s to lose their jobs if their employers discovered they were married or pregnant, so Bernard and Florence kept their marriage secret for as long as possible.[14]

That same year, Bernard was offered a better paying position for the railroad in the refrigeration section of Milwaukee's West Valley Shop Yards, so the newlyweds soon packed up and moved to Wisconsin. In Milwaukee, with both Bernard and Florence in stable jobs with respectable employers, Florence Hand proudly became Florence Maguire.[15]

While Bernard's job prevented him from traveling to Irene's Montana wedding, it did have the perk—enjoyed by Milwaukee Road employees and their families—of a free round-trip pass for Florence. A round-trip ticket in coach from Milwaukee to Miles City cost $35.30 in 1938. Florence did not mind riding coach, since the trip would only take about twenty-four hours. Besides, it had been a long day. Before heading to the station that night, she had worked a full shift at Milwaukee's Misericordia Hospital, a care facility for unwed mothers founded by Canadian nuns. Florence would not have trouble finding sleep.

As the Maguires waited in the station on that quiet June night, the *Olympian* could be heard long before it appeared in downtown Milwaukee, its distant steam whistle blasts signaling its arrival. The locomotive engineer used the air horn sparingly given the late hour. With the bell on the front of the locomotive clanging rhythmically, the eleven-car *Olympian* snaked through the downtown intersections, the ground rumbling under the weight of the Hudson locomotive and its attached tender. The hands of the large, illuminated clock atop the station's 160-foot-high brick tower read ten minutes to one o'clock, as the *Olympian,* wheels squealing, slid under the station's six-hundred-foot-long train shed. Supported by iron columns and girders, the shed covered five tracks and platforms and protected passengers and trains from the elements.

The *Olympian* was scheduled to arrive in Miles City early Sunday morning, at about a quarter to one in the morning. Despite the hour, Florence's parents had told her that they, along with her younger twin brothers, Clarence and Bill, would be at the station to meet her. The family's excitement over her return was clear, and her arrival would be an early Father's Day treat for George. But reunions were a day away. For now, Florence and Bernard said goodbye.

CHAPTER 7

Nothing Faster

Saturday, June 18, 1938

Once the *Olympian* arrived in Milwaukee after its short eighty-five-mile run, the locomotive and train crew—including the engineer, fireman, and conductor—was changed out in a scheduled stop that lasted ten minutes. Depending on the season and the number of reservations, additional sleeper cars were sometimes added to the *Olympian* in Milwaukee, but no additional cars were added on the night of June 18.

On the boarding platform, Florence Maguire presented her ticket to an agent, who then directed her to tourist coach 420, the same car where the Lallas family was seated. Behind coach 420—the second passenger car in the *Olympian*'s consist—were three tourist sleeper cars: the Ipswich, the Choteau, and sleeper C, porter Louis Williams's car.

Also boarding the *Olympian* in Milwaukee were seventeen-year-old Warren "Buck" Jones and his ten-year-old cousin John Baxter. The two boys were headed to Harlowton, Montana, to spend the summer on their grandparents' ranch, located just outside of the small town of Two Dot. The June train trip had become an annual ritual for Jones since his parents had moved to Milwaukee from Montana when he was in elementary school. The cousins were going to be riding in style, since Jones's father had booked them reservations on a Pullman sleeper as a graduation gift for his son. Just a week earlier, he had graduated from Shorewood High School in Milwaukee. In the fall, he planned to attend Dartmouth College in Hanover, New Hampshire. Unbeknownst to Jones, two current Dartmouth students, Dean and Don Hanscom, occupied the tourist sleeper two cars forward.[1]

During boarding, the aisle lights of the *Olympian*'s cars dimmed so as not to disturb the sleeping passengers. Moments after a porter showed Jones and Baxter to their berth and Florence Maguire had settled into her coach seat, two blasts of the locomotive's steam whistle signaled it was time for departure. Gaining speed, the train followed the Menomonee River out of the downtown area and within minutes glided past the historic epicenter of the Milwaukee Road's construction and maintenance yards, originally known as the West Milwaukee shops and later referred to as their Menomonee Valley shops. The company had built its reputation as a competitive, innovative, and forward-thinking railroad in this gritty industrial area. For years, some of the fastest steam locomotives in the world came out of the Menomonee Valley shops. In 1892, engineers from the Milwaukee Road's predecessor company, the Chicago, Milwaukee & St. Paul Railway, figured out a way to use locomotive steam as a source of heat for its passenger cars. Later, it would be one of the first railroads to introduce electric lights in all its passenger cars. The company's engineering and technological innovations set the industry standard for decades.

In 1935, the Milwaukee Road advanced its reputation as an industry leader by introducing a new passenger line that surpassed even the *Olympian*'s reputation for speed and luxury. That spring, tapping into nostalgia for American Indian symbolism, the company introduced one of the first streamlined passenger trains in the United States: the *Hiawatha*. Named after the "swift of foot" hero in Henry Wadsworth Longfellow's 1855 poem, "Song of Hiawatha," it became the Milwaukee's Road's best-known passenger train, living up to the advertising boast, "Nothing faster on rails."[2]

Initially, the company used oil-fired Atlantic locomotives with four driving wheels to pull the *Hiawatha*. An Atlantic could attain a cruising speed of one hundred miles per hour or more during its daily run between Chicago and Minneapolis, lightning fast for a 1930s passenger train. Adding more passenger cars to keep up with the popularity of the route, the company eventually turned to the larger and stronger coal-fired Hudson locomotives, with six driving wheels, to maintain speeds over one hundred miles per hour while pulling ever more passenger cars.[3] The Milwaukee Road could accurately boast that its *Hiawatha* offered the fastest scheduled steam-powered passenger service in the world.

Besides speed, the *Hiawatha* owned the cool factor among competing railroads with its stylish and colorful trains. The company tapped Otto Kuhler, a rising star among industrial designers in the early 1930s and a contemporary of Henry Dreyfuss, to lead the design team. Kuhler convinced the conservative, buttoned-down company leaders to forego the traditional black locomotive in favor of an aerodynamic, silver-gray design with orange and maroon striping. Kuhler covered the entire locomotive with a metal shroud. The bullet-nosed locomotive design also featured silver wings with the number of the engine prominently displayed just below the recessed headlight. A large metal sign reading "The Milwaukee Road" was riveted to the rounded nose of the locomotive. Kuhler had no patience for those confused by the train's appearance: "I did get disgusted every time an uninitiated person asked me, 'Is that a diesel?'" Kuhler also redesigned the observation car, adding a sloped aerodynamic design featuring a multitude of windows for stunning rear-facing views. The company dubbed it the "Beaver Tail."[4]

The Menomonee Valley shops built fifty custom passenger cars for the *Hiawatha*—painted orange and crimson—to match its streamlined locomotive design. Using steel and aluminum alloys, the cars were designed to be substantially lighter in weight than typical passenger cars to help the locomotive maintain the record speeds of its service. Last but not least, Milwaukee Road designers introduced the first stand-up cocktail bar on its *Hiawatha* run, the Tip Top Tap Room. The bar became wildly popular, so much so that within a few years it was moved from a back parlor car into its own specially designed car with porthole windows at the front of the train.[5]

Once out of downtown Milwaukee, the tracks for the *Olympian* turned sharply west toward Minneapolis. Parts of the rail route the *Olympian* followed that night was hallowed ground for the company, running across the original mid-1800s path of the Milwaukee & Mississippi. About eighty miles west of Milwaukee, at about half past two in the morning, the westbound *Olympian* sped past Rio, Wisconsin, site of a terrible Milwaukee

Road train accident half a century earlier. It seems that bad luck followed the tiny town from its beginning. When newcomers, coming mostly from the Ohio Valley, settled the village in the 1860s, they petitioned the U.S. government for a post office under the name Ohio. Government bureaucrats either misread the name, or the ink was smudged, merging the first two letters together into what appeared to be an "R," thus the villagers got their new post office: Rio. The town fathers were aghast and tried to save face by insisting that Rio be pronounced rye-oh.[6]

In the early morning darkness of October 28, 1886, an eastbound Milwaukee Road *Limited* express passenger train traveling about forty-five miles per hour just east of Rio hit a track switch that had mistakenly been left open. The open switch caused the train to suddenly veer off the main track and onto a siding track occupied by a parked freight train that had been waiting for the *Limited* to pass. At full speed, the *Limited* plowed into the freight train, causing its locomotive to derail and its wooden passenger cars, lit with kerosene lamps and warmed with wood stoves, to slam into each other. An open stove door in the baggage car spilled out hot coals and embers, immediately setting the baggage car aflame, which quickly engulfed many other cars in a raging inferno. The violent impact and conflagration killed at least sixteen passengers, most of them pinned inside their cars with no chance of getting out. Passengers in the sleeper cars at the end of the train escaped with cuts and bruises. The railroad struggled to determine precisely how many died in the accident, since the intense fire burned some of the victims beyond recognition.

Newspaper reports indicated that the parked freight train's conductor, H. C. Hankey, was so distraught by the crash and burning passengers that he took to the nearby woods only to be found hours later raving like a madman. The *Chicago Tribune* reported that Hankey was "likely to become a hopeless maniac" because of the accident. The twenty-four-year-old brakeman for the freight train, B. H. Wells, responsible for closing the switch in time, also went missing after the accident, but was found the next day when he tried to draw his salary in Milwaukee. Wells was blamed and immediately jailed for the incident.[7]

Within hours, the company dispatched General Assistant Albert J. Earling to Rio to oversee recovery efforts. Earling, an ambitious man and a rising star within the company, would be appointed president of the Milwaukee Road in 1899. It was during Earling's tenure as president that engineer Frank Merrifield found employment at the Milwaukee Road, eventually becoming certified as an engineer. He would spend the rest of his days passing by towns named for Earling's children and grandchildren.

Not long after the *Olympian* No. 15 sped past Rio, duty called for engineer Frank Merrifield about one thousand miles to the west in Miles City, Montana. The ring of a bedside alarm clock at three in the morning is always cruel, but Merrifield was scheduled to captain the eastbound *Olympian* No. 16 passenger train on its 124-mile run to Marmarth, North Dakota. It was a routine trip for Merrifield; he had held the throttle for many a steam locomotive on the leg to Marmarth and back.

Pulled by a Hudson locomotive, the Chicago-bound *Olympian* No. 16 had departed Harlowton, Montana, at about half past midnight and was scheduled to arrive in Miles City at five in the morning. Merrifield needed to sign on for duty at the yard at least an hour earlier to give him time to talk with the dispatcher on duty and to review any train orders that could affect the trip to Marmarth. Train orders provided important information for the engineer and conductor about track conditions, weather, schedule delays, and other issues on the route.

Merrifield could walk from his home to the station in about five minutes. His tree-lined neighborhood of small, tidy bungalows was bounded by two major railroad tracks traversing eastern Montana: the Milwaukee Road tracks on the northwest side, near the Yellowstone River, and the Northern Pacific tracks to the southeast. In fact, his house was so close to the Milwaukee Road tracks that his windows would occasionally rattle as freight and passenger trains rumbled through town.

The sun rises early in eastern Montana in mid-June, just ahead of the summer solstice, but it was still dark when Merrifield stepped onto his front porch. The weather forecast predicted another day of unusually high temperatures—in the upper eighties and low nineties—for all of eastern Montana, with the possibility of rain and thunderstorms later in the day and into the evening.

Merrifield wore the typical engineer's uniform for a day's work: heavily starched bib overalls over a white or blue starched shirt. The starch protected the clothing from permanent grease and oil stains. Many engineers and firemen wore trousers underneath the overalls for greater protection against any errant hot cinders that could fly out of the firebox. Heavy, black boots protected their feet and were often rendered dull with grease and dirt after years of use. Tradition called for engineers to wear a red or blue bandana tied around the neck and pulled over the mouth and nose if noxious smoke or steam filled the cab. Goggles and large leather gloves also provided vital protection for crew members. Finally, the Kromer cap signified the engineer's status as captain of the train. Like a tree's rings, the stains on Merrifield's cap marked his many years on the job.

The only noise in the train yard at that early hour was the cheery trilling of bands of Allard ground crickets, forewarning warm temperatures to come. In the small dispatcher's office inside the main station, Merrifield and his fireman and partner, Hausmer McCoy, reported for official duty. The dispatcher and telegrapher then briefed the two men on the schedule, weather, status of the eastbound *Olympian,* and any outstanding change orders that could affect the 124-mile trip to Marmarth.

Hausmer McCoy and his wife Della (Knouf) had two daughters, Betty Lou and Ardella. Like the Merrifields, the McCoys had lived in Miles City for many years. They owned a small farm on North Custer Avenue, within spitting distance of the Milwaukee Road yards. During the growing season, the McCoys sold fresh produce in the local markets, a side business that helped the family get through tough financial times in the 1930s. Pushing sixty, McCoy was considered a railroad old-timer. He had secured his license to be a locomotive fireman for the Milwaukee Road on September 5, 1910. Six years after this "firing date," he successfully punched his engineer's ticket. But twenty-two years later, in 1938, McCoy was still shoveling coal. Stuck at number sixty-nine in seniority for engineers operating out of Miles City at that time, McCoy labored under a system still recovering from the Depression. In 1918, an optimistic McCoy had listed his occupation as a railroad engineer on his World War I draft registration card, but he was destined to serve his time out on the rails in the left seat of the cab, firing locomotives, not driving them.[8]

Eastbound *Olympian* No. 16 rumbled into Miles City at about five in the morning, the chugging pistons and drive wheels of the Hudson overwhelming the sound of the crickets. The scheduled stop was for ten minutes, time enough for the crew to be changed out and the locomotive to be handed off to Merrifield and McCoy.

The two men approached the massive locomotive in the morning twilight, making their way through vapor dense with oil and grease and past the six drive wheels that matched their height. They exchanged greetings with the departing cab crew over the gasping steam bursts of the idling 335-ton locomotive. Since the firebox on a hot locomotive was never left unattended, McCoy was first to climb up the steel steps into the cab to check its temperature and the vital steam levels. Like all engineers, Merrifield did a walk-around check of the locomotive, looking for unusual leaks or damaged pipes and valves.

While Merrifield was inspecting his Hudson locomotive in Miles City, another routine inspection was taking place twenty-six miles north—on horseback.

CHAPTER 8

Prairie Monarch

Haughian Ranch, Saturday, June 18, 1938

Dan Haughian Jr. started sweating early on June 18 as he and his horse trotted the dirt paths crisscrossing his sprawling property. Temperatures had soared into the low nineties the day before, and he expected this day to be just as hot. As the sun rose, the humidity stood at about 85 percent. Near the river, the air felt even thicker.

The day's first task for Haughian and Francis Motherhead was to fire up the irrigation pumps and get water to the crops before the heat reached its full intensity that afternoon. A full day's work lay ahead, but that evening promised a reprieve from their labors. The two men, along with Dan's sister Kathleen, had been invited to a dinner and square dance that night in Kinsey. They anticipated a lively Saturday night, followed by a poignant Sunday: Father's Day. Dan Haughian Sr. died from cancer at age fifty-six, years before, but his presence still loomed large in the younger Dan's life. Everything Dan Jr. knew about ranching, horsemanship, and being a man came from his father. The loss left a void.

Born in 1876 to Alexander and Bridget (Doran) Haughian, Daniel Haughian Sr. came into the world shortly before famine gripped his parents' native Ireland. While less severe than the two that preceded it, the 1879 blight nevertheless caused widespread hunger and panic, sparking another wave of emigration. The Haughians remained behind, but Dan Sr. would never forget the hardships his family faced. In his early twenties, he struck out on his own, eventually arriving by boat in Yakima, Washington, where his younger brother Alex soon joined him. Their experience on the family farm in Ireland allowed Alex and Dan to find day work on a large sheep ranch. Before long, the brothers grew restless, tired of receiving poor wages and toiling under someone else's thumb. Acting on a tip from Irish relatives, Dan Sr. made his way to eastern Montana. Arriving in Miles City, he soon acquired a piece of land, fulfilling a lifelong dream of having greater control over his livelihood. For $120, Haughian took ownership of forty acres from a Civil War veteran named H. A. Smith. The land was remote, about forty miles north of Miles City nestled at the base of Little Sheep Mountain, but it included access to fresh water and a small three-room log cabin.[1]

On September 5, 1901, Haughian moved into his new cabin. The ranch sat below the slightly smaller of two 3,500-foot peaks that comprise the Big Sheep Mountains, Montana's easternmost range. Nearby were the headwaters of Custer Creek, named after General George Armstrong Custer, which flowed—like all the other creeks and washes in the area—into the Yellowstone River.[2]

Within a few years, Dan Haughian Sr. had grown his own sizable sheep herds. He sent a letter to his brother, asking him to join him in Montana to help build his business. Alex answered the call, a decision that almost cost him his life. During a freak snowstorm in March 1904, Alex lost his way while herding sheep and went missing for two days and nights. Dan Sr. found his brother buried in a snowbank, half-alive and suffering severe frostbite to his lower legs, and immediately took him to the Miles City hospital by horse-drawn wagon. Traveling the forty miles of rutted dirt roads lying in the back of a buckboard wagon must have been agonizing for Alex, but Dan Sr. saved his brother's life. Alex spent six weeks recuperating in the hospital, losing the heels on both feet to frostbite and gangrene. He recovered enough to return to work for Dan Sr., but from then on served as a foreman instead of a herder.[3]

Lonely on his isolated ranch, Dan Sr. longed for the company of a woman. Before sailing to America, he had become engaged to Maggie Quinn, the daughter of a neighbor. With his ranch established, he set off back to Ireland to marry his beloved and bring her to Montana. He had already crossed the ocean and reached Irish soil before hearing the news that Maggie, tired of waiting for his return, had married another man. Dumbstruck but unwilling to return to America without a wife, Dan Haughian Sr. made the practical decision to court Maggie's younger sister, Susan. He soon proposed to her, and she immediately accepted.[4]

Born in 1887, Susan Mary Quinn was one of sixteen children born to Henry and Susan (Fitzpatrick) Quinn of Kilkeel. Her father was a successful businessman, and the Quinn family employed maids to help with the washing, cleaning, and ironing in their large house.

Shortly thereafter, Dan Sr. returned to Montana and waited for his new bride to join him. Both crossed the Atlantic on the immigrant ocean liner SS *Parisian*, which for almost thirty years made regular runs between Liverpool, England, and Montreal, Canada. Susan arrived in Montreal in October 1905 and spent a week traveling cross-country by rail. In the afternoon of October 31, a weary eighteen-year-old Mrs. Susan Haughian stepped off the Northern Pacific in Miles City, Montana. Little had prepared her for what she saw: rough-looking cowboys, wranglers, bootleggers, and thugs roamed the streets looking for a good time in the many bars, saloons, and brothels that made up the ramshackle downtown. According to family lore, her first words upon arrival were, "Good Lord! What have I done?"[5]

Fortunately, Susan's new husband waited to whisk her away to their ranch in the mountains. Still, her first impressions were not exactly glowing. "My husband hired a team and lumber wagon and filled it with grub," she later recalled, "which I found out meant beans, peas, ham, bacon, canned milk, dried fruit etc. The distance to the ranch . . . seemed endless. We never saw a person or a house on that long, long trail."[6]

With only the company of her husband and his small band of shy sheep herders, the early days of Susan's new life at the Little Sheep Mountain ranch were quiet. Remarking on the wild, open prairie that surrounded the ranch, she quipped, "My husband must have felt like Robinson Crusoe 'I am monarch of all I survey.'"[7]

Small groups of Crow Indians passed by the ranch occasionally during their seaonal rounds in fall and spring. The Haughians' interactions with the Crows were limited, due to the language barrier, but always peaceful.

Susan offered them water and food as a gesture of goodwill. The mail route from Miles City to Jordan, Montana, also went by their ranch. As an enticement to get the mailman to stop and share news from Miles City, Susan would offer him refreshments as he passed by in his horse-drawn wagon.

Life in eastern Montana was a far cry from the life that Susan knew in Ireland. For warmth, the family burned buffalo chips. For washing, they poured lye in the bottom of the water barrel to soften the water enough to create suds. For breadmaking, they bought flour by the ton in Miles City and hauled it forty miles back to the ranch. None of these hardships deterred the Haughians, who immediately set out to start a family. In late 1906, Susan gave birth to their first child, Bridget Teresa. Over the next twelve years, nine more followed, resulting in a brood of five boys and five girls. About a month before each birth, Dan gently loaded his pregnant wife into a horse-drawn wagon and made the daylong trip to the Miles City hospital so that she could give birth surrounded by caregivers.[8]

By 1915, with eight children ranging in age from six months to ten years, Susan lorded over a sprawling ranch home with eight rooms. The Haughians made improvements, adding a new system to light their enlarged home. Carbide lumps placed in water formed a gas that pipes carried to light fixtures throughout the house, where it was lit and burned a flame. "It was rather a dangerous method of lighting," Susan observed.[9]

Eager for social activity, the Haughians built a new barn in 1915, and soon the Little Sheep Mountain ranch became known for hosting parties and dances on Saturday nights. "All the neighbors came to dances, for miles around," recalled Susan. "We had old-time fiddlers, danced many different dances, had jugs of whiskey, big boilers of coffee, sandwiches in washtubs and danced until the sun came up, as the people came in wagons and horseback and could see their way home after daylight."[10]

Like the Haughians, their neighbors were among the tens of thousands of settlers who had streamed into eastern Montana to take ownership of cheap and plentiful land and seize a chance at a new life. Aggressive promotional efforts by the federal government and the railroads themselves had lured waves of newcomers onto the prairie around the turn of the century. Pamphlets filled with hyperbole and half-truths promised homesteaders an idyllic future under the Big Sky. Published in 1900, the Great Northern Railway's "Homeseeker's Guide" for Montana boasted, "The wind never blows when the temperature goes low in Montana. The recorded mean annual temperature of the state is 48 degrees. The average rainfall is twenty inches. Three fourths of the days are bright and sunny, and a great part of the year is characterized by the very perfection of weather."[11]

These promotions worked. In 1909, the General Land Office (GLO) in Miles City recorded 1,200 homestead claims in a single month. At the peak in 1918, more than 14,000 claims were filed on over 3.2 million acres. Half of the newcomers had no farming experience at all, and one-quarter of the homesteaders arriving in the early 1900s were foreign-born.[12]

For a time, conditions in Montana lived up to the rosy promises. This period, known as the "wet years," delivered enough rain to sustain farming and ranching on the dry eastern prairie. In 1917, however, an unrelenting drought started along Montana's Hi-Line, the corridor along the state's northernmost east-west rail line, eventually overtaking about two-thirds of the eastern part of the state by the following year. The summer of 1919 was especially hot and dry, heralding a cruel weather pattern that would largely grip the area for more than a decade, making crop failures common. During this period, the outbreak of World War I and, later, the onset of the Great Depression added to the already overwhelming strain of life on the inhospitable prairie for many families.

On trips to Miles City to get food and supplies, Dan and Susan Haughian passed clusters of homesteader families laboring desperately to claw out a life in the unforgiving, windswept badlands. "The tar-papered shacks were of one layer of boards, roofs shingled or tar-papered, and some had linoleum on the floors," Susan recalled. "The winter cold was so hard on them with the thinly boarded houses."[13]

If battling the weather and isolation wasn't enough, pests and predators took their toll. Bands of wolves and coyotes raided homesteaders' livestock, killing lambs, calves, chickens, and even their family pets. Swarms of grasshoppers ravaged fields and crops. Farmers became desperate, acquiring turkeys by the thousands to eat the insects, but the gobbler experiment failed. Some took a scorched earth approach, incinerating their fields. Still, the grasshoppers came back. Local officials in Prairie

County promoted a poison mash to stop the pests, encouraging farmers to mix bran, arsenic, banana oil, salt, and molasses and spread it around their crops and field. The stench turned out to be more offensive to humans than grasshoppers.[14]

Susan saw the grasshoppers as the last straw for many of her neighbors. Homesteader gardens, she noted, "saved the day for many until the grasshoppers came. They darkened the sun in five minutes and could be seen for a long way up in the sky. They even chewed holes in the shovel and pitchfork handles. Mostly, they didn't stay very long, but could do a lot of crop damage in a short while."[15]

Hundreds of land claims were abandoned by their original owners between 1910 and 1930. By then, 80 percent of the homesteads in eastern Montana had failed. The Haughian family, however, stood among those that remained. As other homesteaders fled, the Haughians bought as much abandoned land as they could afford, gradually accumulating sizable holdings for their expanding herds of sheep, cattle, and horses. In time, the Haughian property spread across 240,000 acres.[16]

For more than three decades, the Haughians had endured Montana's merciless climate. Today's hot, dry weather might be concerning, but Dan Jr. would be damned if he let it get the better of him.

CHAPTER 9

Highball

Miles City Station, Saturday, June 18, 1938

Partners for years, Frank Merrifield and Hausmer McCoy worked well together. The three-hour, 124-mile eastbound journey to Marmarth, North Dakota, was a milk run for them. The mainline track was straightforward: no particularly challenging grades, no urban centers to navigate, and only a couple of major bridges over the Yellowstone River to cross.

In their earlier days, the duo could leap up the metal stairs to the cab of the locomotive, but time and age had conspired against them both. The vertical stairs—like climbing up to a steel treehouse—had become a challenge. It was an awkward ascent for Merrifield, with his left hand in a death grip around the spindly metal handrail and his right hand hooked over the stairs. McCoy, already in the cab tending to the firebox, would have extended a hand to his partner to join him.

Merrifield took his position in the engineer's seat on the right, with McCoy manning the fireman's seat on the left. Their respective positions were a curious vestige of railroading's past: the first locomotives in the United States were designed with British specifications. Even as America quickly overtook Europe in railroading and in building larger, more powerful locomotives, the seat of the engineer stayed where it was.

The Hudson's vestibule-style cab provided some protection for the crew, but the rear was open to the elements. As a result, conditions inside the cab reflected those outside. The firebox gave off a lot of heat, rendering it brutally hot in the summer months, though slider windows on the sides provided some ventilation. The cab could also get viciously cold in winter, despite the firebox. If it was ten degrees and calm outside, and the train was traveling at fifty miles per hour, the "real feel" temperature hovered around negative twenty degrees. With decades of experience driving steam locomotives in eastern Montana, Merrifield and McCoy had seen it all.

Modern diesel locomotives typically have angled windshields equipped with wiper blades that provide a forward view. In the steam era, however, the front of the Hudson cab was a maze of pipes, cock valves, gauges, wires, and levers from floor to ceiling. To get a good look at the tracks ahead, Merrifield and McCoy needed to stick their heads outside the window and sometimes lean out with their upper body. The engineer and fireman were essentially blind to the front end of the locomotive, which, on a Hudson, was over fifty feet forward. For the engineer and fireman, essential equipment included goggles, well-fitting hats, leather gloves, and bandanas that doubled as face masks. Sparks and hot cinders from the firebox and hot steam, ash, and smoke from its forward smokestack presented constant hazards to the operating crew.

Having already pounded the 216 miles of rail from Harlowton to Miles City, the Hudson locomotive waited hot and primed when Merrifield and McCoy boarded for the next leg to Marmarth. As fireman, McCoy's job was to maintain a full head of steam in the boiler so that, from a stop, Merrifield could smoothly throttle forward to accelerate and then maintain speed levels across constantly changing terrain. Even on the relatively flat western plains, railroad grades were rarely level. More often, the locomotive and train had to constantly ascend or descend as they navigated the contours of the land, especially along river corridors. Over the three-hour run to Marmarth, McCoy would be constantly tending to the boiler to maintain proper steam pressure levels for Merrifield, who needed more on the upward inclines and less on the way down.

The two ingredients for McCoy's steam boiler were water and coal, and the Hudson required massive amounts of both. Its tender held twenty tons of coal and fifteen thousand gallons of water. The firebox sat directly in front of the Hudson's cab, a huge cylindrical combustion chamber lined top to bottom with a special firebrick, like a massive pizza oven, that had an eighty-square-foot grate on the bottom. Surrounding the firebox was a vast array of flues and water-filled tubes that, when superheated by fire, created steam. Pressurized to about 225 pounds per square inch, the steam was channeled to tree-trunk-sized cylinders—each of which measured twenty-six by twenty-eight inches—that powered pistons to turn drive wheels on both sides of the locomotive.[1]

As steam locomotives grew larger, faster, and more powerful, the amount of fuel required also increased commensurately. Until the 1930s, most coal locomotives were fed by hand: a fireman, sometimes two, at times joined by the conductor, would furiously shovel coal into the firebox to keep the steam pressure up for the engineer. The work was brutal, and firemen and their labor organizations began to insist that locomotives be outfitted with powered coal augers called "automatic stokers." The federal agency regulating railroads, the Interstate Commerce Commission, took up the issue in 1931, but it would take years to act. In late 1937, the ICC finally issued an order requiring the railroads to retrofit their coal-burning locomotives with automatic stokers within five years. Just six months later, 179 railroad companies banded together and filed a lawsuit trying to block it. But with the handwriting on the wall, some companies, including the Milwaukee Road, began to integrate the technology into their operations.[2]

By alleviating the heavy shoveling, automatic stokers dramatically improved the lives of firemen like Hausmer McCoy. But it did not mean he could sit back and relax on the journey. Regulating the amount of coal pushed into the firebox remained a key responsibility, and the addition of the auger presented new complications. Even though the coal first passed through a crusher that pulverized it, it was not uncommon for the auger to clog and stall, unable to digest larger, harder lumps. This situation would require McCoy to throw the auger into reverse, then forward again—sometimes multiple times—to get the flow of coal moving again. Once inside the firebox, five powerful steam jets blew the flying coal throughout the cavernous grate area to maximize the boiler's heating potential. McCoy needed to manipulate turn valves for each steam jet to adjust the force of the spray and its direction to ensure that he had a fire to his liking. A skilled fireman might also use a steel "scoop" coal shovel to deflect the coal stream into the right spots. As an experienced engineer who operated out of Miles City explained, "Once you got the jets set right, you could go for miles without having to make any change."[3]

Ten minutes after five, their eastbound *Olympian* No. 16 received the greenlight, referred to as the "highball" due to its position at the top of the railyard light post. Merrifield held the reverse lever down in full forward position, and gently notched forward the throttle. As a seasoned operator, he allowed no showboating on his watch. Veteran engineers often did not respect operators who pounded on their engine when leaving town, creating a lot of noise, steam, and smoke. Given his reputation as one of the best, Merrifield would have gently eased the throttle forward, notch by notch, as if handling the stick shift of a sports car.

The Hudson came to life. Its large drive wheels started to turn, and the train soon exited the maze of tracks within the Miles City railroad yards. Using a track that ran parallel to that of the Northern Pacific, they were soon driving north through rich farmland and large ranches, with livestock and horses grazing near the rail path. The train passed beneath clumps of tall, gnarled cottonwood trees, whose gangly limbs stretched out over the rail bed. Less than ten miles east of Miles City, Merrifield eased *Olympian* No. 16 through a bend in the rail northwest toward the Kinsey bridge over the Yellowstone River.

As he throttled back the *Olympian* to enter the "barrel shot" entrance to the bridge, the deep rumble and noisy steam gasps of the locomotive broke the morning silence near the river, scattering bank swallows from their peaceful burrows in the sandstone cliffs. Even though the Yellowstone runs wide and fast in this area, it took just moments for the entire train to traverse the steel bridge and begin its charge up the west side of the river, passing the small, sleeping community of Kinsey.

Leaving the tree-lined dirt streets of Kinsey in its wake, the *Olympian* emerged onto a wide, flat grassland largely devoid of trees and green vegetation, apart from a few fields of early corn planted in the rough soil. For the next twenty miles or so, the rails followed a stubbornly straight line north through Bonfield, Saugus, and Calypso. This stretch of track provided a notable contrast to the arcs and curves of the Yellowstone River as it flowed east on its way to meet the Missouri. Here in the river corridor, the enormity of the Yellowstone River valley, carved in ancient times, is breathtaking. Bracketed by multicolored badland buttes and cliffs on either side, and miles wide in places, the valley expands and narrows with the meandering river.

As it approached the Saugus station, a small, weather-worn wooden shack, the *Olympian* pounded across lands newly owned by Dan Haughian Jr. He had built his small ranch, constructed from pieces of a railroad section house, near the river on the east side of the track. At that point, Dan Jr. and his family had not yet claimed the hundreds of acres of rolling badlands in the area that would spawn the Haughian's Badlands Cattle Company, an enterprise that continues to operate today. Frank Merrifield, in the engineer's seat, had a direct line of sight to Haughian's ranch as the train passed by at about half past five that morning. It is likely that Merrifield and Haughian were acquainted with each other, given the small size of Miles City in the 1930s and the fact that both men and their families had lived in the area for decades.

The only bridge of any consequence in the twenty-four-mile stretch of track on the west side of the river between Kinsey and Calypso was in Saugus. Designated as bridge AA-438 by the Milwaukee Road, the 180-foot wood and steel structure was also known as the Custer Creek bridge. One of the larger washes on the west side that fed into the Yellowstone River, Custer Creek was a dry ditch for most of the year. After the bridge, the rail bed narrowed dramatically due to a sizable badland butte stubbornly abutting the shallow river waters. The engineers and construction crews who built the line thirty years earlier blasted away just enough of the ancient sandstone to safely lay track.

Once through the narrow passage, the *Olympian* burst onto a broad grassland plain as it headed toward the tiny hamlet of Calypso. The mounded peaks, buttes, and cliffs of the Terry Badlands appeared on the horizon directly ahead, as did the three-section, steel-framed bridge connecting Calypso with Terry, a twin to the structure downstream at Kinsey.

About a mile before the graceful steel arches of the Calypso Bridge, Merrifield briefly throttled down the Hudson. The engineer looked to tip his cap and wave to Lou Goplen, the section foreman who managed this stretch of track and lived in a small house nearby. Such an early morning greeting, along with a short blast from the locomotive's steam whistle, was a sign of respect. Merrifield understood the vital role that men like Goplen played in ensuring not only his own safety but that of his crew, passengers, and cargo. Within minutes, the *Olympian* was back on the east side of the river, just south of Terry, the seat of Prairie County. Originally called Joubert's Landing until the Northern Pacific Railway came through in 1881, the town had been renamed to honor General Alfred Howe Terry, a U.S. Army officer who led campaigns against the Lakotas and the Nez Perce during the 1870s and 1880s and served as Custer's commanding officer at the time of the Battle of Little Bighorn.

As an express train, the *Olympian* would only stop in Terry if there were passengers to drop off or pick up. There were no such passengers that morning, so Merrifield cruised past the Terry station at about six o'clock. To the north, he again eased open the throttle, following the river parallel to U.S. Highway 10. At Bluffport, the Milwaukee Road tracks arced sharply southeast and traced the gentle riverbed contours of O'Fallon Creek toward Mildred.

A FEW miles back, Lou Goplen had watched the eastbound *Olympian* No. 16 pound past him. He had been up well before the sun that morning patrolling his section of track on a "speeder," a gasoline-powered track car. The small cart could zoom to speeds of thirty miles per hour and carry as many as eight track workers and their equipment. Like Merrifield and many other employees in the area, Goplen had followed the rails from the Upper Midwest to the Dakotas to Montana. Born in 1902 in Pipestone, Minnesota, to Augustus ("Gus") and Albertina ("Tina") Goplen, Louis Edward Goplen took after his father, who made his living working the rails as a track laborer.[4]

Barely into his teens, Lou left his family and Minnesota to look for work and adventure. He ended up in Haynes, North Dakota, and soon had a job working on a section crew for the Milwaukee Road, then the Chicago, St. Paul & Pacific Railroad, which had recently laid track through the area. Before the arrival of the railroad, Haynes had been known as Gadsden, but in 1907 the town was renamed after George B. Haynes, who was at that time the president of the railroad. Perched on endless prairie, a sea of grass extending in all directions, the town straddled the North and South Dakota state lines, sitting just south of present-day U.S. Highway 12. In 1920, it had a population of 121, including Christine Miller, Goplen's future bride. They married on May 30, 1921.

In later years, Goplen liked to tell friends that he worked the rails in just about every town between Mobridge and Miles City. It was not unusual for railroad workers to move frequently for better work opportunities and more money. Just before the Great Depression, with three young children in tow, Goplen's work took the family to Lacomb, Montana, between Ismay and Mildred. In 1934, the Goplen family moved again, thirty-six miles west to Calypso, where they lived in a small section house supplied by the railroad. The Goplen home was sandwiched between the Yellowstone River and the mainline tracks, with a view of the Calypso Bridge arches from the backyard. It was a busy stretch of rail with numerous freight and passenger trains passing by each day.[5]

In 1938, at thirty-six years old, Goplen was the boss. As section foreman, he managed a ten-mile stretch of single track between milepost 1,085, just east of Calypso toward Terry, to milepost 1,095, one mile west of the Saugus station toward Miles City. The wooden mileposts demarcated distances on the track from its starting point in Chicago, meaning that within Goplen's section stood the exact midpoint of the Milwaukee Road's 2,188-mile run from Chicago to Tacoma.

Goplen's job required that he knew every feature—each grade, curve, siding, signal, culvert, and trestle—of this section in detail, including the 180-foot bridge spanning Custer Creek. A much sturdier concrete and steel structure had in 1914 replaced the original single-track bridge built in 1907. Anchored on the east and west sides with abutments, the steel-reinforced floor of the bridge sat on six piers supported by a combination of steel girders on the east side, and hefty precast slabs over two feet thick on the west end. To provide the necessary support for increasingly larger, heavier, and faster trains, the slabs were "heavily reinforced for tension, compression and shearing stresses."[6]

Custer Creek flowed during spring runoff and when an exceptional rainstorm drenched the Little Sheep Mountains to the northwest but ran dry most of the year. Still, the bridge was built with water in mind. The Milwaukee Road drove the abutments and piers anywhere from six to fifteen feet below the bed of the creek. To help minimize erosion and the scouring effects of water passing by the piers under the bridge, the company reinforced each of the piers on the outside with riprap rock. The bridge had no guardrails.[7]

The Milwaukee Road carefully maintained its infrastructure, especially the company's many bridges and trestles. In addition to Goplen and his crew, teams of professional engineers regularly inspected all Milwaukee Road bridges. The company considered structural repairs or upgrades to be specialty operations. It brought trained crews on-site by railcar to do the work. The company had inspected and reinforced the Custer Creek bridge as recently as 1937.

Goplen had two men working for him on the ten-mile Calypso section in 1938. In the difficult times of the 1930s, such a small team was not uncommon. Section crews like Goplen's patrolled the mainline track and maintained it by securing rails and ties. Each individual rail was thirty-three feet long, weighed about one thousand pounds, and required twenty oil-treated fir ties underneath. A single spike on each side of the tie, which sat atop two feet and two inches of gravel ballast, affixed it to the rails. Crews employed a tool called a gandy to maneuver and align individual lengths of rail, an awkward proposition that gave rise to the term "gandy dancer." In addition to securing rail to ties, section crews kept busy clearing vegetation along the right-of-way, fixing fences and signs, clearing ditches of debris, filling water stations, and clearing snow and ice from station platforms and from switches along the railway. This work was demanding for even the toughest of men. The company often assigned heavy construction such as laying new rail spurs and sidings or installing new ballasting to larger "floating gangs" that deployed to sites as needed.[8]

Patrolling his section, a twenty-mile round trip, could take Goplen several hours in his motorized track car. He had been around long enough to remember when a patrol would take much longer, when section crews relied on their own muscles instead of internal combustion engines to move a platelayer's cart—also known as a gandy dancer cart—across the track. Along the way, he and his men would often stop and walk to conduct a more detailed inspection of rail conditions. It was not unusual for Goplen to patrol his section on his own, but he preferred to have at least one laborer with him to handle the unexpected. On the speeder, they carried shovels, pickaxes with multiple heads for different jobs, a ballast fork, rail tongs, hacksaws, track jacks, drills, and a track gauge.[9]

The arrival of the motorized track car was one of many improvements that had transformed life along the tracks in what was considered the "golden age" of American railroads. For an engineer like Frank Merrifield, the changes couldn't have been more obvious. Between 1905 and 1935, locomotives made impressive leaps in size and speed as companies actively competed for passengers and freight revenue. Since punching his engineer's ticket almost thirty years earlier, Merrifield had piloted just about every major class of steam locomotive used by the Milwaukee Road.

In this era, steam locomotives with iconic brand names such as American, Prairie, Mikes, Mallet, Atlantic, Pacific, Mountain, Hudson, and Northern ruled the rails from coast to coast. In the early 1880s, Walt Whitman adoringly described one such machine as a "fierce-throated beauty," a characterization that still rang true as their power and size grew. Driving wheels grew in number and size, increasing speed and endurance; pistons and cylinders expanded to the size of tree trunks, boosting power; additional wheels were added beneath the cab to support ever larger fireboxes to produce more steam; and innovations such as superheaters, which upped steam capacity, added new life to older boilers. The design and size of tenders, which carried water and fuel, also advanced significantly during this time, allowing trains to pull more cars and travel longer distances between refueling stops.[10]

When Merrifield earned the right in 1907 to wear the Kromer, the engineer's hat, he likely trained on an American-type locomotive. The Milwaukee Road was flush with Americans at the turn of the century, owning about five hundred in its steam locomotive inventory. Economical to operate and highly adaptable, Americans could be used for passengers, freight, or switcher assignments in railyards. With four driving wheels, their power and reliability made them the dominant model used by U.S. railroads up until the 1890s, when heavier loads and longer trains demanded larger and more powerful locomotives.[11]

Merrifield spent his career with the Milwaukee Road almost entirely west of Minneapolis and as far west as Harlowton. By 1910, he was piloting locomotives out of Miles City, then a recently designated division headquarters. The Milwaukee Road's newly opened 1,400-mile Puget Sound Extension presented new challenges for the company, forcing it to consider what type of locomotive was best suited to speed across the flat prairies of the Dakotas and climb the challenging mountains grades of Montana, Idaho, and Washington. Knowing the limitations of its fleet of American-type locomotives and always mindful of the competition, the company experimented with various models, investing heavily in its search for an engine that could reliably and economically pull its new *Olympian* the entire distance to Tacoma.

In 1910, the same year that Frank Merrifield relocated to Miles City, the Milwaukee Road took ownership of about 160 Pacific-type locomotives. The early *Olympian* passenger trains were pulled the entire 2,188-mile distance from Chicago to Tacoma by Pacifics, also called F4s, which boasted a set of six driving wheels, each measuring sixty-nine inches. In fact, it was a Pacific steam locomotive, number 3004, that pulled the very first *Olympian* through Montana in May 1911. Reliable and tough, Pacifics were used to cross the mountains of the Northwest until 1916, when the Milwaukee Road introduced all-electric locomotives called "Quills" to take the *Olympian* over the challenging mountain runs between Harlowton and Avery, Idaho.[12]

The early Pacifics were just over seventy feet long and fourteen feet, nine inches tall, tugging a tender with seven thousand gallons of water and ten tons of coal. They were hand-fired, meaning firemen like Hausmer McCoy would spend their shifts shoveling tons of coal into the firebox to keep up steam pressure levels for the engineer. New superheater technology for boilers, introduced in 1912, gave the next generation of Pacific locomotives, called F5s, a significant operating advantage over earlier models. According to railroad historian Bill Wilkerson, superheated boilers significantly improved the efficiency of coal and water consumption and provided substantially more "tractive effort," which meant better capabilities in sheer pulling power. Wilkerson described these Pacifics as "the biggest little engine we had." They were "built for speed and would turn out high speed performance mile after mile with the right size train." The newest class of Pacifics were used on the run from Mobridge to Harlowton from 1912 to 1930, until they were gradually replaced with the newer F-class locomotives, the Hudsons, known as F6s.[13]

Baldwin Locomotive Works first began delivery of the beefier Hudsons to the Milwaukee Road in 1928. The company originally intended to use Hudsons for passenger service between Chicago and Minneapolis, but so impressive were the new locomotives' sturdiness and speed that management soon reassigned them to longer runs between Minneapolis and Harlowton. As a result, the railroad sent a fleet to the Trans-Missouri Division in Miles City, home base for Frank Merrifield. Underscoring its reliability, a new Hudson locomotive completed ten round trips between Minneapolis and Harlowton—a distance of over eighteen thousand track miles—during a period of one month in 1933 without any days lost for servicing. It was no wonder that railroad management loved the fast and low-maintenance Hudsons.[14]

The last locomotive Merrifield would pilot was truly a steel giant on the rails, the Northern, with eight driving wheels. The massive Northern, an S2, stretched 110 feet from tender to cowcatcher and weighed some 444 tons with a fully loaded tender. Thirty Northerns were delivered to the Milwaukee Road in 1937. Designed primarily for heavy, long-distance freight runs, the Northern was thirty feet longer and about twice the weight of a Pacific locomotive. Its all-steel tender was enormous, with a capacity for twenty-five tons of coal and twenty thousand gallons of water, almost three times the capacity of the tender pulled by the earlier version of the Pacific. The Northern was a monster, one of the largest and most powerful steam locomotives ever used by the Milwaukee Road. In fact, it was so big, it was not allowed to enter Chicago's Union Station.[15]

As fate would have it, Frank Merrifield would be handed the throttle of a shiny new Northern locomotive, number 220, in Marmarth, North Dakota, on Saturday evening, June 18, 1938. Given his experience handling locomotives of all types and sizes, he likely settled right into the engineer's seat without a second thought. Hausmer McCoy, however, having not yet fired a Northern, might have been less confident.

A few hours earlier, Lou Goplen, like any trained section boss, had his eye on the unusually hot weather. Thunderheads had approached the Calypso area from the west on Friday afternoon, but no rain ever came. The clouds cleared overnight, but the start of Saturday looked like a repeat of the day before. Humidity weighed down the air that morning and the sun rose quickly in the eastern sky, lighting up the rippling waters of the Yellowstone River like a ribbon of gold.

CHAPTER 10

Morning

Saturday, June 18, 1938

In the early morning hours of Saturday, June 18, a thirty-eight-year-old rancher named Frank LaRoque was tending his sheep in the eastern foothills of the Rocky Mountain Front near Choteau, Montana, when lightning struck him and several members of his flock. Paralyzed and unable to move or call for help, LaRoque lay in the cold rain for two days and nights, until he was found alive in a ditch, surrounded by a mass of dead sheep. His scalp had been seared and his clothes had been ripped off his body and pulverized by the blast. "The bolt had followed the zipper on his coat and had literally torn his shoes to pieces," reported the *Great Falls Tribune*.[1]

LaRoque never regained consciousness and died in a local hospital within days. He and his sheep were among the first victims that day of the strong, sudden, and highly localized storms that occur on occasion in Montana, particularly in the months of June and July. For instance, during Lewis and Clark's expedition in 1805, Meriwether Lewis took note of the wild and unpredictable weather as the Corps of Discovery attempted to navigate treacherous waters near what would become Great Falls: "the same cloud will discharge hail alone in one part hail and rain in another and rain only in a third all within the space of a few miles."[2]

Pushed by the jet stream, which flows west to east, large cold air masses from Canada and the Pacific Northwest can collide with warmer, moisture-laden air pushed up from the Gulf of Mexico, spawning massive storms. Montana's exceptionally diverse terrain, especially the Rocky Mountains, produces friction between the air and the land, causing storms to break apart into severe, localized downpours. The violent storm system that pummeled Montana from the morning through the early evening of June 18 owed to this phenomenon.[3]

That same morning, about three hours east of Minneapolis, Louis Williams rested on a small stool in the back of tourist sleeper C of the westbound *Olympian* No. 15. It was hardly comfortable, but it allowed him to both relax his legs and be at the ready if anyone needed him in the night. To remind passengers of his name, a card that read "Louis" hung on the wall near his stool. Being called by your own name was hardly a given for porters like Williams. In fact, this nameplate and the name tag he wore on his uniform were new developments in the industry.

Porters suffered many indignities in their work, but one of the worst was being called "George," an offensive throwback to a time when enslaved people were given the names of their masters. After the Civil War, George Pullman staffed his sleeper cars with freed people, many of whom had been domestic slaves in the South. Passengers began derisively referring to the porters as Pullman's "boys," and, eventually, as "George." This dehumanizing tradition only began to fade away in the 1930s, just as Williams began to work as a porter.

Even early on in his career, Louis Williams had good reason for optimism about his future. He had an opportunity to join the first Black labor union in the United States, the newly formed Brotherhood of Sleeping Car Porters, which represented porters and railroad attendants. Recognized in 1937, the Brotherhood's motto, "Stands for Service Not Servitude," made its core purpose clear.

The idea for a union protecting the rights of train porters had emerged decades earlier but gained traction in the 1920s thanks to the efforts of Black labor activist A. Philip Randolph. Randolph's relentless campaign for the Brotherhood often met brutal resistance from Pullman and its client railroad companies. Before the union was recognized, Randolph and his supporters endured years of threats, intimidation, and violence by thugs. In the early part of his campaign, an advertisement in *The Messenger*, a literary magazine founded by Randolph, underscored the Brotherhood's principal demands for change, along with an appeal to join:

> IF:
> You are tired of being treated like children instead of men;
> You think you should work shorter hours;
> You think your wages should be larger;
> You are tired of doubling back;
> You are sick of Company tyranny;
> You have a backbone instead of a wishbone.[4]

In addition to demanding that the porter's name be posted on a card in each car, the Brotherhood pushed Pullman and its client railroad companies to increase monthly pay from $100 to $150, to abolish the tipping system in favor of a living wage, to cap monthly working hours at 240 instead of 400, and to allow porters a minimum amount of sleep: four hours on the first night out (instead of three) and six hours for each consecutive night.

Pullman rules for sleeping were nothing short of abusive. Pullman allowed, but did not guarantee, three hours of sleep on the first night out and nothing for the rest of the trip. This meant that Williams would need to be on duty for fifty-five hours of the *Olympian*'s fifty-eight-hour journey to Tacoma. Unlike the train's white crew members, the rulebook dictated that a porter could only sleep in the men's lounge in a designated smoker car, since a buzzer was in the smoker to alert the porter if he were needed. The lounge, however, was less than ideal, since passengers often used the lavatory throughout the night. Further, the company considered slouching or lying down in any seat a fireable offense. This meant porters had to sit upright to sleep or retreat to an uncomfortable stool in a back corner of their assigned car.[5]

After it was finally certified in 1937, the Brotherhood made progress on some of its demands, notably monthly pay rates. Yet while Pullman agreed to increase the pay for porters to $175 per month, resistance on the part of railroad companies meant that it took years before porters saw any real change in their take-home pay. Indeed, in 1938, Louis Williams earned about $100 a month, not counting tips, which was considered good pay for a Black man at the time. Conductors, however, almost all of them white, earned three times as much. Even the men that washed the train cars earned more than porters.

Moreover, Pullman required its porters to cover a number of job-related expenses, which reduced their net income. They paid for their uniforms, which cost about fifteen dollars each, and most porters typically kept two. They bought their own meals while working and even paid for their own shoe polish. Porters found particularly upsetting a Pullman policy that made them financially responsible for anything that went missing in their assigned train car, including soap, towels, combs, pillows, and blankets. No protest was tolerated; the cost was simply deducted from their pay.

The first preparations for breakfast would soon start in the diner car directly behind Williams's tourist sleeper, signaling the beginning of the busy part of his day. Perched on his stool, he reviewed a list of the passengers who desired a wakeup call and those who preferred to sleep as long as possible. With the first call for breakfast at just after six o'clock, Williams would be ready to "make up" the sleeping berths back into sitting coaches as passengers used the lavatories or went to the diner car for breakfast. For now, he could savor these last few minutes of rest, knowing he would be on his feet until the people under his care went back to sleep that night.

Breakfast on the *Olympian* was a fine dining experience. The smell of coffee and freshly baked rolls acted as an irresistible wakeup call. At about a quarter after six, a dining car waiter playing a melody from a hand-held chime walked from car to car announcing seating for the upcoming breakfast. In 1938, the *Olympian* used a forty-eight-seat diner car, and there were three calls for each meal. The first seating for breakfast was at half past six, the last an hour later.

Immaculately dressed in white, a steward stood ready at the diner door to greet arriving passengers and show them to a table. Once seated, he—in 1938, all dining car stewards were men—handed each passenger a detailed menu, along with a small form and pencil to write down their order. The diner car served its food on fine china, custom made for the *Olympian*. Silver cutlery and crisp, white linens adorned every table, along with a small vase of freshly cut flowers. The railroad was immensely proud of its first-rate breakfast service. It even offered all patrons a mailing envelope for the menu card.[6]

EARLY morning clouds had begun to give way to sunshine as the train thundered westward to Minneapolis. The sun cast playful shadows on the gold and emerald-green fields of the gently rolling Minnesota landscape. The occasional barn and farmhouse would suddenly appear and just as quickly vanish in the wake of the train.

Around the same time a few hundred miles west, passengers on the *Olympian* No. 16, chugging eastward out of the Yellowstone River valley, watched as the topography and scenery changed dramatically. Groves of cottonwood trees and greenery along the river gave way to semiarid badlands with rough-cut, deeply eroded rock formations and multicolored sandstone canyons. A modest uphill rail grade toward Fallon required more steam from McCoy before the train hooked southeast following the path of O'Fallon Creek toward Mildred.

The sun was fully up by this point, brilliantly illuminating a gentle, rolling valley of prairie grass tinged with gold and shades of brown. Bright green spires of cottonwood trees along O'Fallon Creek pointed the way to Mildred. Soon, the town's tall coal dock and water tower emerged in the distance, and Merrifield started to ease back the throttle of the Hudson.

McCoy, constantly monitoring water levels in the boiler, signaled to his partner that the train would need a water stop in Mildred. Having set off from Miles City topped off with fifteen thousand gallons of water in its tender, the Hudson would have easily consumed several thousand gallons in the sixty miles to Mildred. McCoy could control the amount of water being injected into the engine at any given time, but he needed a minimum of about five thousand gallons of water in the boiler—almost a third of its reserve—to safely operate the 340-ton beast. Bill Wilkerson, a Miles City engineer, later underscored the importance of maintaining the boiler by quipping that minimum water levels must be followed "if you wanted to grow old." If the levels became dangerously low, he added, a boiler alarm would "raise the dead five miles away, especially ex-railroad men." If not heeded, the locomotive could literally blow apart. Leaving nothing to chance, Merrifield slowed the *Olympian* to a crawl so he could precisely position the tender between the coal dock and water tower that faced each other on either side of the tracks.[7]

The town of Mildred, with only a few hundred residents in 1938, would hardly elicit a momentary glance from *Olympian* passengers when their train stopped in the community. Even drivers of the few stray automobiles or trucks that cut through town on old U.S. Highway 12 (now the Ismay Road) rarely gave the forlorn community a second look. Marked out in the dirt, the townsite had been divided into lots before any structures were built. Named after the daughter of a Milwaukee Road employee, Mildred became a magnet for homesteaders and immigrants in 1908 when the company laid rails for the Puget Sound Extension in the area.

One early settler named B. T. Vance recalled that when he arrived in 1908, Mildred consisted of crude meandering paths trampled in the grass by wagons and cattle. A weather-beaten converted boxcar served as the local train station. Vance indicated the relative ease of navigating from one part of town to another: you just pointed your horse in the general direction, and off you went.[8]

The quiet isolation that characterized Mildred in 1908 might have discouraged some, but not people like Vance. The allure of cheap, open land and the opportunity to carve out a new life were powerful motivators. After first visiting the area, Vance quickly returned by train to Winona, Minnesota, picked up his wife, paid twenty-five dollars to rent an "immigrant" train car—essentially a crude empty boxcar—and packed it with his life's belongings. He loaded in lumber, tar paper, and buckets of nails, enough to build a "claim shack" on land he would soon own.[9]

Not known for comfort, immigrant rentals were assigned the worst, most worn-out boxcars or wooden coaches. Most had flat roofs, wooden benches for seats, no running water, a hole at one end of the car serving as a toilet, and a potbelly woodstove for heat. Trains pulling these ragged cars received the lowest priority on the tracks, even behind freight and local trains. This meant the immigrant trains were often "sidetracked," sent to wait on an adjacent set of rails while other trains passed, making a long trip even longer.

In Mildred, Vance and his wife made their way to the Pope Ranch, several miles northwest of town, where they spent their first night on the prairie. The next step for the Vances—and all the homesteaders arriving in droves—was a bumpy buckboard ride to join the queue at the General Land Office in Terry. The Vances eventually selected a quarter section—160 acres of land—west of Mildred and filed the necessary papers. The Vances endured intense heat, wind, and violent storms while living in a tarpaper shack on the flat prairie.[10]

Mildred became an "official" town on May 20, 1908, with the opening of a U.S. Post Office. The first structure to be built in the town, however, was the tall, lonely Milwaukee Road water tank that now fed Merrifield's train. The coal dock that sat across the track was also an early addition. Three carloads arrived daily from the Milwaukee Road's coal yard in Roundup, Montana. And every day, the dock operator—jokingly named "snowball"—would offload the coal from railcars into a holding bin using a large bucket with a power winch. It was dirty, dangerous work.

The young children of Mildred in the 1920s and 1930s would grab a bucket and search for loose chunks of coal on the tracks and around the coal dock to take home to their families. As local historian Art Brown later claimed, "The good citizens of Mildred, including church deacons, were very cooperative in helping the railroad unload the coal. The difference was the people unloaded their share at night, and the railroad unloaded what was left in their coal dock during the day." For the most part, the railroad bosses looked the other way. Only when locals got too brazen with their "nightly pickins"—for example, by hitching a ride on a coal car so they could throw its cargo to neighbors ready with buckets and sacks below—did the railroad opt to prosecute.[11]

Mildred's status as a fuel and water stop for passing steam locomotives guaranteed a measure of prosperity for the community's future—at least for a few decades. As Merrifield and McCoy pulled *Olympian* No. 16 east out of Mildred on their way to Baker and Marmarth, they steamed past a series of less fortunate small towns that lacked important rail infrastructure. The immigrant communities of Lacomb, Ismay, Westmore, and Plevna were reeling from a decade of drought and the Great Depression. When the Milwaukee Road built its main line through the area in 1906, engineers working with A. G. Baker, the man in charge of the new track's construction from Marmarth to Miles City, reported just one ranch between Ismay and Terry. At that time, Ismay was called Burt, after a Minnesotan named George Burt who moved to the area with his family in 1895. When the U.S. Post Office planned to open a branch in the town after the railroad arrived in 1908, the agency would not accept the name Burt, concerned it would be confused with Butte. They chose Ismay, a joining of Isabelle and Mae, the daughters of Milwaukee Road president Albert Earling.[12]

The residents of Ismay nearly abandoned the town's name in 1912. That year, Bruce Ismay, chairman of the White Star Line, which owned the *Titanic,* became a world-renowned scoundrel when news accounts alleged that he had pushed his way past women and children to take a place on one of doomed ship's lifeboats. Although it was mere coincidence that the town shared its name with a disgraced shipping executive, many residents insisted that Ismay should change its name; a bare majority nonetheless voted to keep it.

Beyond Ismay, the *Olympian* followed Arthur Baker's chosen route along Sandstone Creek toward Plevna, site of the next station. Named by Bulgarian immigrant railroad workers dreaming of their homeland, Plevna means "city of churches." When *Olympian* No. 16 steamed through that morning, Plevna counted just under three hundred residents—roughly its population apex. Today, it is half the size. But with four churches (Catholic, Lutheran, Evangelical, and Baptist), about one for every thirty-eight residents, the town still lives up to its name.[13]

If there was a place on the *Olympian*'s route where Merrifield could lay on the steam, it would have been between Plevna and the town of Baker. Once known for the seemingly endless bison herds, Baker sits on an ocean of prairie grass. By the time the Milwaukee Road carved its rail line through the area in 1908, commercial hide hunters had exterminated bison from the region. Before then, the few residents who toughed it out on this lonely stretch of prairie called their community Lorraine or Sandstone Flats, since Sandstone Creek was the nearest local source of water. The arrival of the railroad brought prosperity to the town, which soon boasted a hardware store, banks, a grocery store that also served as the local post office, a clothing store, restaurants, a shoe shop, a drugstore and barbershop, and, of course, several saloons. Locals even recalled a tamale stand on Main Street and a Chinese restaurant called Lew Jim's, where you could get a full-course meal with pie and coffee for thirty-five cents.[14]

By 1913, the Milwaukee Road had renamed its new station after the man in charge of charting the railroad's route across the prairie, Arthur Baker. Needing a local source of fresh water for its steam locomotives, the Milwaukee Road dredged and created a man-made lake on the southern edge of the community that they called Lake Baker, later changed to Baker Lake. The Milwaukee Land Company used the lake as a key selling point in its marketing blitz to lure homesteaders to the area to try their hand at a promising new farming technique called "dryland farming."

A man-made lake and the railroad's boosterism notwithstanding, plenty of reasons explain why Baker's surrounding environs remain generally desolate: a lack of moisture, harsh winters, and wind. These factors would combine to eventually bankrupt eight out of ten homesteaders in the area within twenty years. Only its supply of natural gas, first discovered in 1915, saved Baker from becoming another Montana ghost town.

✦

PERCHED high in the engineer's seat, piloting the flying *Olympian* east toward North Dakota that morning, Frank Merrifield was in his element. He never tired of having a locomotive throttle in his hand. Born in a Wisconsin town named after a railroad executive, it seemed Merrifield was destined for a life on the tracks.

As a young man in the early 1900s, Merrifield left the family farm and relocated to Green Bay, Wisconsin, where he found work shoveling coal into a locomotive firebox. He earned his fireman certification in 1902, at the dawn of railroading's golden age. To be considered for a promotion to engineer, a fireman needed three years of service or had to log at least thirty-six thousand track miles working on freight trains. It was not uncommon for some ambitious men who did not mind being away from home to log that many miles in a year or less, but Merrifield followed a different path. A year after becoming a railroad fireman, he married Nora

Cunningham, who gave birth to their daughter, Lorelei Elizabeth, in 1905. Wanting to spend time with his new wife, and then his young child, Merrifield instead took the full three years to qualify for advancement.[15]

Graduating from fireman to an engineer did not happen automatically. Candidates had to pass three written tests and take an oral exam, which required knowing the railroad operating "book of rules" cover-to-cover. Passing those hurdles earned an engineer's certification, which started a "date clock" by which one began building seniority within the company. Senior engineers typically received the assignment to pull passenger trains. The competition to get an engineer's seat on freight trains, meanwhile, proved less intense because the work paid less.[16]

Frank Merrifield achieved his dream on November 3, 1907, earning the right to wear the engineer's Kromer hat and laying down his seniority day mark. While few opportunities for engineer jobs existed in Green Bay, the Milwaukee Road's plan to build the Puget Sound Extension changed everything for the Merrifields. This massive construction project and expansion of the railroad's service territory created many new openings for men interested in working as firemen, engineers, and other jobs on the railroad. The Merrifields soon left Wisconsin in hopes that Frank could land a coveted position pulling passenger trains.[17]

As the Milwaukee Road began to lay its rails across the prairie on its way to Puget Sound, the Merrifields first moved to Mobridge, South Dakota. By the time they arrived, the small, isolated town on the eastern bank of the Missouri River had rapidly transformed into a boomtown. In addition to mountains of railroad building equipment arriving in the community around-the-clock, Mobridge teemed with legions of rough men looking for a paycheck and a good time on their days off. For Frank and Nora Merrifield, Mobridge soon became the site of tragedy, as they lost their two-year-old daughter Lorelei in 1908.[18]

The Milwaukee Road eventually offered Merrifield, who had been looking for an opportunity to leave Mobridge, an engineer's position in Miles City, Montana. The railroad company had big plans for Miles City, due to its strategic location near the midpoint between Chicago and Tacoma. It became the headquarters for its new Trans-Missouri Division, responsible for 530 miles of railroad and track operations between the

Missouri River and Harlowton, affectionately referred to as "Harlo" by railroad men. Frank Merrifield would spend the rest of his career operating out of the Trans-Missouri Division, enjoying a degree of security in his employment that was not uncommon for many company employees at the time. There, he made the much-anticipated transition from freight trains to passenger trains.

While the move to Montana brought stability to Merrifield's professional life, it did not do the same for his personal life. Frank and Nora's marriage did not last, and she moved back to live with family in Michigan after they divorced. In May 1920, the forty-year-old engineer married again to Winifred E. Martin, an Englishwoman half his age who had found her way to eastern Montana. The marriage was short-lived. In February 1926, Merrifield married for a third time, again to a much younger woman. Mary ("Marie") Hunter had just turned twenty-two when she accepted Merrifield's proposal.[19]

Born on April 16, 1903, in Vancouver, British Columbia, Marie's parents abandoned her as a child. She spent her formative years living in a series of foster homes. Unloved, miserable, and mistreated by her foster families, Marie conspired with a fellow foster child to leave their hopeless life behind. Together, they crossed the border into the United States. Riding the trains, Marie eventually found herself in Miles City looking to start a new life when she met Frank Merrifield.[20]

To outsiders, the marriage of Frank and Marie seemed steady enough in the early years. Marie had five children, one of whom died at childbirth, in relatively quick succession. The growing family, however, and the work involved in managing a busy household shrouded tension in their relationship. There was an edge to Marie, who possessed a short temper. She took to smoking cigarettes, rolling her own, and gained weight. She had been hardened by her years as a foster child. Having no role model as a mother, she applied a tough-love approach to her own children. "She had a loud voice that carried well," remarked her youngest daughter, Phyllis Marie. Hugs and tenderness were not offered. Her children later admitted to fearing her.[21]

Despite Frank's steady work as a locomotive engineer, money was tight in the Merrifield household. Marie taught herself to sew and spent long hours in front of the machine making crude house dresses for herself and basic clothes for the children. She also had a green thumb, and carefully cultivated a backyard garden that produced potatoes, corn, beans, and tomatoes. She canned her own tomatoes, storing them in the garage for the colder months. The family bought fruit by the crate, which Marie rendered into jams and jellies. They raised rabbits that she skinned for cooking and eating. And Marie baked a lot of bread, including cinnamon rolls, which were a household favorite. "She worked like a man," observed Phyllis Marie, "and she paid for it with a bad heart."[22]

Marie's true passion, however, was flower gardening. She particularly liked growing colorful dahlias. "She babied them, tilled around the plants, watered, and fertilized" the dahlias—and even spent time talking to them—recalled Phyllis Marie. Marie's flowers added color and elegance to an otherwise unremarkable Miles City house that sat on a small lot across the street from the Sacred Heart High School.[23]

CHAPTER 11

Devoted Agent

Minneapolis, Minnesota, Saturday, June 18, 1938

Devout Catholics, Paul and Marcella Gehrig of Minneapolis, Minnesota, observed a daily regimen of prayer. On their knees both at sunrise and routinely before bed, they would recite a short devotional giving praise and thanks to God. It was a practice they both enjoyed and took seriously. Before departing on the morning of Saturday, June 18, 1938, for a two-week summer vacation in California's Yosemite National Park, the Gehrigs likely said a prayer to guide and protect their family on the journey out West.[1]

Paul Gehrig had booked reservations for Marcella, their five children, and their twenty-year-old niece Helen on the Milwaukee Road's westbound *Olympian* No. 15. On its way from Chicago, the *Olympian* was scheduled to arrive in downtown Minneapolis by about nine o'clock that morning. A special coal agent for the Milwaukee Road, the forty-five-year-old Paul knew the station quite well. He had already logged twenty-eight years with the railroad, starting as an apprentice telegrapher in 1910. He landed a job as a freight solicitor in 1918, just as America was entering World War I, a position he would hold for twelve years.

In that role, Gehrig spent most of his time on the road, traveling through the Midwest and the Dakotas selling space on Milwaukee Road freight cars to businesses, governmental agencies, farmers, and ranchers. According to one experienced railroad employer, the most important qualifications for a successful freight solicitor were to "smile, tell the truth, cut out the drinks, be neat in your appearance, keep moving and don't be afraid of working hard, and some day you will find that your company has come to the conclusion that you are too good a man for a small field and has added to your territory."[2]

Always on the hunt for good salespeople, the Milwaukee Road placed a premium on articulate employees who looked good in a suit. Gehrig fit the bill, but not without an extraordinary amount of effort. Raised by German parents in Cologne, Minnesota, Paul Gehrig did not learn to speak English until the eighth grade. The family spoke German at home, as did the teachers at St. Barnard's, the Catholic school he attended in Cologne. Entering high school, he realized that he needed to learn English and learn it well if he had any hope for getting ahead in America. He studied the language, spoke slowly and deliberately, and almost eliminated his German accent. His youngest son, Louis, said his father often tripped on pronouncing words beginning with the letter "w"; water, for instance, became "vater."[3]

Working on the freight side of the business gave Gehrig a central role in the railroad's operations. In 1937, freight hauling comprised 82 percent of the Milwaukee Road's revenues. While it boasted 970 passenger cars in its inventory that year, the company listed 55,174 freight cars, including 27,734 boxcars, 13,709 coal cars, and 5,435 cars equipped to haul automobiles and trucks.[4]

Milwaukee Road–owned freight cars logged sixteen million track miles in 1937, carrying almost everything imaginable: 173,500 carloads of agricultural products such as flour, wheat, corn, oats, potatoes, and sugar beets; 128,000 carloads of animals, including cattle, horses, hogs, sheep, and goats; and 37,000 carloads of refrigerated meats; 246,000 carloads of mining products, including coal, gravel, sand, and crushed stone; 141,300 carloads of timber products, including logs, cut lumber, lath, shingles, and pulpwood. The list goes on and includes freighting tons of fuel, iron, steel, cement, and thousands of freight cars loaded with automobiles and car and truck parts.[5]

During his years as a freight solicitor, Gehrig also became familiar with the coal and energy side of the business. With more than one thousand coal-fired steam locomotives in its 1937 inventory, the Milwaukee Road was itself a major consumer that hauled millions of tons annually from the

Bull Mountain coal strip in Roundup, Montana, which the company took control of in 1908 as it mapped out the rail path for its Puget Sound Extension. It also created subsidiaries, including the Republic Coal Company, to mine the coal. Bull Mountain supplied coal to the Milwaukee Road through World War II, when the company began to retire its fleet of coal-fired steam locomotives in favor of diesels.[6]

In recognition of Gehrig's strong work ethic and performance on the freight side of the business, the Milwaukee Road tracked him for future advancement. In 1930, he was promoted to the position of special coal agent. The new role required the Gehrig family to move from Duluth back to Minneapolis, headquarters for the Milwaukee Road west of Chicago.

Like Bernard Maguire and certain other employees, Gehrig was able to secure free train passes for members of his family. Gehrig made decent money but was by no means a wealthy man. For the family vacation to California, a free ride on the *Olympian* was a huge benefit. The cost for seven round-trip reservations on a tourist sleeper—niece Helen was booked on a coach car—to Spokane, Washington, in 1938 was about $360, the equivalent of roughly $6,700 today. Gehrig had mapped out the family's travel plans months in advance. This was a particularly meaningful trip for the Gehrigs as their eldest children, Lee and Barbara, would be leaving home at the end of the summer. Twenty-year-old Lee hoped to attend college at the University of Minnesota. Eighteen-year-old Barbara dreamed of becoming a nurse. Their other children included Paul Jr., age sixteen; Jack, age thirteen; and the baby of the family, Maureen, age eight.[7]

As the Gehrig family drove into downtown Minneapolis, they made their way toward one of the most prominent structures in the city, the towering 140-foot-tall clock tower of the Milwaukee Road Depot train station. Locals set their house clocks and watches to the clock tower, which was visible from across the city and sat atop the station itself. Built in 1899, the elegant, three-story brick building was a busy place in the 1930s, with many days seeing as many as twenty-five or more passenger trains arrive and depart.

The Gehrigs bustled into the station just after half past eight in the morning. A stickler for punctuality, Paul preferred to arrive at the station far in advance of a scheduled train departure. But he usually traveled by himself, so herding a large family with a small mountain of luggage certainly added to the challenge of navigating the busy depot. Inside the station's first floor a grand waiting room, ticket offices, a telegraph office, and the popular Interstate Restaurant greeted passengers. Office space used by Milwaukee Road employees occupied the second and third floors.[8]

After taking the *Olympian* No. 15 to Spokane, the Gehrigs planned to catch a Union Pacific train as far as Portland, Oregon, and then a Southern Pacific train for the final leg to Oakland, California, with a scheduled arrival on the morning of Tuesday, June 21. They then planned to rent a car and drive east to Yosemite.[9]

Tickets in hand, the family made their way outside to the covered train platforms to wait for the arrival of the *Olympian*. The station's magnificent, 625-foot steel-trussed train shed was impressive. It still stands today, one of the few train sheds of its era remaining in America. Like its counterpart in downtown Milwaukee, the Minneapolis shed sported large steel, cylindrical smokestacks to vent the clouds of ash, smoke, and steam belched by arriving and departing locomotives. Paul Gehrig had reserved two sleeping berths for the family on the tourist sleeper Ipswich, the first sleeper car in the *Olympian* consist. As she was not immediate family and thus not eligible for the free fare, Helen chose to book a less expensive seat in coach car 420, located directly in front of the Ipswich. The coach car seats did recline for dozing or sleeping at night. Florence Maguire and the Lallas family rode in the same car.[10]

Many of the tourist sleepers that the *Olympian* used in the 1930s were relatively new. Designed and built in Milwaukee Road shops, the heavy, all-steel cars rivaled Pullman sleepers for space, comfort, and amenities. Air conditioning was now standard, an improvement that required replacing the older windows that could slide open with sealed, break-resistant windows throughout. Company engineers had also improved the car's suspension system to ensure the smoothest ride possible for passengers.

Tourist sleepers had six sleeping sections on each side, twelve total, all oriented toward the middle of the car. Located at the front end of the car was the spacious and comfortable ladies' lounge. Serving as both a lavatory and a sitting room, the lounge offered plush sofas and chairs, dressing tables with lighted mirrors, two sinks, a "toothbrushing station," and a drinking fountain. The men's lounge was considerably smaller and located in the rear. Having ridden many trains, Paul Gehrig knew to choose berths as close to the middle of the car for the quietest ride, on the north side of westbound trains for the best views, and, perhaps most importantly, as close to the ladies' lounge as possible for his wife and the girls. The Gehrigs' berths were across the car's central aisle from one another. Paul and Marcella took the northside berth with their daughters Barbara and Maureen. The three boys had the southside berth across the aisle. With the worries of planning and packing for a large family behind them, Paul and Marcella could finally relax. Avid card players, Paul loved poker and Marcella bridge. They could look forward to playing a few games together and with their children on the long train trip. Their summer vacation had just begun.[11]

Unknown to the Gehrigs and other passengers, a new Northern locomotive—number 220, with eight large driving wheels—chugged out of the roundhouse and was hitched, along with its massive tender, to the westbound *Olympian*. Typically there were three Hudson locomotives in service in Minneapolis assigned to pull the *Olympian* to Harlowton, but for some unknown reason one was not available that morning. Stubbornly dependent on steam power and impressed with its brute strength and pulling capabilities, the Milwaukee Road purchased over fifty Northern locomotives in the late 1930s. Management hoped their ability to haul bigger and heavier freight loads over longer distances would offset the financial drain caused by new federal rules that required so-called granger railroads to haul farm products, including grain, at prices far below actual costs.[12]

The Northern—also called an S2—measured over 110 feet in length and weighed about 444 tons when its all-steel, welded tender was full of twenty-five tons of coal and twenty thousand gallons of water. All told, the Northern was about one hundred tons heavier than a Hudson with attached tender. When pulling passenger trains, the Northern was rated to haul up to eighteen cars compared to the eleven-car capacity of the Hudson. With its seventy-four-inch diameter driving wheels, the Northern did not have the speed of a Hudson, which could roar across the rails between eighty and one hundred miles per hour. But since speeds for passenger service were generally restricted to seventy-five miles per hour, the Northern could substitute quite handily for its faster counterpart. That Sunday, the locomotive's assignment was to pull eleven *Olympian* cars 914 miles to Harlowton—a walk in the park for the mighty engine.[13]

At 9:25 A.M., the *Olympian*'s conductor could be heard yelling "all aboard." Moments later, locomotive 220 began to pick up speed, heading west out of the Minneapolis station. Engineers familiar with the Northern admired its distinct, powerful-sounding exhaust, especially when pulling out of a station. The four sharp exhausts per revolution of the driver wheels would rattle windows a block away. The powerful machine made heads turn, according to Milwaukee Road engineer Bill Wilkerson: "If the exhaust didn't get their attention, 285 pounds of steam pressure going through the Hancock 5 chime whistle sure would."[14]

By a quarter to ten, the shiny black and green Northern locomotive had hit its stride on the rails, cruising at about sixty-five miles per hour. The sun had risen fully, and the forecast called for a hot day. The next major trip marker for the *Olympian* was the Missouri River and the town of Mobridge, South Dakota, about 384 rail miles west. According to schedule, it would pull into Mobridge, located on the eastern banks of the Missouri, at just after six that evening.

CHAPTER 12

To the Missouri

By 1880, Alexander Mitchell, the hard-charging president of the Chicago, Milwaukee & St. Paul Railway, had set his sights on the Missouri River as the next major prize in his campaign across the continent. Other railroads were already pushing west, and Mitchell did not want his company to fall behind. He approved plans to aggressively extend rail lines into Iowa, Minnesota, Nebraska, and Dakota Territory.

Around this time, Mitchell and his board of directors created a new arm of the railroad, the Milwaukee Land Company, to buy land along its routes for sale to western emigrants. On especially promising parcels, Mitchell envisioned establishing actual townsites. His new land company encouraged farming as well, promising settlers that it would reimburse their land purchases if the land was broken and cultivated within a year. The land company also bought forested tracts and sold them to timber companies for harvest, as long as they used Mitchell's railroad to transport their lumber, of course.

With Mitchell calling the shots and his very able general manager S. S. Merrill—nicknamed the "old man"—executing on the ground, the 1880s saw more fast-paced growth for the railroad as it leapfrogged across the western states and territories. By 1879, the company had secured the first of multiple rail beachheads along the Missouri River. Unexpected events, however, interrupted these plans and rattled the company. S. S. Merrill died in 1885. Two years later, in 1887, the seventy-year-old Alexander Mitchell suffered a fatal heart attack while on a business trip to New York City. Beginning with just 270 miles of rail in 1866, Mitchell had expanded his empire to over 5,000 miles of track in seven states by the time of his death.[1]

Mitchell's successor was forty-two-year-old Roswell Miller. In hopes of carrying on the railroad's legacy of expansion, the young and talented Miller pushed new rail extensions forward in many states. The destiny of settlements along the way hinged on where the company decided to chart its path. The history of two South Dakota locales—Mobridge and Evarts—provides a classic example.

Thanks to the railroad, Evarts, a frontier cow town on the east bank of the Missouri, about twelve miles south of present-day Mobridge, would grow into one of the largest cattle shipping points in America. With its tracks terminating at the river, the Milwaukee Road encouraged cowboys and cattlemen as far away as the Black Hills to ship their livestock through Evarts. The company built an enormous, fenced enclosure for the herds, six miles wide and eighty miles long. Every fall, tens of thousands of cattle would be funneled through the "strip" directly onto hundreds of parked railroad stock cars. In the fall of 1904, trains shipped forty thousand head of cattle east from Evarts to the major meat packing operations in Chicago.[2]

When company engineers arrived in Evarts a few years later with plans for building a railroad bridge across the Big Muddy, they chose a more favorable location about twelve miles to the north. There, the river channel narrows as it gently bends to the west, forming a small peninsula—a perfect natural landmass for setting the foundations of a new rail bridge. This new location would eventually be named Mobridge. Evarts's fate was to follow the well-worn path of many boomtowns gone bust: abandoned, it all but melted into the prairie and disappeared.

In 1938, at about the same time the Gehrig family in Minneapolis waited at the station to board westbound *Olympian* No. 15, Frank Merrifield and Hausmer McCoy were slowing eastbound *Olympian* No. 16 for an on-time arrival in Marmarth, North Dakota, 575 miles to the west. The train's brakes squealed as it came to a stop just before eight in the morning.

Located in the southwest corner of the state and sheltered from extreme weather by high bluffs and hills, Marmarth served as a dividing line between the badlands of North Dakota to the east and the rolling, grassy prairie of Montana to the west. Nicknamed the "City of Trees" due to the dense stands of cottonwoods that thrive in the area, westbound travelers saw Marmarth as an oasis as they emerged from the gray and brown hues of the barren and dusty badlands. Without the replenishing waters of the Little Missouri River hugging the east side of town, the desolate area may have never been settled.

The area first received public attention in the 1880s when Teddy Roosevelt traveled to North Dakota and the Little Missouri River to hunt, fish, and take stock of his life. He fell in love with the badlands, and ended up buying a local ranch, the Chimney Butte Ranch, also known as the Maltese Cross Ranch. Roosevelt eventually built a log cabin on the property and returned frequently. He even penned one of his first books at the ranch: *Hunting Trips of a Ranchman*, published in 1885. Roosevelt apparently killed his first buffalo and grizzly bear while camping in the area.

Neva, the forerunner to Marmarth, was a speck of a town located across the river to the east. The hub of settlement moved to the west side of the river in 1906 when the Hunter Brothers, owners of the local OX Ranch, deeded 160 acres to the real estate company owned by the Milwaukee Road, which was laying the rail path for its Puget Sound Extension. Farmers and ranchers stuck on the east side experienced real hardship after the move. For a decade, getting to town meant crossing the river on a crude, wooden ferry, until the construction of a steel bridge across the Little Missouri in 1916.

The first Milwaukee Road train arrived on Christmas Day 1907. The new town was renamed Marmarth after Margaret Martha Fitch, granddaughter of the railroad's president, Albert Earling. With the Milwaukee Road's support, the fledgling community became a gateway for waves of homesteaders. It soon had all the amenities one might expect to see in a small midwestern town, including water and sewer systems, paved streets, concrete walkways, a city park, a school system, electric streetlights, and a railroad hospital. By 1918, Marmarth was home to two banks, several hotels, six restaurants, a hardware store, a gas station, churches, grocery stores, an undertaker, a local newspaper, the 187-seat Mystic Theatre, a Ford dealer, a jewelry shop, and, according to the local newspaper, the finest opera house west of Minneapolis.[3]

As Marmarth grew, so did the Milwaukee Road's presence in town. It expanded its facilities and personnel, adding three section crews, a roundhouse, a sidetrack for short-order repairs on cars, an icehouse, car repair crews, and a coaling station and water tank. The railroad also built fifty acres of stockyards to accommodate the major ranches located in the area, including the OX and the 777 Ranch. The vast facilities included eighty-six loading and sorting pens and fifteen chutes. As local resident Earl Ekholm recalled, "It would take up to forty hours to unload, feed, water and reload the stock on the train." In 1934, at the peak of the company's stock shipping days, almost one thousand Milwaukee Road–owned railcars were loaded with cattle in Marmarth and shipped to the major meat markets and processors in Chicago and Omaha.[4]

By 1938, however, Marmarth was barely hanging on. Its population had dropped below 700 residents from its peak of about 3,500 in 1910. The town had been hollowed out due to a steady decline of residents and businesses, an outmigration that began during the drought that started in 1918 and lasted over a decade. As beaten-down ranchers began to abandon their properties, fleeing farther west in search of new opportunities, a nationwide strike of railroad shop workers and machinists in 1922 accelerated the exodus. The two-month labor stoppage was financially devastating to railroads across the country, including the Milwaukee Road. Sixty-five Marmarth shop workers took part in the strike, and in retaliation railroad management did not rehire them when the walkout ended. These good-paying jobs moved elsewhere, mostly to Miles City and Mobridge. Because they were represented by different unions, railroad engineers, firemen, and conductors did not participate in the strike.

Though the town's fortunes had faded, Frank Merrifield and Hausmer McCoy nonetheless visited Marmarth regularly to hand off the eastbound express train to another crew for its next leg of roughly 190 miles to Mobridge. The *Olympian* required multiple fresh crew changeouts in the course of its run between Puget Sound and Chicago. Labor regulations restricted the number of hours a train crew could be on duty each day. A crew change included the locomotive engineer, fireman, conductor, and brakemen. Mail and baggage clerks, porters, and the dining car staff, including the steward, waiters, and cooks, stayed on the train for the duration of the scheduled journey.

Before ending their shift, Merrifield and McCoy needed to sign a register in the dispatcher's office at the station. With that administrative detail done, they had over twelve hours to kill before they would sign in again after eight that evening to pilot the westbound *Olympian* No. 15 back to Miles City. It made for a long day. Even though Marmarth continued to be an important location for the Milwaukee Road, the railroad dormitories for overnighting crews or layovers like Merrifield's and McCoy's had been shuttered for years. The two remaining hotels in town, the St. Charles and the Yellowstone, were the only options. Neither had a restaurant.

Since they had been up and working since well before sunrise, Merrifield and McCoy were ready for a good breakfast. Fortunately, they had easy access to the Interstate Restaurant, located inside the Marmarth station. The "Beanery," as railroad crews called it, was under contract to feed hungry Milwaukee Road workers arriving in Marmarth anytime of day or night.[5] It was also open to the public. Located in the center of the station, bookended by the men's and women's waiting rooms, the Beanery had a semicircle, diner-style eating bar. The establishment also had a more traditional dining room with tables set off to one side. While the food wasn't fancy, it was good.[6]

Merrifield and McCoy would not arrive back home until after one in the morning on Sunday, which also happened to be Father's Day. For Frank Merrifield, the holiday must have been fraught, as the veteran engineer had a deep secret: he had a mistress in Marmarth. This was no casual affair. It had lasted for years, and at least one new Merrifield child had come into the world as a result.

Indeed, there were two Merrifield families, in two states, separated by 124 rail miles. If McCoy didn't know outright what was going on, he must have wondered why his partner would wander off for hours at a time during their downtime in Marmarth. Merrifield's double life had scandal written all over it. If revealed, it would have humiliated his family, especially Marie in Miles City, and he ran the risk of losing his job. Knowing this, Merrifield must have gone to great lengths to cover up his infidelity.

Regardless of Frank's precautions, the two women in his life would soon have a surprise meeting.[7]

CHAPTER 13

Perfection of Details

Aboard Westbound Olympian *No. 15, Saturday, June 18, 1938*

Hearing twins Don and Dean Hanscom stir on Saturday morning, porter Robert Nolan would have gently made his presence known at their berth on the *Choteau* and asked if they were interested in breakfast. The boys had the choice of joining others in the dining car or, if they preferred to sleep in, of having breakfast brought to their berth. For an additional charge of twenty-five cents, any passenger could have meals delivered on the *Olympian.*

Donald and Dean were not identical twins, but even their friends would occasionally confuse them. Both looked considerably younger than their age, almost boyish. Dean, at five foot nine, was slightly taller than Donald and thin as a scarecrow. Donald had broad shoulders and wavy dark hair, casually thrown back in the manner of a young Gary Cooper. Dean had more of a pompadour, likely requiring copious amounts of then-popular Brilliance hair oil to keep his dirty blond mane under control.

Like many twins, the Hanscom boys were inseparable. Both had played football at Bronxville High School in New York, and both had been journalists for the school newspaper. At the urging of their father, both twins had applied to and were accepted at Dartmouth College, becoming members of the class of 1940.[1]

Having just completed their sophomore year, the Hanscom boys were fully initiated Dartmouth men. Throughout their first two years,

Don and Dean shared a room on the third floor of Russell-Sage, a classic brick dormitory with dark green shutters. The melodious carillon bells of nearby Baker Library pealed on the hour, calling all students, including the twins, to class. It was a quick walk from Russell-Sage to Webster Avenue, also known as "Fraternity Row." Membership in a Dartmouth fraternity—never a "frat"—was highly sought-after. The "order of loyalty" among Dartmouth men was "College, Class, Fraternity," suggesting the prominent place of these social clubs in student life. First-year students could not join fraternities and had to wait until their second year to rush. The Hanscom boys did so in the fall of 1937, at the beginning of their sophomore year. A testament to the twins' popularity on campus, Kappa Sigma welcomed them both. In addition to their involvement in Greek life, Donald and Dean were serious students and interested in world affairs. They looked forward to moving into the new fraternity house on Webster Avenue in the fall of their junior year.[2]

Departing Minneapolis, the *Olympian* began a 914-mile leg to Harlowton that constituted just under half of the distance of its journey to Puget Sound. As an express, the *Olympian* made only seven scheduled passenger stops between Minneapolis and "Harlo," as railroad men called it: two in Minnesota, two in South Dakota (including Mobridge), one in North Dakota (Marmarth), and two in Montana (Mildred and Miles City). In addition to taking on or dropping off passengers, each stop meant a crew change and the replenishment of coal and water.[3]

All westbound Milwaukee Road steam locomotives ended their duty in Harlo, where the all-electric Quill locomotives built by General Electric took over, pulling the westbound *Olympian* up and down multiple mountain ranges to Avery, Idaho. In Harlo, the steam locomotives would be serviced while the tenders were refueled and filled with water, then turned around and hitched to eastbound *Olympian* passenger trains. Back and forth they went.

Before the Hudson arrived in the late 1920s, locomotives needed to be changed out sixteen times on the 2,188-mile trip from Chicago to Tacoma. Thanks to the improvements in durability and power, only five or six locomotives were needed by the early 1930s. In fact, a single Hudson could cover the entire 914-mile run between Minneapolis and Harlo, resulting in huge savings for the company. Steam locomotives demanded plentiful amounts of fuel and water to operate, and in the run from Minneapolis to Harlo, workers replenished the water supplies ten times, and coal supplies six.[4]

Like other railroads that operated across long distances, the Milwaukee Road erected coaling towers or coaling stations in many communities. These were often the tallest structures in town and could be seen for miles across the western plains. Most of the Milwaukee Road steam locomotives operating in the 1930s used soft anthracite coal supplied from company-owned mines and delivered by freight trains with sometimes fifty or more coal-filled hopper cars. For the most part, the trains' workings went unseen by passengers, who blithely enjoyed the trip, anticipating timely departures and arrivals.

The next scheduled passenger stop for the *Olympian* was Aberdeen, South Dakota. Making good time that morning, the train charged through western Minnesota. The lush, alternating green and gold scenery of Minnesota farm country mesmerized passengers. Endless fields of wheat, beans, and early corn stretched unbroken until Granite Falls, where the track met the Minnesota River. Hugging the river's eastern shore, the train hooked northwest toward Montevideo for a scheduled six-minute passenger stop and crew change.

The first call for lunch on the *Olympian* came as the train approached Granite Falls. A dining car waiter sounded the lunch chimes, starting from the luxury parlor car in the back of the train and working his way up the aisle, past the Pullman sleepers, the tourist sleepers, and last, the tourist coaches in front. From her seat in coach, Florence Maguire would have heard the melodic chimes as the waiter chanted, "First call for lunch. First call. Dining car is back, please," making his way forward.[5]

Life on the elite transcontinental *Olympian* revolved around mealtimes, and, in 1938, the food and service were exceptional. As George Rector, the Milwaukee Road's director of cuisine, explained, "Care in the perfection of details is the chief 'ingredient' in our recipe for making the Milwaukee Road trains famous." This had not always been the case. Prior to Pullman's rolling restaurants and the standard of excellence set by Fred Harvey, passengers often brought their own food. Some railroads began to put an "e" to denote an "eating stop" on train schedules. There, food hawkers pushed carts up to the train and sold food and drinks to passengers through their windows. At most stations, the food was awful and of poor quality. Often, leftovers from one train would be put out for the poor souls on the next train that stopped.[6]

Following the lead of George Pullman and Fred Harvey, the Milwaukee Road went to great lengths in the early 1900s to vastly improve the quality of food served to passengers on its trains. Dinner service on express trains from Chicago to Milwaukee, managed for more than two decades by steward Dan Healy, earned national acclaim for the railroad's high-quality cuisine. The Pullman Palace Car Company honored Healy in 1931 by naming their latest diner car after him and painting "Dan Healy" in gold on the flanks of the car.[7]

In the late 1920s, the Milwaukee Road hired George Rector as its director of cuisine. A celebrity chef, restaurant owner, and author of numerous best-selling cookbooks, Rector personally taught the railroad company chefs his recipes and techniques in a specially outfitted diner car, set up as a classroom on wheels. The chefs, cooks, and waiters were "drilled in all aspects of food service under simulated dining-car operating conditions." Proud of its diner cars and food experience, the company offered its patrons his latest book, *The Rector Cookbook,* for free.[8]

The forty-eight-seat *Olympian* diner car, introduced in 1936, was the largest-capacity single-unit food service car of any railroad. With three seatings for each of the three daily meals, the diner could serve as many as 175 passengers. The cars sported plush carpeting, wood veneer walls, recessed lighting in an arched, painted-white ceiling, a spacious floor plan, and air conditioning. A steward seated passengers at tables with crisp white linens, a small vase of real cut flowers, silverware, and custom-designed china with painted patterns of birds and flowers.

As the last seating for lunch was called, the *Olympian* had about forty miles to travel before crossing the Minnesota River into South Dakota. The express sped past a small station with a sign reading "Watson." Few passengers, except perhaps Paul Gehrig, would have taken any note of the small farming town. Even the humblest of communities along the railroad served as influential stops in the lives of railroad men, and Watson had been where Gehrig first started building his career along the tracks.

Paul Gehrig delighted in telling friends that he was Harvard man. After eliciting the quizzical look or expression of surprise he was hoping for, he would clarify that he did not attend Harvard University, but he did spend the summer of 1918 on campus in Cambridge for signalman training with the U.S. Navy. In May of that year, he had joined the service with hopes of becoming a radio operator. An article covering Gehrig's enlistment in his hometown newspaper, the *West Valley Journal,* exclaimed that "Paul is a bright young fellow with a lot of pep and ambition and should make good without question."[9]

Born in March 1893, Paul Peter Gehrig was one of nine children born to George and Bertha (Guettler) Gehrig of Cologne, Minnesota. George and Bertha's parents emigrated to America from Germany in the mid-1800s, ultimately finding their way to Cologne, a farming and grain-milling town settled by other German transplants. Located forty miles southwest of Minneapolis, the Cologne of Paul Gehrig's youth never had more than a few hundred residents. George Sr. started out as a farmer, but eventually turned to sales work for a local butcher shop. Given the relative isolation of the community, German was the primary language spoken by Cologne residents in its early years, including the Gehrigs.

Life in Cologne changed when the Milwaukee Road laid tracks through the town. A favorite pastime for residents, young boys especially, was to hang out at the local station to watch the trains. The flat, open landscape rendered the train's trail of smoke and ash visible until it disappeared over the horizon.

An advertisement for the Milwaukee Road deployed folksy language to convey the sense of awe and wonder a young boy like Paul Gehrig might have felt watching its trains pass through Cologne:

> Son, if you walked those tracks west, you would walk into a country so big, you'd feel knee high to a grasshopper. You'd see Indians sure—and cowboys, too – but you'd see lots of other things. Miles and miles of grain, more sheep than you ever counted – cattle-galore; sky-scrapin' mountains that look like they had a hunk of ice cream on top of 'em. You'd see rushin' water turnin' factory wheels and changin' yellow waste country to land as green as our pasture; apples half as big as your head and trees as tall as Jack's bean stalk. You'd

> meet friendly people livin' on farms and ranches and in up- and comin' towns and cities that ain't much older than you. Finally—you'd wind up lookin' out over the Pacific ocean.[10]

In 1909, at age seventeen, Gehrig took his first job as a laborer and apprentice telegrapher with the railroad at the Cologne station. How exciting it must have been being able to walk to work, to earn money for the first time, and to learn a valuable new skill like telegraphy. Paul was smitten. He had found his life's vocation.

During this time, Paul also started playing baseball. "Town ball," as locals referred to it, was a hugely popular pastime in Minnesota. On Sunday afternoons across the state, crowds packed bleachers to watch the games and cheer on their team, made up of members from the local community. Gehrig played infield and pitched for the Cologne Silver Leafs, sponsored by Silver Leaf Feed, a local milling company. Throughout the summer season, the Silver Leafs played against other area squads, including Norwood, Waconia, Plato, and Hydes Lake. Tournaments took place in nearby Glencoe.

Paul met his future wife, Marcella Hund, a young beauty from the neighboring community of Mapleton, while playing ball for the Silver Leafs. Marcella's parents, Roman and Barbara (Kiffe) Hund, had also emigrated from Germany, arriving in America in the 1880s. After a knee injury ended Gehrig's ball playing for the Silver Leafs, he and Marcella married and began building their family. Their first child, Leo, known as Lee, was born just weeks before the Navy shipped Paul Gehrig off for training. After his return in 1919, Gehrig received his first real promotion with the Milwaukee Road to the position of station agent in Watson, a speck of a town in the western hinterlands of Minnesota, closer to the Dakotas than to Cologne or Mapleton.

As the *Olympian* passed Watson that day, Gehrig may have reflected on his career on the rails. Other passengers may have overlooked the town. Or, perhaps, in the words of one local history, they might have agreed that Watson boasted "the clearest sounding name, the easiest written name, the best-looking station name on the C. M. & St. P. railroad between Chicago and Puget Sound."[11]

CHAPTER 14

The Dispatcher Taketh

Saturday, June 18, 1938

Roughly two hundred miles southeast of where Frank LaRoque and his flock of sheep lay stricken in Choteau, Montana, a violent cloudburst and heavy, localized rain drowned four hundred sheep at the Lammers Ranch near Harlowton. About eight miles east of the Lammers Ranch, rain and hail accompanied by intense gusts of wind broke the south-facing windows on the main house at the Winnecook Ranch. The fast-moving storms also flattened hundreds of acres of the Winnecooks' hay crop, resulting in a substantial loss and dealing a blow to the family's finances. The storms did not linger. Instead, the torrent moved steadily eastward, descending abruptly on homes, ranches, and communities, inflicting maximum damage before quickly moving on to pound the next town.[1]

Meanwhile, as the westbound *Olympian* No. 15 crossed through open prairie and the seemingly endless fields of corn and wheat in eastern South Dakota, the engineer signaled the fireman to lay on the steam. The relatively flat terrain of this section of Milwaukee Road track was perfect for pushing the eight powerful driving wheels of the Northern locomotive to a cruising speed of seventy-five miles per hour.

The Milwaukee Road was one of the earliest railroad companies to start laying track through South Dakota in its territorial days. It first entered Dakota Territory in 1872, extending a line from Sioux City, Iowa, south to a small settlement called Vermillion, located near the river of the same name, in the territory's extreme southeast. The Milwaukee Road's rail toehold in the territory became fortuitous after the discovery of gold in the Black Hills two years later, triggering a massive expansion of the territory's rail network to 2,456 miles of track by 1885.

When rail is laid, people follow. A flood of settlers, fortune seekers, swindlers, bandits, and outlaws descended on the fertile eastern half of the future South Dakota like a swarm of locusts beginning in the late 1870s, a period known as the "Great Dakota Boom." With the population exploding, the number of platted townsites skyrocketed from just 6 in 1870 to 213 in 1880. About half of the new towns were registered to railroad companies. By 1910, the Milwaukee Road dominated the rails in South Dakota, controlling an impressive 1,800 miles of track that connected almost every corner of the state.[2]

As westbound *Olympian* No. 15 sped toward its next scheduled stop in Aberdeen, communities with distinctly English names like Webster, Bristol, Andover, and Groton flashed by in the blink of an eye. These tiny locales were all railroad towns, created and registered by the Milwaukee Road's predecessor companies in the 1880s as part of the push to the Missouri River. The company strategically established these "ten-mile towns"—a reference to the distance between them—and built sidetracks near each town to allow trains speeding along the same single track to pass by one another. The idea was to avoid a "cornfield meet," in which two trains moving in opposite directions collided.

Cornfield meets were not uncommon in the late nineteenth century. Fortunately, improvements in communications and increasingly sophisticated train timetables made such horrible events a rare occurrence by the 1920s and 1930s. Before World War II, dispatchers and telegraph operators sprinkled throughout these ten-mile towns, sitting in station offices along the mainline route, dictated and choreographed all train movement. Detailed company-issued timetables governed the movement of all trains. And "train orders," issued only by dispatchers, superseded the timetables as needed to make allowance for delays, unexpected locomotive breakdowns, poor track conditions, bad weather, bridge construction projects, or crews working on the mainline track. Passenger trains generally received priority status over freight trains on the mainline. Express trains such as the *Olympian* took top priority, relegating all other trains onto sidings so they could continue their breathless pace to Tacoma or Chicago.

At about 3:40 P.M., between Aberdeen and Bath, two *Olympian* trains headed in opposite directions—westbound *Olympian* No. 15 and eastbound *Olympian* No. 16—roared by one another. The entire section between Minneapolis and Aberdeen was double tracked. A short greeting of steam whistles and hand waves momentarily broke the monotony of the prairie landscape with a whoosh and multi-second shudder as the trains flew past. According to the schedule, the eastbound *Olympian* No. 16 would make a Saturday evening stop in Minneapolis before pushing on to Chicago for an early morning arrival on Sunday, June 19.

About ten minutes after crossing over the James River, *Olympian* No. 15 pulled into Aberdeen for a passenger stop and a crew change. Incorporated in 1881, Aberdeen was named in honor of the Scottish birthplace of Milwaukee Road president, Alexander Mitchell, who also had a private railcar of the same name. A true rail town, prior to 1900 Aberdeen had nine different rail lines converging on the community "from all directions, much like the spokes of a wheel," earning Aberdeen its nickname: the Hub City.[3]

Aberdeen was also home for a time for Frank Baum, author of *The Wizard of Oz*. Baum was said to have drawn on his memories of South Dakota for the imagery of wicked weather pummeling a "land of plenty." The citizens of Aberdeen would gain national attention during World War II when they established a "Pheasant Canteen" with support from the Milwaukee Road, supplying free pheasant sandwiches to over a half million soldiers passing through town by rail en route to Chicago and, eventually, deployment to Europe.[4]

While stopped, a smattering of passengers climbed off the *Olympian* into the intense heat and humidity of the afternoon. Some sought refuge and a measure of coolness in the Aberdeen Depot, a stately brick station said to be the largest of its kind in all of South Dakota. The skies were overcast, and the temperature had climbed to eighty-four degrees. But the hot summer winds that can blow and scorch the treeless prairie and its residents had not yet started. It was only mid-June, after all.

Even though air conditioning was increasingly common on passenger trains in 1938, few homes, businesses, or railroad stations boasted this luxury. As the oppressive afternoon heat settled over Miles City like a heavy blanket, around the same time *Olympian* passengers stopped in Aberdeen, folks tried to cool down the old-fashioned way—by opening windows and pulling electric fans out of closets. For days, afternoon temperatures had soared into the high eighties and lower nineties in communities along the Yellowstone River.

Dave Hagerty had just begun his evening shift in the Miles City station. As a chief dispatcher for the Milwaukee Road, he was responsible for managing and directing all train movements within the 124 miles of mainline track between Miles City and Marmarth. On any given day, with dozens of freight and passenger trains on the move, the railroad's latest, carefully detailed timetables could be thrown to the wind due to weather, mechanical issues, track problems, derailments, and accidents. Dispatchers like Hagerty calmly and professionally straightened everything out. Given the stresses and enormous responsibilities of the job, it was no wonder that a train dispatcher's office was commonly referred to as a "battle station."

A deeply experienced railroad man, the fifty-two-year-old Hagerty had spent a decade dispatching trains out of Miles City and was seasoned in the art of managing complicated traffic schedules. His career began when he was only a teenager, hired by the Soo Railroad as a messenger boy and apprentice telegrapher. He changed employers and relocated often over the years, motivated by better pay and positions. Hagerty became a train dispatcher with the Great Northern and Northern Pacific railroads, before relocating to Miles City in the late 1920s to work for the Milwaukee Road.[5]

Despite the demands of his job, Hagerty had another passion: politics. He served in the Montana State Legislature as a representative for two terms, between 1933 and 1937. His interest in government opened doors for him, as during the Depression he was appointed chief relief administrator for several Montana counties, doling out federal dollars to families in need and recruiting eligible men to work for the Works Progress Administration. While working part-time for the government, the widowed Hagerty met his future wife, Lucille Donovan, a senior case worker assigned to work with him. They married in February 1937.[6]

As dispatcher, Hagerty relied on company-issued timetables for basic information on the comings and goings of train traffic. These paper manuals were updated frequently and date stamped, and contained far more detail than what was posted for the traveling public. Scheduled "meets," embedded into the timetables in boldface type, allowed opposite-direction trains or lower-priority trains to share the track by simply waiting in a siding for the other train to pass. Moving onto a siding also applied to slower, local trains when express trains such as the *Olympian* needed to blast by to remain on schedule. Any alteration to the timetable governing train movements required an official "train order," which could only be issued by dispatchers. "What the timetable giveth, the dispatcher taketh" was an old railroad saying that underscored the authority wielded by dispatchers like Hagerty while at their battle stations.[7]

Miles City, as a railroad division office, had a team of telegraph operators who helped Hagerty manage rail traffic in the area. Even though telephones were in widespread use in the 1930s, railroads still leaned heavily on the Civil War–era telegraph system, which used the dots and dashes of Morse code to communicate orders and convey train movements and track conditions. Through a web of wires attached to poles running parallel to the track, the telegraph provided Hagerty a means to quickly communicate vital messages to the crews of outbound or inbound trains. This could include basic information about weather and track conditions, but also red-flag warnings such as time changes for arriving or departing trains and reroutes caused by derailments or accidents, the effects of which could ripple across the entire rail system. There was a strict, military-like precision associated with translating a train order. The receiving operator had to repeat back word-for-word the dispatcher's transmission before an order could be considered "complete." Using carbon paper, multiple copies of the order would be made and then posted for the incoming train.[8]

A train order, also called a "flimsy" or "tissue," a reference to the onion skin paper used in earlier days, stayed in effect until it was superseded by another order. There were two basic types of train orders, a Form 31 and a Form 19. A 31 order required a signature of the train crew, usually the engineer or conductor, and was used when the dispatcher had absolute confidence that the train crew had actually read the order. The 19 did not need a signature.[9]

Trains on the move were alerted of change orders by a station signal board, which usually took the shape of a tall wooden pole, fifteen to twenty feet in height, erected near the main building. Sometimes, the signal board was attached to the side of the station, or even mounted on its roof. Mechanically operated green and red metal blades were positioned at the top of the signal board to convey important information to a train crew. The four-foot-long signal blades were illuminated at night for visibility. A green blade, similar to a green traffic light, signaled the engineer that he could proceed past the station without stopping. A red blade lowered to a horizontal position always meant stop, and alerted the incoming train that a train order was waiting.[10]

The train crew, including the engineer, fireman, conductor, and brakemen, knew to be on the lookout for the red blade or red light as they passed through towns. If an order was delivered to a location that was already a scheduled stop for the train, the engineer or conductor would simply walk to the telegraph operator's office and pick up the order. If it was not a scheduled stop, the train would conduct a "fly-by" pickup, in which the fireman or engineer would grab the order from the end of a long bamboo pole held by the telegraph operator. A fly-by pickup was dangerous, especially at night or during bad weather conditions. Loose brake shoes were known to take flight and loads that shifted on a moving train could easily kill a person standing next to the rail.

Over time, methods for the "hand up" improved, including prepositioning the order in a metal "hoop" before the train passed, allowing the crew to "grab-and-go" by reaching through the hoop. Methods advanced so much that even a wild animal could pull it off. In the 1940s, a very observant elephant named Jumbo, riding on a Ringling Brothers circus train, had seen the conductor grab an order out of the metal hoop when the train slowed down. The next time the train slowed down, Jumbo spotted the hoop, snaked his trunk out of the car and grabbed the order like a seasoned professional. Fortunately, orders were produced in triplicate and the telegrapher on duty was able to run out in time to hand off another copy to the conductor as the caboose rolled by.[11]

Officially on duty at his battle station desk, Hagerty strapped on a metal, hands-free mouthpiece that looked like an old, modified ear trumpet. The base of the mouthpiece sat on his chest, just below the knot in his tie. If things got busy, the mouthpiece allowed him to multitask by quickly barking out orders and directives without holding the telephone earpiece.[12]

Hagerty had been briefed by the outgoing dispatcher on significant events during the day, including changes to the master schedule and timetable. Westbound *Olympian* No. 15 was running late. Otherwise, most of the issues that evening were routine, except for reports of fast-moving rainstorms accompanied by high winds, thunder, and lightning moving east across Montana. But Hagerty wouldn't learn of the extent of the damage—the devastation at the Lammers Ranch in Harlo and the loss of a large herd of sheep by drowning—until days afterward, as the grim details made their way into the newspapers.

As the day progressed, the large storm system continued to roll across Montana, toward Miles City and its next unsuspecting victims. Torrential rains engulfed Roundup, the site of the Milwaukee Road's Bull Mountain coal mine, located on the Musselshell River, that afternoon. With the ground already saturated from rain events in previous days, flash floods carried away sections of U.S. Highway 87, the route connecting Roundup with Billings, cutting off the town's access to the south for days. Parts of the mainline Milwaukee Road track in town were swamped as well, reported to be under two feet of water. Meanwhile, local officials nervously eyed the bridge spanning the swollen Musselshell River, concerned it might share the same fate as the highway.

About thirty-five miles east of Roundup, the citizens of Melstone dove for cover from wind-driven hail that, according to terrified residents, sounded like a gatling gun. Icy droplets shattered windows in homes and businesses, stripped trees of their leaves, and pockmarked cars and trucks parked on the street. Soon enough, the unsuspecting denizens of eastern Montana communities like Miles City and Terry would find themselves in the storm's path. Meanwhile, in the parlor car of westbound *Olympian* No. 15, oblivious passengers ate cookies and sipped tea in quiet conversation.[13]

CHAPTER 15

Build It Fast

> It was a world almost without a feature;
> An empty sky, an empty earth; front and back,
> the line of railway stretched from horizon to horizon,
> like a cue across a billiard-board; on either hand,
> the green plain ran till it touched the skirts of heaven.
> —ROBERT LOUIS STEVENSON, *Across the Plains* (1892)[1]

Just before the first call for dinner at half past five, the *Olympian* passed the small town of Selby, South Dakota, about twenty miles east of Mobridge and the Missouri River. Selby sat on the one-hundredth meridian, an almost mythical line of longitude often referred to as the easternmost edge of the "Great American Desert." Within a span of miles, the landscape changes dramatically: annual precipitation plummets, trees become sparse, and ranches start to outnumber farms. The *Olympian*'s journey into the American West had begun.

American explorer John Wesley Powell described this transition in an 1890 article for *Century Magazine*:

> Passing from east to west across this belt a wonderful transformation is observed. On the east a luxuriant growth of grass is seen, and the gaudy flowers of the order Compositae make the prairie landscape beautiful. Passing westward, species after

> species of luxuriant grass and brilliant flowering plants disappear; the ground gradually becomes naked, with "bunch" grasses here and there; now and then a thorny cactus is seen, and the yucca plant thrusts out its sharp bayonets. At the western margin of the zone the arid lands proper are reached.[2]

Powell spent much of his later career educating the public and federal policymakers about the West's arid climate and its implications for future settlement and development. He argued that the farming techniques and crops used in the East were not necessarily transferable to the West. Sadly, Powell's research and eerily prophetic thinking fell on deaf ears, among the consequences of which was the dramatic bust of the homesteader boom a few decades later.

Nicknamed the "Big Muddy" due to the vast amount of earthen sediment it carries, the 2,350-mile Missouri River carves a path through the center of South Dakota, dividing it into eastern and western halves. A major tributary of the Mississippi River, the Missouri proved a formidable barrier to the builders of America's transcontinental railroads. Even though America's first transcontinental railway, the Union Pacific, completed in 1869, ran from Omaha, Nebraska, to Sacramento, California, it operated without a bridge over the Missouri for its first three years. America's eastern train network literally stopped at the river's eastern bank, in Council Bluffs, Iowa. Ferry boats and barges carried passengers and luggage to a separate train waiting on the other side in Omaha. In winter, when the river froze, temporary rail tracks were laid across the ice to hasten the transfer, but shifting ice made winter crossings perilous.[3]

The breadth of the Missouri and its fast, shifting currents befuddled America's best bridge designers. In March 1872, a half-mile-long bridge made of iron and wood, perched about sixty feet above the muddy water between Omaha and Council Bluffs, opened to daily train traffic. Celebrated as a monumental engineering achievement, the bridge lasted only five years before a vicious windstorm destroyed it. Lesson learned, the bridge was quickly rebuilt, this time with stronger materials.

The Milwaukee Road's track corridor intersected the Missouri in Dakota Territory, five hundred miles north of Council Bluffs. Upon reaching the river, the company was confounded by an entirely different set of complicating circumstances: the sixty-million-acre Great Sioux Reservation, which covered almost all of present-day South Dakota west of the Missouri River and parts of what is now North Dakota, Wyoming, and Nebraska. The Sioux Nation had long opposed any trains crossing their land and had successfully blocked most railroad construction plans into the western Dakotas for decades.

Politicians and developers itching to gain access to these lands, however, constantly attacked federal laws and treaties protecting the reservation. Starting in 1887, a series of new federal laws and policy changes fueled by anti-Indian sentiment targeted these lands, resulting in a massive shrinking of the reservation boundaries. Huge new tracts of land in the so-called West River region became available, triggering a miniature land-boom for settlers and speculators. Plans for extending railroad tracks across the territory, sidelined for years, were dusted off and reexamined. The timing of the Milwaukee Road's decision to build its Puget Sound Extension was hardly coincidental.

When Roswell Miller became president of the Milwaukee Road in 1888, it was a surprise appointment that raised eyebrows in railroad circles given his young age, forty-two, and the fact that he was a relative newcomer to the company. Yet Miller soon earned a reputation as a "suave, genial man" who led the sprawling organization with confidence and discipline. And like his predecessor, Alexander Mitchell, Miller advocated for expanding the railroad farther west, perhaps even to the Pacific coast.[4]

As president, Miller made the wrenching decision to move the headquarters and office staff to Chicago in 1890. For a half century, Milwaukee had been home to the railroad, helping it transform into a Midwest powerhouse. Despite intense local pride, Milwaukee was no Chicago, and never would be. Chicago was fast becoming the largest railroad hub in the United States, home to the Milwaukee Road's primary competitors, including the Great Northern, Northern Pacific, and the Chicago, Burlington & Quincy, and offered easy access to money, resources, and political power. Although the headquarters and front offices moved to Chicago, the company's fabled manufacturing, maintenance, and engineering shops remained in the Menomonee River Valley west of downtown Milwaukee.

Five years after Miller took over, the company had to grapple with the Panic of 1893, a deep economic recession that froze banking across the country and devastated the railroad industry. About a quarter of the operating railroads in the United States—eighty-nine separate companies, representing about forty thousand miles of owned track—went bankrupt during the recession. Moving quickly, wily financiers like E. H. Harriman, J. P. Morgan, the Rockefellers, and others feasted on the bankrupt remains, greatly enriching their railroad holdings and empires. Even the legendary Union Pacific Railroad, builder of the first transcontinental railway, went belly-up during the panic. Harriman eventually scooped up the Union Pacific and also bought controlling shares of the formidable Southern Pacific Railway a few years later. By the early 1900s, he owned and controlled the largest amount of track mileage in the United States.

With good management, agility, and a bit of Scottish luck, the Milwaukee Road was able to sidestep the convulsions that rocked the railroad world in the 1890s, emerging in 1900 as an admired blue-chip company with an estimated worth of about $250 million (about $7.8 billion today). Roswell Miller relinquished his role as president in 1899 and became chairman of the board of directors. Leadership of the company then fell to Albert J. Earling, a career employee. Thirty-three years earlier, Earling had joined the Milwaukee Road as a telegrapher at the age of seventeen. A protégé of Alexander Mitchell, he quickly rose through the executive ranks while remaining popular with rank-and-file employees. Upon becoming president, Earling immediately faced some excruciating decisions. Unless the company could continue to grow its rail assets and balance sheet, it would likely face a merger or hostile takeover and cease to exist as an independent rail operator. Its primary competitors, now controlled by James J. Hill and J. P. Morgan, were eager to take over the assets of the Milwaukee Road.[5]

Morgan and Hill were formidable adversaries. Morgan, who essentially controlled the country's banking system in the early 1900s, had allied himself with Hill, a ruthless Canadian known as "the empire builder" who made his mark in the railroad world by transforming his company, the Great Northern Railway, into a transcontinental powerhouse. With Morgan's money, Hill controlled most rail lines in the northern half of the western United States by the early 1900s.

Instead of buckling under the pressure, Earling and the Milwaukee Road brought forth a bold initiative. On November 28, 1905, the company announced a plan to extend its rail lines all the way to the Pacific Ocean. The decision to build the Puget Sound Extension was ambitious, and not without financial peril. Hill's Great Northern and Northern Pacific railroads already had mainline track headed to the Pacific and were actively scooping up freight and passenger lines in the growing states of Montana, Idaho, and Washington.

The Milwaukee Road faced another key obstacle in that, unlike the Northern Pacific and Union Pacific transcontinental railroads, it had no government land grants. The company would have to either buy land for the rail line or purchase existing railroads, a hugely expensive endeavor. The early cost estimates for the Puget Sound Extension were a whopping $60 million in 1906. Although it had anticipated the support of financial markets for this bold move, the company instead encountered skepticism. Carl Snyder, a respected financial analyst and longtime admirer of the company, was aghast. He panned the proposed route as bizarre and inexplicable and warned investors that the route chosen provided no competitive advantage for the company.

Despite the concerns, Earling and the company pressed ahead, dispatching teams of surveyors out to the Dakotas, Montana, and Idaho to map out the future rail route. Construction began four months later in April 1906. The company selected Mobridge, South Dakota, as the point to span the Missouri and connect its operations. Even though bridge-building techniques had advanced significantly by the early 1900s, it took the company a full year to span the river with a wooden bridge on pontoons, which could swing open to allow the passage of boat traffic on the Missouri.

The Milwaukee Road used this crude, early bridge for two years to support the construction of the Puget Sound Extension across the Dakotas into Montana. Special work trains, teeming with hundreds of immigrant laborers, assembled in Mobridge and dispatched across the river to carve grades and lay track across the prairie. An endless procession of freight cars, brimming with food for the laborers, steel rail, wooden ties, tons of bolts, spikes and plates, and all assortments of railroad building materials supported the construction. Before passenger service began on the new line, the company replaced the wooden bridge with a steel design in 1908.[6]

In keeping with its "build it fast" motto, the company hired one construction company, the McIntosh Brothers of Milwaukee, to manage construction of 718 miles of the new rail line, from Mobridge to Butte, Montana. The construction crews reached the eastern prairies of Montana, near Baker, on December 30, 1907.[7] It took just three years for the 1,400-mile Puget Sound Extension to be completed, an astonishing accomplishment. This feat was even more amazing considering that the route crossed five major mountain ranges in three states. The ceremonial golden spike was driven into a railroad tie on May 14, 1909, near Garrison, Montana, and on July 4 of that year the company started passenger service on the new line. Two years later, on May 28, 1911, the company unveiled the *Olympian,* a new luxury express passenger train with daily runs from Chicago's Union Station to Seattle and Tacoma. An advertisement for the *Olympian* in 1912 touted it as being the shortest line to the Pacific with the best scenery.[8]

By the time the Milwaukee Road launched the *Olympian,* the company was a major player among U.S. railroads. It owned 7,300 miles of mainline rail and about 1,200 locomotives, 518 passenger cars, 100 sleeping cars, 24 parlor cars, 20 dining cars, and 435 baggage and mail cars. For its freight business, it owned 30,000 boxcars, 8,700 flat coal and ore cars, 1,850 refrigerated cars, and 700 work, wrecking, and tool cars. Once fully operational, the Milwaukee Road referred to the Puget Sound Extension as its "Northwest Passage," as its freight trains began to haul loads of goods from the far reaches of the Pacific: "raw silk, wood, oil, tea, cotton, porcelain and wool from China and Japan; pelts from Siberia, and hemp and coconut oil from the Philippines." It also tapped into the productive industries of the Northwest, hauling "finished lumber, crude oil, grain, wool, livestock, zinc, fish, agricultural products, wood pulp, paper, posts, piling, manganese, copper, and copper products."[9]

The enormous risks taken with the underwriting of the Puget Sound Extension appeared to have been worth it for Earling and the company in the early years, but the final numbers were staggering. While estimates for the extension stood at $60 million in 1906, by the time it was completed three years later, the actual costs amounted to $257 million. Despite the company's optimistic revenue predictions associated with increased freight and passenger traffic, the enormous amount of debt soon proved impossible to absorb. By 1920, the company's debt load had ballooned to about $400 million, almost four times its size in 1910. Many factors contributed to the runaway costs, foremost among them the railroad's inability to secure federal land grants along its mainline track corridor. Other events like the opening of the Panama Canal in 1914 worsened the Milwaukee Road's financial position. In addition to fierce competition for freight hauling from other railroad companies, it now faced competition from shipping. Railroads initially downplayed the effect the canal would have on their business. Hill, the owner of the Great Northern, bragged that he would cut his freight rates so low that lily pads would soon fill the waterway of the canal.[10]

The 1917 entry of the United States into World War I added to the industry's woes. To support the war effort, the federal government seized control of all railroads, operating them at a loss until they were released back to their owners in 1920. Two years later, a poorly timed coal miner and shop men's strike not only added to the company's expenses, but also sank revenues due to disrupted service. Around the same time, a post-war recession undercut the Milwaukee Road's eastbound freight market, reducing freight tonnage and revenues by about 30 percent. By that time, too, Americans had new transportation options. The exponential production of cars, trucks, and passenger buses all combined to decrease rail passenger travel and curtail revenue.[11]

Facing mounting debts and increasing regulatory pressures, the company, once admired by investors, had few options left. The company filed for federal bankruptcy protection and receivership on March 17, 1925. In twenty-five years, it went from being one of the strongest railroads financially to one of the weakest. In receivership, the company was allowed to continue its operations while it reorganized its finances and assets. When the line emerged from federal protection in 1928, its name officially changed to the Milwaukee Road, and Henry A. Scandrett, who had started his career with the Union Pacific Railroad in 1901 as a claims adjuster, became its new president.

Looking to shake off the recent financial problems, Scandrett and his board of directors were bullish about the reorganized company's prospects. Unfortunately, the Great Depression hit the Milwaukee Road hard. In 1931, the company's overall revenues dropped about 22 percent. To make matters worse, passenger revenue continued to slide as the automobile only grew in popularity. Total passenger rides on the Milwaukee Road dropped from 20 million in 1920 to 6.7 million in 1930. Management had to cut salaries and wages for all employees.[12]

Rocked by an operating deficit of over $16 million dollars at the end of 1934, the company was again forced to seek federal bankruptcy protection. Its second bankruptcy filing occurred on June 29, 1935. The Milwaukee Road remained in bankruptcy for almost ten years, not emerging until 1945 after the end of World War II.

CHAPTER 16

Sioux Ceremony

Mobridge, South Dakota, Saturday, June 18, 1938

During the summer months, a small advertisement appeared in the brochure detailing the timetable and schedule for the *Olympian*. It touted "Indian Ceremonial Dances" that would take place between June 16 and August 31. "When the OLYMPIAN makes a brief stop at MOBRIDGE, SO. DAK.," it read, passengers could "step out on the platform and see painted and completely costumed Indians perform ancient and authentic tribal dances. Don't Miss it!" The schedule in the summer tourist season noted an extended stop of twelve minutes in Mobridge, enough time for passengers to watch the dances performed by members of the Standing Rock Sioux Tribe. What had begun informally with a small group of fully costumed dancers had become such a popular attraction that the Milwaukee Road began promoting the event and added time to the stop.[1]

George Lallas recalls his father, Tom, showing him and his siblings the Milwaukee Road's advertisement for the dances. One can imagine the excited Lallas children positioning themselves by the exit door of their coach car as the *Olympian* slowly pulled into Mobridge Station. Porters instructed passengers where to walk on the platform and reminded everyone to be back on the train in twelve minutes. A photograph taken by passenger Maurice Odquist shows other *Olympian* passengers joining the Lallas family on the Mobridge platform. George fondly remembers watching the performance and being fascinated by the sound of the drums and chanting. The dancers, according to one account, were "dressed in the most gorgeous of ceremonial outfits: full eagle-feathered headdresses, buckskin fringed leggings and skirts with beadwork, small bells and porcupine quills sewn in intricate designs, and exquisite handmade moccasins with still more beadwork on their feet."[2]

Esther Lallas had given each of her children some coins to toss onto a blanket lying on the platform to encourage passenger donations. Delighted, the Lallas family walked quickly back to coach 420 and reboarded. Porters reminded returning passengers that the second call for dinner in the diner car had just sounded.[3]

Just before departing Mobridge, all the clocks on *Olympian* No. 15 and the watches of its key train personnel were turned back one hour to Mountain Standard Time. Railway men from the past would have marveled at the simplicity of coordinating time and railway schedules in the 1930s. Some fifty years earlier, a passenger enduring a cross-country trip by rail would have been required to change their watch at least twenty times. Railroads pushed hard to establish standard time zones in North America, greatly simplifying the lives of most Americans in the process. As journalist Stephen Fried explained, "The fact that this new national standard of time was put into place by the railroads, and not the government, gave a fair indication of who was really running the country."[4]

After crossing the Missouri, the *Olympian* steamed past McLaughlin, the childhood home of Florence Maguire. Her memories of the ocean-like prairies of the Dakotas were bittersweet but still resonated. Since the 1870s, the Hand family had called Dakota Territory home. After emigrating from Ireland, the Hands established themselves as farmers, ranchers, businessmen, and railroad workers in a foreign country. Hand County, located in the heart of today's South Dakota, was named after a cousin, George H. Hand, who became territorial secretary in 1880. In that year, about 150 people occupied the county's 1,440 square miles, making it a terribly lonely place.

Florence's grandfather, George J. Hand, spent time tilling the land in the Dakotas but eventually gave up the plow to become a dairyman, moving his family to Mobridge, a new rail town bustling with Milwaukee Road workers. Florence's parents first met in Mobridge. Rose Hand's father, Charlie Haffeman, had been working as a carpenter in Wisconsin when he answered the call of a Milwaukee Road recruiter looking for skilled labor to build the company's first bridge across the Missouri River in 1906. He liked the work and soon relocated his family to the frontier rail town. The Haffemans also figured that the dry air in the Dakotas could benefit their sixteen-year-old daughter, Rose, who suffered from tuberculosis. Until they could save enough money to build a house, the family lived in a large, handmade tent that Charlie Haffeman stitched together on a sewing machine. Rose recalled that at the time Mobridge had "a few hundred families," a single dirt street, and no sidewalks.[5]

George and Dave Hand, an enterprising duo, owned one of the businesses in town: Hands Butcher Shop. Their supply of beef came from members of the Standing Rock Sioux Tribe on the west side of the river. Since the bridge across the river was not yet built, this arrangement required an intrepid round-trip rowboat excursion across the fast-flowing Missouri. The Hands purchased, butchered, and quartered the beef on the west side, then rowed it back to Mobridge. Tethered to trees on the east side, their horses and wagon stood ready to bring the fresh beef back to the shop.[6]

One day, Rose's mother dispatched her to the Hands Butcher Shop to buy some meat. While making the purchase, she noticed on the countertop a photo of a handsome young cowboy, standing by his pony with a lariat in his hand. "Who is this good looking cowboy?" she inquired. The clerk, Joe Delaney, responded that it was one of his bosses, George Hand. Always one to take charge of a situation, Rose took the photo from the counter and told Delaney, "You tell him a pretty girl stole his picture." A few weeks later, Rose and George met at a Fourth of July dance. "He really looked better than his picture," Rose recalled. After three years of dating, Rose Haffeman and George B. Hand married on April 30, 1912. Florence was born the following year.[7]

Looking to farm, George Hand left the meat business and, in 1915, bought a quarter section of land in McLaughlin, about thirty miles west of Mobridge. At the time, McLaughlin was the largest town inside the Standing Rock Indian Reservation. Most of the five hundred residents of McLaughlin were tribal members, many of whom were greatly impoverished and had been displaced by the shrinking of the reservation. The Milwaukee Road had put McLaughlin on the map in 1907 when, as part of its Puget Sound Extension, it laid tracks through the area and built a coaling station and water tower to feed steam locomotives as they traveled across the plains. Large stockyard pens and grain elevators would eventually be added to support local farmers and ranchers.[8]

Renting out their Mobridge home for ten dollars a month, the Hands relocated to a two-room tarpaper shack that George built on their land, which was about five miles outside of McLaughlin. Plentiful rain in their first few years yielded strong crops of flax, barley, and oats. Gaining traction as a farmer, George invested in a small herd of milk cows, and soon they owned about twenty calves. With another baby on the way, a bigger house seemed in order, so George built his family a four-room log cabin with a sod roof.[9]

The joyous occasion of Irene's birth in 1917 was marred by two events that in some ways marked the beginning of the end of the Hands' farming ambitions. A blizzard swept through McLaughlin, wiping out most of the family's cattle. On that same day, while working to save his herd, George accidently stepped on a steel spike in the yard. The rusted steel went through his boot and penetrated his foot. He almost died when the wound became infected.[10]

To make matters worse, the following year, the flu pandemic of 1918 ravaged many Dakota families, including the Hands. Rose Hand, pregnant again and with lungs already damaged by childhood tuberculosis, was stricken, and had to be taken to Mobridge to recover with relatives. George also became sick. They both recovered, and fortunately Rose's pregnancy was not compromised. She gave birth in May 1919 to twin boys Clarence and William. The Hand family, however, would not entirely escape the killer pandemic. George's brother Dave, Dave's wife, and one of their children all died within days of each other due to the flu.[11]

Like so many other homesteaders, the Hands' early farming success abruptly ended when the precipitation that had initially boosted their crops dried up. Sandstorms replaced rainstorms as an unforgiving drought settled across the Dakotas. Irene Hand recalled that the prairie surrounding McLaughlin became so parched during the summer that their front yard grass died, leaving nothing but packed dirt. "You could sweep our front yard," she remembered. Many times, swarms of grasshoppers devoured crops that survived the drought. Then there was the wind, which blew all the time, occasionally carrying snow into the family's home. The miserable conditions left little margin for error, and any small mistake could spell disaster. Once, a gate was left open, resulting in the disappearance of a herd of newly purchased cows and calves. Searching for days on horseback as far as North Dakota, George Hand never found the unbranded cows.[12]

No matter how hard he tried, it seemed that Florence's father was not cut out to be a farmer. He started to look for another job that would provide a steady paycheck to support his growing family. He fortunately found one working nights for the small local power company in McLaughlin. Money was still tight, but the Hands were not alone in this on the hardscrabble prairie. "We didn't ever realize that we were poor," Irene Hand explained. "Even the bankers lost money."[13]

Despite the hardships, Florence and her sister Irene had many good memories living on the lonely prairie. The girls loved having a yard full of cows, chickens, hogs, and horses. George taught Florence how to tack up and ride a horse. To attend grade school, Florence rode her pony five miles into McLaughlin by herself. If the weather turned bad, she stayed overnight with her grandmother and aunts.

Just as the Hands had achieved a fragile life balance, forces beyond their control upended it. In the summer of 1923, a mysterious disease temporarily paralyzed the entire right side of Irene's six-year-old body. Little was known about polio at the time, and she required frequent doctor visits and constant care. The family could hardly afford the doctors' bills. Out of necessity, Rose Hand leaned heavily on ten-year-old Florence to help care for her ailing sister and the two boys, now toddlers. With this kind of responsibility, Florence grew up fast. Like her mother, Florence became strong-willed, and gracefully accepted the new family responsibilities. Irene recalled that Florence always liked to be in charge.[14]

Eventually, the Hands had to declare bankruptcy, losing both their McLaughlin and Mobridge homes to the bank. Devastated by the setback, and despite his bad fortune, George Hand remained a proud man. Determined to set things straight again, he refused donations from neighbors and did not want help from the government, which offered only meager assistance. He wanted the family to avoid the stigma associated with "living on the county."[15]

George Hand packed the family and their remaining possessions into his pickup truck and headed back to Mobridge. There, the Milwaukee Road hired him as a night policeman. He worked there until the early 1930s, when the company reassigned him to Miles City and the family moved to Montana. Irene mostly recovered from polio, but the disease took its toll. Irene's right arm was paralyzed and limp for the rest of her life.[16]

As she passed through McLaughlin that day, twenty-four-year-old Florence Maguire probably had her mind on other things than how childhood hardships had shaped her as a person. But she would soon find out. Like her parents, she was a survivor.

Tom Lallas, meanwhile, was again alone with his thoughts. The Sioux dances had provided his family with a much-needed escape from the uncertainty that shrouded their return to Washington. With the Greece escapade a bust, he had spent many hours on the journey brooding about leaving his prosperous business and wondering what he should do once he got back to Bellingham. Walking to the smoking room at the rear of coach car 420, he chain-smoked his Lucky Strike cigarettes. He also drank as much coffee as his stomach could stand, since he needed to stay awake and alert on the trip to Tacoma.

While in Greece, Lallas underwent a medical procedure to remove a cyst from the back of his neck. While under anesthesia, he had a dream that frightened him. An unknown person appeared to him and warned that his family would suffer a tragedy on the train ride home. The premonition was so vivid, he even quietly told Esther about it and vowed not to shut his eyes while riding the *Olympian* home. Making things worse, Anna's stomach pains had grown since leaving New York, and Thomas and Esther were eager to get back to Bellingham to have their daughter checked by their family doctor.[17]

CHAPTER 17

Smell of Rain

Saugus and Calypso, Montana, Saturday, June 18, 1938

Late Saturday afternoon, the air around Dan Haughian Jr.'s ranch thickened. With no wind, an ominous stillness set in. In a repeat of similar weather activity on Thursday and Friday, dark clouds had begun to gather in the northwest over the Big Sheep Mountains. They rolled and boiled skyward, poised to unleash hell on the Yellowstone River valley. The smell of rain was in the air. Precipitation had threatened every afternoon, but, other than a smattering of light showers, nothing substantial had come of it. The crushing heat showed no sign of relenting, and the humidity—remaining above 80 percent for the entire day—added to everyone's discomfort.[1]

Local farmers and ranchers like Haughian fretted about the debilitating heat. Rainfall, how much and when it would come, was always at the front of their minds, especially during planting season. Rumors of drought, an annual occurrence in the prairie towns of eastern Montana, swirled in bars, in churches, and on front porches.

On the final tour of his alfalfa fields for the day, Haughian would have kept one eye on his vital irrigation pumps and the other on the gathering thunderclouds. The fact that his mother, Susan, had traveled back to the family farm—at the base of the mountain now directly under the clouds—was concerning. His own plans for the evening were also in question. But first, he had to finish his rounds and get his horse, who occasionally spooked at the rumbles of thunder echoing through the river valley, back to the barn.

The dinner and dance that Dan, his sister Kathleen, and Francis Motherhead planned to attend that evening would be held at the community center in Kinsey, about halfway to Miles City. Named after an early homesteader, Kinsey had only about seventy residents in 1938. Yet its hotel, general store, post office, and lumberyard made it one of the larger towns on the west side of the river. Every Saturday night, the community center would host a local country band with a caller for square dancing.

Dan and Kathleen had learned to dance from their parents, who regularly threw wild, all-night dance parties at the family ranch with fiddlers, plentiful jugs of whiskey, big boilers of coffee, and washtubs full of sandwiches. The revelers would dance until the sun came up, preferring not to travel at night. Bachelors Dan and Francis enjoyed the dancing and the music in Kinsey, but they were primarily interested in the eligible ladies who would attend. Having finished his chores and given his horse some extra grass, the cowboy was due for a shave, wash, and a fresh set of clothes.[2]

Within the hour, the trio squeezed into the cab of Dan's truck. As they headed toward Kinsey, short squalls of rain and wind gusts shook the cab. The precipitation soon transformed the hard-packed dirt and red clay roads into slippery mud. This "gumbo," as locals called it, was notoriously sticky and difficult to walk or drive through. In 1805, Meriwether Lewis, traversing the future Montana with his Corps of Discovery, referred to it as an "impassable glue."[3]

Their fourteen-mile ride to Kinsey followed a road that bent and turned with the meandering path of the Yellowstone River. Bouncing along behind them in the bed of Dan's truck that night was a ten-foot wooden ladder. Whether Dan was always in the habit of carrying a ladder is unclear, but its ten feet would soon make the difference between life and death. With back tires spinning, the truck lurched forward. It crossed the train tracks and turned south as potholes in the road filled with water and the shower picked up into a steady rain. Rumbles of thunder rolled down the small clay hills, and wind gusts buffeted the truck as it crawled toward Kinsey.

Just northeast of Kinsey, a line of thunderheads over the Big Sheep Mountains dispersed, and it seemed to be raining buckets in and around Terry, including in the badlands west of town. Terry's streets quickly transformed into muddy rivers. Residents reported that as much as two inches of rain dropped in the span of an hour. The basement of the historic Masonic Temple, located in the heart of downtown, filled with four feet of water. Flooding wiped out small bridges across Cherry Creek and washed away the dirt and concrete footings supporting both ends of a relatively new bridge four miles north of Terry.[4]

Across the Yellowstone River in Calypso, the rain pounding on the roof of Lou Goplen's house sounded similar to a passing freight train. Goplen had predicted that storms would pass over his section that day, but the rain came much heavier than he expected. He knew that several freight trains would be traveling his designated ten-mile stretch of track in the coming hours. He also knew that westbound *Olympian* No. 15—which, at the time, was still making its way through the Dakotas—would come through just after midnight, headed for Miles City, Harlowton, and ultimately Tacoma.

Heavy rain could cause all sorts of problems for railroad section men like Lou Goplen. A deluge of water could easily clog and wreck culverts protecting the mainline track. The carefully laid bed of gravel ballast and wood ties could wash away, causing the steel rails to sag, an imminent threat to passing trains. Federal authorities advised that when "violent rain or windstorms, or a sudden rise in streams occur," railroad workers needed to "carefully examine condition of the track, bridges and culverts," and report them to the chief dispatcher if they appeared unsafe. Fog was also a danger. Goplen's ten-mile section of track was possibly the lowest land between Terry and Miles City. Haze rolling off the gnarly clay hills of the badlands had a habit of settling over the mainline track like a curtain, causing visibility issues for the locomotive crews straining to see any signs of danger ahead.[5]

With the rain now blowing in sheets, Goplen did not wait for the dispatcher's call—he knew a patrol was necessary to check for water-related track problems and signs of damage. Quickly suiting up in rain pants and suspenders, heavy-duty rubber boots, and a bulky rain jacket, he trudged the fifty yards to his speeder, parked in a small shed off the mainline track. The walk would have been hard going, since the red clay gumbo stubbornly stuck to his boots with every step. The air, thick with humidity, would have caused Goplen to perspire heavily under his heavy, awkward rubber rainwear.[6]

Despite the rain, the speeder's gasoline-powered engine came to life immediately. Goplen throttled the track cart forward, turned onto the mainline, and headed for the tiny Calypso station a short distance away. The Milwaukee Road listed Calypso as a "non-agency station," meaning that it was too small to staff with an agent, and only local trains made occasional stops. A siding block phone at Calypso had a direct line to the dispatcher's office in Miles City. Goplen could not "occupy" the track with his speeder until he received verbal permission from chief dispatcher David Hagerty. There were important safety issues involved, especially at night. Goplen needed to know of imminent train traffic in his area, called a "line up," so he could be safely in a "hole"—off the track, on a siding—when a train passed. On the phone at about ten minutes before eight, Goplen recommended a limited patrol of the Calypso area due to the heavy rains. Hagerty approved the request.[7]

About forty minutes later, the two men spoke again. Concerned about new reports of rain throughout the area, Hagerty instructed Goplen to widen his patrol to include his entire ten-mile section of track, which stretched from Calypso to Saugus, just past Dan Haughian Jr.'s ranch. Despite his instruction to expand Goplen's patrol, Hagerty likely had no specific concerns. Having worked the battle station desk at Miles City since 1928, Hagerty was a veteran dispatcher, and using all possible caution was simply best practice.[8]

Around nine o'clock that night, about eighteen miles northwest of where Goplen was on patrol, fifteen-year-old Helen Warner tried her best to keep calm while comforting three terrified young children. It wasn't easy. Their automobile was stuck on a flooded coulee, while a violent thunderstorm raged around them, sending rain whipping into the car.

Just hours earlier, Helen had been enjoying a leisurely dinner at her mother's house in Terry along with her sister, Lucile, and her family. During the meal, dark storm clouds formed on the western horizon, and deep bellows of thunder came from the badlands. No rain had yet fallen at the Warner house, but the family knew it was imminent. Despite Helen's mother pleading with Lucile's husband, Jimmy, to wait out the storm and spend the night, he stubbornly insisted on driving back home to Kinsey. Lucile stayed the night with her worried mother, while Helen and the children squeezed into the two-seater 1926 Chevy touring car with Jimmy at the wheel.

Jimmy had options for driving back to Kinsey. The safest route would have been via U.S. Highway 10 on the east side of the river, a straight shot to Miles City. Instead, he decided to take a popular shortcut through the badlands on the west side of the Yellowstone River. Knowing the route well, he was confident they could make it home safely before the storm hit.

It would be a car ride Helen Warner never forgot. Within ten minutes of leaving her mother's house, they were heading west on Cherry Creek Road when the wind gusts began to steadily increase, rocking the small car. By the time Jimmy turned south onto Cap Rock Road, he'd already lost the race against the impending storm. As they drove by the headwaters of Custer Creek, in the foothills of the Little Sheep Mountains, Helen panicked. As she later recounted, "The section of Custer Creek we could see off to the left quickly turned into a raging river, at least a half a mile wide taking everything in its path. Large trees were floating down the river." The typically dry small streambeds and shallow coulees that cut across the dirt road at regular intervals had become fast-flowing rivers of muddy water. Despite Jimmy's frantic efforts to find the best path forward, their car was soon swamped. It became hopelessly stuck up to its running boards in the slick gumbo.[9]

Even with the windows up, intense bursts of rain kept finding their way inside the car. Helen wrapped her heavy, blue flannel nightgown around the children, trying to keep them dry and warm. Jimmy had wisely strapped two rolls of binder canvas onto the front fenders of his Chevy before they left Terry. During a break in the rain and constant lightning flashes, he leapt out and tied the heavy tarps over the back and roof of the car to provide more protection from the downpour. Jumping back into the car fully soaked, Jimmy admitted to Helen that the safest thing to do was stay put for the night.[10]

Helen and Jimmy were witnesses to the last of three violent thunderstorms that pounded the headwaters area of Custer Creek, all within about six hours. Locals recalled seeing a large mass of black clouds looming over the landscape. Frank Hamlich, a local rancher, took note of the series of storms, and later told the local paper that the last one, which hit at around nine o'clock, was the most severe. He was awed by the size and power of the storm, noting, "There was the most unusual movement of clouds in the distance . . . appearing to be a cyclone." Measuring six inches of rainwater in a sprinkling can in his backyard, Hamlich said it was the worst series of storms he had ever seen in the thirty-three years he had lived in the area.[11]

What Hamlich likely observed that evening was a line of thunderheads forming over the Big Sheep Mountains. In the world of meteorology, these mushroom or anvil-shaped clouds are called cumulonimbus clouds, a super-sized relative of moisture-laden nimbus clouds. Since they can grow to over four miles in height, the wind speed at their tops can be fierce, shearing off their heads, forming their unique anvil shape. Thunderheads typically form at low altitudes, under twenty thousand feet, helping them load and carry water more easily. The closer these cloud formations are to the earth's surface, the more likely they are to carry water.

At the time, such formations were commonly known as "cloudbursts," given their penchant for dumping an enormous amount of water in a localized area, but today they would more likely be called a downburst or microburst. Microbursts are often packed with an explosive cocktail of unstable air, water, and tremendous energy. The hot, humid conditions that occurred during the mid June 1938 heat wave in eastern Montana provided the perfect conditions for these storms.[12]

The Warners found themselves stuck at the upper end of the substantial watershed drained by Custer Creek. About ten miles across at its widest point, it spans roughly 160 square miles in total. The flooded, angry headwaters of Custer Creek had only one place to go: down the twenty miles of gently sloping prairie foothills to the Yellowstone River.[13]

Earlier that evening, aboard westbound *Olympian* No. 15, passengers took in the impressive monotony of the lonely prairies of western South Dakota. The three separate calls for dinner on the train had come and gone, but a small group of passengers lingered in the diner car while the waiters cleaned around them and began resetting the tables for the next day's first call for breakfast. While passengers digested yet another fine meal, the *Olympian* thundered past the stations of small prairie towns named Cadillac, Watauga, Keldron, and Thunder Hawk.

After a brief stop for coal and water in Lemmon, South Dakota, the *Olympian* accelerated through the tiny towns of Petral and White Butte before turning north and crossing the state line into North Dakota. The next scheduled stop was Hettinger, where Louise Woolsey of Miles City was waiting to board. Woolsey was on her way home from Minneapolis, where she had traveled to attend her daughter's graduation from Macalester College earlier in the week. Her daughter, Mary Louise, had planned to join her for the trip back home but decided to stick around in Minneapolis to spend time with her college friends following the graduation.[14]

Woolsey took the opportunity on her return to stop in South Dakota for a few days to visit relatives. Fanning herself to stay cool with a Milwaukee Road brochure, Woolsey was surprised to see a friend from Miles City walk onto the platform of the station, Mary Elizabeth Arnold. The two ladies chatted as they waited for the *Olympian,* scheduled to arrive in Hettinger just after eight that evening. Their plans, so casually changed, proved fateful for Mary Louise Woolsey and her mother.[15]

CHAPTER 18

First Order

Saturday, June 18, 1938

Knowing that westbound *Olympian* No. 15 would soon be arriving in Marmarth, North Dakota, on its way to Miles City, chief dispatcher Dave Hagerty instructed his telegrapher to immediately send an order to the Marmarth station. Issued at about a quarter to ten that night, it read: "Order 51. Heavy rains reported from Bluffport to Bonfield. Section men patrolling track." This precautionary order covered about thirty miles of mainline Milwaukee Road track along the Yellowstone River, including all of Lou Goplen's ten-mile section from Calypso to Saugus.[1]

Hagerty issued the order as a lower-priority "Form 19," which did not require a signature of acknowledgment by the crew. Even though it was a read-only order, Hagerty wanted to be sure that Frank Merrifield and the *Olympian*'s conductor, Chris McGee, had advance knowledge of the bad weather they would encounter on the return trip to Miles City. Like Merrifield and Hausmer McCoy, McGee had spent the day in Marmarth waiting to take the westbound *Olympian* back home to Miles City. Christopher Columbus McGee—his father named all his boys after famous explorers—was an experienced railman. He started work for the Milwaukee Road as a brakeman in 1902 before ascending to the position of conductor. McGee was the conductor on the first passenger train that pulled east out of Miles City thirty years earlier, in 1908.[2]

The conductor was the highest authority on a passenger train. In earlier days, the title of "captain," a throwback to the maritime era, was used instead. The conductor issued and took passenger tickets, careful to keep records of all those onboard. He then tucked the tickets into a small, leather satchel bag, tethered to his side by a shoulder strap. The conductor also supervised all the employees on the train. The engineer, fireman, brakemen, flaggers, porters, and dining car stewards all worked under the watchful eye of men like Chris McGee. The conductor was ultimately responsible for the entire train, including the safety of all passengers and crew. He might be called to settle arguments, wrangle unsupervised children, or intervene if a passenger became intoxicated. In the event of an emergency, the conductor was in charge. And it was McGee who shouted "all aboard" at passenger stops and signaled Merrifield when it was safe to depart.[3]

Waiting at the Marmarth station, Merrifield and McCoy had signed in for duty. While waiting on the platform for the *Olympian,* the telegraph operator approached both men and handed Merrifield the order from chief dispatcher Hagerty. The two men reviewed the order and instructed the telegrapher to share it with McGee. Merrifield noticed that McCoy appeared agitated after he had learned that a new Northern locomotive was pulling the *Olympian,* rather than the usual Hudson. Even though McCoy had been firing passenger trains for decades and had an engineer's certification, he had not yet had a chance to fire on the Northern. Merrifield tried to calm him down by reassuring him that a Northern was not altogether different from a Hudson. Sensing McCoy's uncertainty, he suggested that he ask a fellow fireman, Henry Shipley, who had experience firing the powerful, new locomotive, to join him in the cab until he got the hang of it. McCoy seized on his partner's recommendation and strode off to find Shipley.[4]

Henry Shipley and Hausmer McCoy were friends, beginning their Milwaukee Road firemen careers together in 1910. Like McCoy, Shipley was trained and certified back in 1916, but did not have a serious shot at becoming an engineer because of his low seniority. Their time on the rails had taken them in different directions. McCoy found his groove firing for passenger trains, while Shipley preferred freight trains.

At fifty years old with graying hair and steel-blue eyes, Henry Shipley did not have an ounce of fat on his wiry five-foot-eight-inch frame. The grueling physical demands of a fireman's job had kept him in shape over the years. He had also been on a routine "milk run" that Saturday, firing for a freight train from Miles City to Marmarth. Needing a ride back home to Miles City, he requested to "deadhead" on the westbound *Olympian* No. 15. Deadheading was a common railroad practice for ferrying off-duty crews and employees between stations or terminals. It meant a free ticket and seat, usually in the coach car. Shipley had secured a seat on tourist coach 4441 that night, the first passenger car in the *Olympian* consist. Several other off-duty employees, including members of Shipley's freight crew, were also deadheading back to Miles City in coach 4441. They included William Shearer, a veteran engineer; Chauncey Tarbox, a conductor; Jerry Clifford, an engineer; and John Umhoeffer, a retired conductor.[5]

McCoy was worried about his ability to properly fire the Northern, but there was no consideration given that night to another vitally important difference between the two locomotives: weight. At close to 450 tons including its loaded tender—almost one hundred more than the Hudson—the Northern was a monster.

Just as westbound *Olympian* No. 15 departed Marmarth, about one hundred miles to the west, Milwaukee Road freight train 263 approached Saugus. Moving nimbly due to a slick track and a heavy load, freight train 263 was chugging its way toward Miles City on the west side of the Yellowstone River. Its engineer, identified in later reports only as "Davis," throttled back the locomotive to about thirty miles per hour as the train crossed the short concrete and steel bridge that spanned Custer Creek. Having hit heavy rains while passing through Terry, Davis was aware of the storms lingering in the area and knew that Hagerty had issued a cautionary order due to the weather.[6]

While crossing Custer Creek, Davis wanted to be sure to get a good look at the water levels beneath the bridge. As he stuck his head out of the cab, he estimated that the creek had about three to four feet of water moving through it—nothing to be concerned about. Davis had passed over the bridge hundreds of times before, rarely seeing much water in the streambed, even after rainstorms. The veteran engineer also made a mental note that the track approaching the bridge looked good.[7]

Clear of the bridge, Davis throttled the locomotive back up and accelerated toward Miles City. About a mile down the track, safely parked in a "hole" near the Saugus station, Goplen and a section laborer named Eastwood waited for freight train 263 to pass. The duo had reversed direction after completing their patrol of ten miles of track as far south as milepost 1095 in Saugus. Now heading north toward Calypso, they continued their methodical inspection of the track.[8]

Davis would have seen the small headlamp on Goplen's speeder cutting through the mist as he passed the trackwalkers and exchanged a hand wave in greeting. Goplen and Eastwood pulled back onto the mainline track and headed east toward Custer Creek. They planned to stop and conduct a more thorough inspection of bridge AA-438, the only bridge of any significance in Goplen's section. Davis would find out the next day that his freight train 263 was the last to successfully cross the bridge at Custer Creek.

Around the same time, concerned about the worsening weather, Dan and Kathleen Haughian and Francis Motherhead left the dance early to return home. The rain and the wind seemed to be coming in surges, primarily from the northwest in the direction of the Big Sheep Mountains. The road conditions had deteriorated while they were in Kinsey, resulting in slow going for Dan's truck. Low-lying sections were washed out in many areas. Fog had settled in, and visibility was poor. At times, the truck's windshield wipers could hardly keep pace with the rain.

With the ranch in sight, the truck approached the mainline tracks for the Milwaukee Road just as Goplen's speeder came into view. After crossing the rail, Haughian stopped his truck and hopped out to greet the trackwalkers. The two men knew each other. Haughian's ranch marked the southern end of Goplen's ten-mile section. Goplen and Haughian had a brief conversation, likely discussing the condition of the roads and the nasty weather, during which Goplen indicated that the mainline track appeared to be holding up well despite the rain.[9]

After the meeting, Goplen and Eastwood drove the speeder about a mile to the north, crossing the Custer Creek bridge, where they parked the track car on the east-side abutment. Each took a side of the bridge and spent time on their knees with flashlights to examine its underside. Using their flashlights, Goplen and Eastwood could see muddy water flowing rapidly under the bridge, about six or seven feet below the main girders. This flow seemed about right considering the heavy rains pounding the area that evening. Satisfied with their inspection of the bridge, the two men resumed their patrol and headed toward Terry. Goplen would later tell investigators that the amount of water he and Eastwood witnessed flowing in Custer Creek "did not suggest any possibility of trouble" for trains crossing the bridge, including the speedy *Olympian.*[10]

With Merrifield, McCoy, and Shipley in the cab, the eight massive drive wheels of the Northern S2 locomotive slipped momentarily on the rails before gripping and slowly gaining speed on its way to Mildred, then Miles City. *Olympian* No. 15 had been losing precious time all afternoon as it crossed the Dakotas. It was now nineteen minutes behind schedule as it pulled out of Marmarth. There is a saying in the railroad industry that it is harder to make up time on a fast track than a slow one, and the *Olympian*'s delay seemed to prove that true.[11]

As they left Marmarth, *Olympian* conductor Chris McGee ordered Merrifield to test the train's air brakes, a procedure called a "running brake test." The test was standard practice, typically done at the beginning of a run with a new crew. Merrifield had control of two brake systems, one for the locomotive and the other for the entire train. With a steady, experienced hand, Merrifield slowly moved the brake handle forward for the train until he could feel the grab of the brakes. Satisfied that the brakes were working properly, he levered back the handle to the running position. The test had taken seconds. It was so smooth that only McGee and the other employees on the train knew what had occurred.[12]

The widespread adoption of air brakes, an invention dating back to the 1870s, had transformed railroad safety. As Bill Wilkerson described them: "Air brakes on a train are the most complicated, simple system ever devised by man." Before air brakes, employees called brakemen used guts and muscle to slow trains manually. When signaled by a special toot of the steam whistle, the brakemen hurriedly climbed atop each car and turned a large wheel that applied a brake shoe to the car's wheels. Unsurprisingly, it was not a very effective method for stopping a one-thousand-ton train. As spectacular crashes mounted and droves of passengers and brakemen died in the middle of the nineteenth century, a businessman named George Westinghouse stepped forward with a new idea for halting the forward progress of the massive trains.[13]

Westinghouse's innovation used pressurized air to force a brake shoe against the wheel of a train car. A steam-driven compressor located in the locomotive filled a tank with pressurized air. Connected to the train cars through flexible hoses, the pressurized system could simultaneously activate all the cars' wheel brakes. The engineer controlled the air pressure with a valve in the cab. Full pressure kept the brakes open, while a release of pressure applied the brakes. Westinghouse designed this seemingly counterintuitive system as a fail-safe method to stop a train. If an air hose happened to break, or cars were separated in some type of accident, pressure would be released, and the brakes would slam shut. Still, with air brakes fully applied in an emergency, it could take a modestly sized passenger train like the *Olympian* an entire mile—or longer—to come to a full, screeching stop.

With the brake test complete, Henry Shipley offered Hausmer McCoy some pointers on how to operate the Northern's coal auger, supplying Merrifield all the steam pressure he needed to accelerate west toward Montana. It was only six miles to Montline, the state boundary line that separated North Dakota from Montana, and another fifty-seven miles to Mildred, where the *Olympian* would stop briefly so Merrifield could top off the tender's coal supply and replenish its water.

Merrifield flicked on the locomotive's powerful headlamp. Due to the steel-gray skies and storms in the area, nightfall had fallen early in the extreme western edge of North Dakota. The headlamp vibrated with the movement of the train, casting ghostly shadows against the desolate badlands, making the landscape appear even harsher.

Merrifield would have enjoyed handling the new, powerful Northern locomotive. Built for heavy freight work, and barely six months old, locomotive 220 was clearly overpowered for the task of pulling an eleven-car *Olympian* consist. Although most familiar with the Hudson, he was sure to like the feel of the locomotive as it effortlessly navigated the curves and topography of the steel rail approaching Montana.

CHAPTER 19

A Thousand Miles

When the *Olympian* entered Montana at about half past ten that night, the only sign was a simple mile marker with the number 1,001, indicating the distance from its starting point in Chicago. The *Olympian* had another 1,187 miles to go before reaching Tacoma, Washington. After crossing the state line, the rail bed straightened in a northwesterly direction, allowing Merrifield to throttle up the locomotive to a cruising speed of sixty-five miles per hour. About fifteen minutes later, the *Olympian* steamed past the town of Baker. With a population of about 1,300 in 1938, it was the first sizable community the train passed in Montana.

A few minutes later, a mile or two outside of Plevna, the rail route that A. G. Baker plotted in 1906 turned decidedly northwest toward Terry. Baker's decision to swing the line northwest is curious, since less than twenty years later a team of government surveyors chose a more direct route to Miles City when planning construction of U.S. Highway 12. The path for the new highway cut out a full third of the rail distance from Plevna to Miles City, some thirty miles. The straightening of the road also stranded the small railroad towns of Westmore, Ismay, Lacomb, Mildred, and Whitney.

Just after eleven o'clock, the *Olympian* charged through sleepy Ismay, where the mainline rail corridor picks up the path that follows O'Fallon Creek for the next forty miles to Terry and crosses the Yellowstone River. As the *Olympian* sped toward Mildred, the mainline rail momentarily nicked the northeastern edge of Custer County and then entered Prairie County.

Between Ismay and Mildred, the *Olympian* started hitting rainstorms, coming in waves from the west. The steel rail ahead, as seen through the locomotive's headlamp, was now slick with rain. The weather quashed any hopes Merrifield and McCoy had for making up lost time on the way to Miles City. In fact, the *Olympian* would be lucky to not lose additional minutes on its schedule in the remaining seventy-five miles. McCoy seemingly had calmed down since leaving Marmarth and was growing more comfortable with firing the new locomotive. Henry Shipley's patient coaching was working.

The air became thick and humid as the *Olympian* approached Mildred. Despite sealed windows on the train, the smell of wet sage, pungent and aromatic, drifted through the coach cars and sleepers as passengers slept.

Around the same time, Lou Goplen and his partner, Eastwood, had arrived back in Calypso after completing their three-hour patrol of the mainline rail, a round-trip of about twenty miles. Within sight of his lonely section house, Goplen found a few spots along the track where storm water had displaced some of the gravel ballast beneath the rail. The heavy rains had also left pockets of standing water on the rail bed. This discovery immediately raised the specter of a "soft track." A one-thousand-ton train passing over a depressed section of steel rail could cause wheel lift on one side, a perilous situation that, depending on the speed of the train, could set forces in motion leading to a derailment.

After examining the sections of track further, Goplen knew he had to inform Hagerty, the dispatcher in Miles City, about the problem. Using the siding phone at the Calypso station, Goplen called Hagerty to update him on their patrol findings and the local weather. Their conversation focused on the soft track in Calypso. He never mentioned the water flowing in Custer Creek beneath bridge AA-438.[1]

Even in the driving rain, the red "stop" light was still visible on the Mildred station signal board. A new dispatcher's order awaited the arrival of the *Olympian*. Merrifield gently throttled back the train, slowing it down to almost a crawl as he eased the massive tender behind the locomotive in position to get topped off with coal and water. It was not unusual during the weekend nights of summer for a small crowd of Mildred residents to gather near the track to get a glimpse of the Milwaukee Road's finest as it briefly stopped. But not that night. The platform and station lights were on, but it was ghostly quiet.

Making his rounds through the passenger cars, conductor Chris McGee had also seen the red light. He waited for the train to stop before he jumped off and quickly walked to the station to retrieve the order from the on-duty telegraph operator. Like Merrifield, McGee had been anticipating another train order, given the warning they had received in Marmarth about heavy rains in and around Terry. Hagerty's new Form 19 order, number 395, read: "Do not exceed 20 miles per hour between switches at Calypso account of soft track."[2]

Based on his conversation with Goplen, Hagerty had telegraphed the directive to Mildred about thirty minutes earlier. McGee interpreted the order to mean that parts of track around Calypso could be underwater. Calypso was several miles south of Terry, on the west side of the Yellowstone River. McGee quickly returned to the train to share the information with Merrifield and McCoy.

As McGee approached the cab, he met Henry Shipley, who was climbing down the stairs. Shipley informed McGee that, in his opinion, McCoy had the firing procedures completely under control for the new locomotive. Since his coaching was no longer needed, he headed to his seat on the first tourist coach to try to get some sleep before their arrival in Miles City. As Shipley walked off in the dark, McGee climbed up into the cab and shared the "go slow" order with Merrifield and McCoy.[3]

McGee made a habit during night runs to check the powerful headlamp of the locomotive and did so as he exited the cab that night. Satisfied the light was working properly, McGee walked back to the last tourist coach car with his lantern lighting the way. Standing in the coach doorway, McGee waved his lantern in a large arc motion from his knee to his shoulder, signaling to Merrifield in the cab that the train was set to go. The station's signal board changed to green, the "highball," and McCoy gave Merrifield the thumbs up sign signaling that the locomotive's steam pressure was where it needed to be to depart the station. Merrifield gave two short blasts on the steam whistle and gently notched the throttle forward. The eight drive wheels began to turn, and *Olympian* No. 15 headed west once again in a plume of steam.[4]

The *Olympian* departed Mildred at 11:47 P.M. It had lost another minute during the stop and was now twenty minutes behind schedule. The Mildred station telegraph operator noted the exact time the *Olympian* departed and sent the details in a dispatch to Hagerty. From the telegraph operator's office, the lights of the *Olympian's* last car, the parlor car, were visible for a few fleeting moments as the train left the station. Soon, it was dark again at the station, with the rain and wind the only sounds.[5]

AS the crow flies, it is about twenty-two miles from the headwaters of Custer Creek in the Big Sheep Mountains to the Yellowstone River. Just before it connects with the river, the creek passes through Saugus and flows under bridge AA-438. Custer Creek bends and cuts wildly through the deeply creviced badlands. The smooth, eroded rock under the dirt and prairie grass offers minimal friction to flowing water, allowing it to accelerate during a thousand-foot drop in elevation to Saugus. Numerous other smaller creeks feed into Custer as it makes its way to the river. That night, the heavy rains had engorged every streambed on the west side, exponentially expanding the volume of water cascading down the prairie foothills.

Investigators later determined that the titanic amount of rain released by the series of storms Saturday evening had carved an entirely new watercourse into the hillside that fed into Custer Creek, dramatically increasing the peril below. The river of mud and water accelerated as it descended, ripping down full-grown trees and collapsing entire hillsides. As the flow expanded into a boiling stew of trees, stumps, sagebrush, and ripped-up fence posts, it devoured and destroyed everything in its path.

Witnesses recalled the raging waters of Custer Creek, now monstrous in size and closing in on Saugus and bridge AA-438 at a terrifying speed, beginning to roar like an unearthly beast. For thirty years, since 1908, the small bridge spanning Custer Creek had allowed safe passage for thousands of trains.

WITH Mildred behind it, the *Olympian* wove its way toward Terry, following the northwesterly path of O'Fallon Creek. The *Olympian* would occasionally stop in Terry to drop off or pick up a passenger, but not on this night; it was full steam ahead to Miles City. Barely slowing down, it rumbled by the quiet station just after midnight, still running about twenty minutes behind schedule. The new estimated time of arrival in Miles City was one in the morning on Sunday, June 19.

At about twenty minutes after midnight, the *Olympian* arrived at the narrow "barrel shot" entryway of the Calypso Bridge. It took just seconds for the entire eleven-car train to emerge onto the sparsely populated west side of the Yellowstone River.

In addition to the approximately 165 passengers, there were eighteen Milwaukee Road employees and several contracted personnel on the train. Aside from Merrifield, McCoy, and a few other crew members still at work preparing for the upcoming stop in Miles City, almost everyone else onboard was asleep or sitting quietly in the dimmed cars of *Olympian* No. 15. One of those passengers still awake was Thorston Thoreson, from Dawson, Minnesota. Gazing out his window, he watched the last vestiges of the storm outside as the *Olympian* made its way through eastern Montana. "It was a black morning through which the train was rushing," he recalled. "The wind was blowing into a roar. Nothing but flashes of lightning showed us what was going on out in that open, isolated country beyond the windows."[6]

As the train approached Goplen's section house in Calypso, Merrifield eased back on the locomotive's throttle, slowing down to about twenty miles per hour. Despite being eager to close the last thirty-four miles to Miles City as quickly as possible, Merrifield and McCoy followed Hagerty's "go slow" order. The locomotive's headlamp pierced the darkness, illuminating the glistening ribbon of steel track that lay ahead. Merrifield and McCoy spotted a lantern swinging methodically in the distance. It was their colleague, Goplen, signaling the location of the soft track. The rain had stopped. Faint, distant flashes of lightning offered reminders of the storm system now beginning to move away.

Both men craned their heads outside as they approached Goplen and his swinging lantern. Training their flashlights at the rolling wheels of the locomotive, the men examined the condition of the track as the *Olympian* chugged forward. There were spots on the track where sitting water reached the outside edges of the locomotive's seventy-four-inch driving wheels. If the track were to sink at all because of the rains, it certainly would have done so under the crushing weight of the Northern, its tender loaded with water and coal. The track appeared safe and beneath it the thick bed of gravel ballast held firm.

Clear of the spongy section, Merrifield throttled up the locomotive to a comfortable cruising speed of about fifty miles per hour. The speed limit for passenger trains was sixty-five in this area, but the veteran engineer played it safe. Goplen stood by the tracks and watched until the lights of the *Olympian*'s parlor car disappeared into a fog bank near where Deer Creek empties into the Yellowstone River. The crickets resumed their trilling, the sound of the rippling river gradually filling back in as the *Olympian*'s chugging faded in the distance.

Goplen fired up his speeder and headed home to end a long day. With his track car tucked in for the night, he trudged back through the muck to his simple home by the river. After cleaning up, he crawled into bed, careful not to wake his wife, Christine.

That night, an employee with the Northern Pacific Railway in Miles City had drawn the short straw, assigned to monitor nighttime train movements from a small control shack in a place called Zero on the east side of the Yellowstone River. Zero lived up to its name, consisting of not much more than a few switching signals, a weed-infested rail siding, and herds of lazy cattle from the nearby Kalfell Ranch. In 1882, Gottlieb Kalfell had staked a claim on 160 acres of land near Camp Creek adjacent to the newly laid tracks of the Northern Pacific. As the number of homesteaders grew, the Northern Pacific established a new shipping depot nearer to Kalfell's ranch and called it Zero. Gradually, however, the punishing life of ranching and farming on the prairie led to a steady exodus from the area. By the mid-1930s, Kalfell's ranch was again mostly alone in a sea of grass.[7]

From his shack next to the Northern Pacific's mainline tracks, the night monitor had commanding views of the Yellowstone River and the Milwaukee Road's rail corridor on the opposite side of the river. He could also see lights at Dan Haughian Jr.'s ranch directly across the river in Saugus. In fact, Gub Kalfell, Gottlieb's son, who was friendly with Haughian, used a small, wooden home-built boat to cross the Yellowstone for visits.[8]

With a railroad watch and detailed timetable, the Northern Pacific employee in Zero knew the comings and goings of all the nighttime trains between Terry and Miles City. In the days of steam locomotives, an experienced railman could identify the type of engine pulling a train by its headlamp. He could also tell the train's speed by how its headlamp moved. Seen from across the river, the beam illuminated the pale gray trunks and fluttering leaves of the giant cottonwood trees that sprouted next to the Yellowstone. It cast large shadows on the sandstone outcroppings that framed the corridor of the mainline track.

As an employee of the Northern Pacific, the fact that the Milwaukee Road's *Olympian* was running late that night was not his concern. Then again, as the minutes of his watch clicked away, he may have been curious about the continued darkness on the west side of the river. At about half past midnight, however, the headlamp of Merrifield's locomotive made its appearance, and the Northern Pacific employee watched the dancing light as it moved south toward Saugus and Haughian's ranch.

Then the light disappeared. The west-side track was suddenly dark again. Puzzled, the monitor took out field glasses to see if he could still see the train moving. Perhaps the headlamp failed for some reason. As he searched again with his binoculars, he could see train car lights on what looked like the east end of the Custer Creek bridge. The lights were not moving. Had the train stopped at the bridge for some reason? Alarmed, he picked up the railroad phone in his shack and called the Northern Pacific dispatcher in Miles City.[9]

The Northern Pacific dispatcher immediately called his counterpart at the Milwaukee Road. Hagerty's shift had ended at midnight, and Neil Grogan was now manning the station. Before signing on, Grogan and the on-duty telegrapher had been briefed on all the events of the evening, including the weather and soft track issues. Dispatcher Grogan was also aware that *Olympian* No. 15 was running late.

The last communication Miles City had regarding the *Olympian* was a message sent from Mildred when the train departed. Concerned about the report of possible trouble, Grogan and his telegrapher began to work the phones for information. Calls went out to the Terry station and to Goplen in Calypso. No connection. After several unsuccessful tries, Grogan concluded that the telephone lines were down.

Outside the Miles City station, a small crowd had gathered in the refreshing coolness of the night, waiting for the *Olympian* to arrive. George and Rose Hand, along with their twin sons, Bill and Clarence, had driven downtown to greet Florence at the platform. Inside the dispatcher's office, however, anxiety had begun to take hold. Was the *Olympian* halted for some reason on the track? Had something gone horribly wrong? The train was not due in Miles City for another twenty minutes. Lacking hard information, and not wanting to jump to conclusions, Grogan continued to make calls. With all eyes on the station's master clock, time slowed in Miles City.[10]

CHAPTER 20

Pileup

Saugus, Montana, Sunday June 19, 1938

Having passed the soft track in Calypso without incident, Merrifield and McCoy figured it would be smooth sailing to Miles City, about twenty-eight miles to the south. The rain had mostly stopped, and the night skies began to clear. Except for a gradual bend in the track about eight hundred feet before bridge AA-438 over Custer Creek, the mainline rail on the west side was a relatively straight shot to the bridge in Kinsey that would return the train to the east side of the Yellowstone River.

A single headlamp positioned on the nose of the locomotive provided a minimum of 1,500 feet of visibility. As the light beam straightened after the bend and illuminated the track to the bridge, Merrifield and McCoy must have been stunned by what they saw ahead: a massively engorged Custer Creek. The normally dry wash was the size of a small lake, boiling with trees, stumps, and debris. They could see the track across the short bridge, but the raging slurry of silt—a record twenty feet deep—flowed madly under the span, inches below the rail. Cruising at just over fifty miles per hour, it took the *Olympian* about ten seconds to travel the remaining eight hundred feet to the bridge abutment on the east side. Once on the bridge, the locomotive and tender would cross the 180-foot span in less than three seconds.

The *Olympian* did not make it. Unknown to Merrifield and McCoy, the tremendous forces exerted by the fast-moving water tunneling under the bridge had torn away tons of riprap rock protecting the bridge's concrete piers. The shock of the 440-ton steam locomotive and tender pounding across the bridge was all it took to trigger a catastrophic collapse. As the locomotive reached the halfway point across the bridge, the structure started to buckle. The first three concrete piers groaned and then rotated on their foundations, destabilizing the fifty-foot steel plate girders holding up the track. The movement of the piers was enough to cause the locomotive's tender, filled with heavy coal and water, to tip to the right and come off the tracks, plunging its front end through the two-foot-thick concrete floor of the bridge and into the water. The downward momentum of the tender dragged the back end of the locomotive, where the cab sits, down with it, forcing the nose of the massive locomotive to lift into the air while still traveling across the bridge at great speed.

The derailment of *Olympian* No. 15 triggered a series of disastrous events that resulted in four distinct crash areas spread across both sides of Custer Creek and on the destroyed remains of the 180-foot bridge. The first area involved the lead cars of the train, including the locomotive, tender, U.S. Mail car 1201, and the express baggage car. All landed on the west side of the bridge, either on or near the concrete abutment, demolishing it, and gouging out a deep hole of mud and rock on the northwest embankment of the swollen creek.

The second crash area involved the next three passenger cars, filled with sixty to seventy sleeping or dozing passengers. The engine had dragged the cars partway across the bridge at high speed before they violently separated from the baggage and mail cars. Twisting sideways, the cars jackknifed against each other before coming to a stop near the west side, pinned between the pulverized remains of several bridge piers. The three cars remained upright throughout but landed entirely within the raging waters of Custer Creek.

Among them were tourist coach car 4441, which included Henry Shipley; tourist coach car 420, also known as the smoker, where the Lallas family was seated along with Paul Gehrig's niece, Helen; and the tourist sleeper car Ipswich, where the seven members of the Gehrig family had adjoining berths. The entire front end had ripped off of coach car 420, a testament to the astonishingly violent forces at work during the wreck. A sizable chunk of its steel roof was peeled back like a sardine can. The

Ipswich's underside chassis, which held its wheels, was torn off as it slammed through the bridge and its piers.

The third crash area involved the next two tourist sleeper cars, the Choteau, also known as the middle sleeper, and sleeper C, porter Louis Williams's car. The Hanscom twins, along with the three Clancy ladies, were in their sleeper berths on the Choteau. Its front coupling tore away from the Ipswich, stranding the car on fragments of rail close to the middle of the bridge. It teetered precariously over the raging creek waters. Behind the Choteau, the front half of Williams's sleeper car hung over Custer Creek while its back half clung to the track on the east bridge abutment.

The remaining cars of *Olympian* No. 15—the diner car, two luxury Pullman-Standard sleeper cars, and the observation car at the rear—had miraculously stopped short of the bridge on solid ground. This, the fourth crash area, saw the least amount of physical damage

Death came quickly for Merrifield and McCoy. As their massive locomotive plowed through the bridge, it sheared off the concrete tops of three piers and rapidly decelerated. The tender, mail, and baggage cars behind it smashed forward, catapulting the locomotive toward the west bank of the creek. As it launched into the air, the locomotive twisted to the west before crashing hard on the embankment, carving out an enormous ditch in the mud and rock. A rail from the bridge pierced the locomotive's smokebox like a javelin through tinfoil and stuck out its front end near its nameplate. Less than six months old, the shiny new Northern locomotive was demolished, lying crumpled on its right side, hissing and smoking.

Remaining stubbornly attached throughout, the tender had accompanied the locomotive on its death leap. Unlike the engine, it had landed upright on top of the destroyed west bridge abutment, showering the passenger cars that trailed it with tons of black dust and chunks of coal.

In the U.S. Mail express car, behind the locomotive and tender, was mail clerk Milton Norberg. Based in Aberdeen, South Dakota, Norberg was a U.S. Post Office employee contracted to man the "rolling post office" for the Milwaukee Road. He pulled duty on the *Olympian* weekly, often shuttling between Minneapolis and Harlowton. Norberg usually had the mail car to himself, particularly after the latest round of Milwaukee Road layoffs and budget cuts. This particular evening, however, Norberg was sharing the mail car with his colleague, fifty-four-year-old Fred Raschke, from St. Paul. Dragged by the tender and locomotive, the mail car skidded across the top of the water as the bridge disintegrated. When the steel coupling connecting it to the tender sheared off, the car pitched sideways through the air before smashing on top of the locomotive. As it tore across the cylindrical smokebox of the locomotive, the midsection of the mail car crumpled, almost splitting into two pieces, and disgorging mail and packages. The steel wheels and undercarriage of the mail car crushed the locomotive's cab before skidding to a stop upright and diagonal to the smoldering wreck beneath it. Both Milton Norberg and Fred Raschke died instantly.

Behind them, in the express baggage car, baggageman Charlie James had been eager to get to Miles City, his hometown. With several days off waiting for him, James looked forward to spending them with Vera, his wife and partner of fifteen years. James was tired. The forty-seven-year-old had been tossing bags for the railroad for almost thirty years, and he had been on duty for the better part of a week, riding the *Olympians* from Miles City to Minneapolis and back. He had followed the Milwaukee Road to Miles City in 1909, just as the Puget Sound Extension was being built. The same year, he was hired as a bag handler and had been doing the job ever since. On this trip, a corpse, on its way to Tacoma, Washington, for burial, lay silently in a lightweight coffin in the mail car. If James were like many other railroad men, he would have worried that a corpse on a train brought bad luck.[1]

Helplessly tethered to the mail car, the baggage car was "ripped apart and torn open like paper" before smashing sideways against what remained of the west bridge abutment. The weight and momentum of the careening baggage car caused it to burrow under the rear wheels of the tender, levering the back end of the tender skyward in a surreal pose that would haunt rescuers. Charlie James, the veteran Milwaukee Road employee working in the baggage car, did not make it home to Miles City that night. He too died in the wreck, succumbing to multiple fractures and a crushed chest, leaving behind his beloved Vera.[2]

After helping McCoy in the cab from Marmarth to Mildred, Henry Shipley had returned to his seat in tourist coach car 4441, the first

Olympian passenger car behind the baggage car, alongside his deadheading mates. He had fallen asleep while the *Olympian* made its way to Miles City. The sudden crash sent Shipley flying into the lap of one of his colleagues, Bill Shearer, a veteran locomotive engineer. A series of impacts tore several seats from their floor anchors and sent them flying through the car. Broken glass sprayed the passengers flung from their seats as the car windows buckled and exploded. The car careened from side to side, before coming to a final, crunching stop, still upright but now in the raging water of Custer Creek near the west bridge abutment, closest to land on the west side. The lights in the car flickered out.

For a moment, there was an odd silence in the darkness. Then a collective wail. Cries of pain and shock rang out, mixed with frantic calls to loved ones. Like everyone else, Shipley was momentarily stunned. But he understood that the train had crashed. Extracting himself from a tangle of luggage, suitcases, shoes, and articles of clothing, he reached into his pocket and was relieved to find his flashlight. At first, Shipley thought the train was still on solid ground, but when he clicked on his flashlight, he was horrified to see that the car had somehow landed in a river. Water roared past the car on both sides, just below its windows.[3]

"Boys, we're in the old Yellowstone!" he yelled. Shearer saw the water and took a few minutes to realize it was Custer Creek. He later recounted to reporters being shocked by the raging current, thinking to himself: "Why, I have put a train over these tracks thousands of times and I never saw more than a bucket of water in the creek at once."[4]

Aiming his flashlight around the car, Shipley tried to get his bearings and find a way out. Passengers later recalled that Shipley's flashlight had a calming effect and rendered him the leader of the escape effort. He beamed the light toward the front of the car and the dormitory-style rooms of the dining car employees. It was crumpled. Shipley did not know it at that moment, but the baggage car had flattened the coach's front when it crashed on top of it, blocking any possible escape in that direction.

Turning to the rear, the path to the back door and vestibule looked passable. Picking his way to the back of the car, checking on passengers as he went, Shipley was able to pull the rear door open and look outside. The roar of the engorged Custer Creek set him back on his heels. Fortunately, the rear of the coach had landed close enough to the west bank that Shipley believed he could either jump or wade through the waist-high water to reach land.[5]

Immediately behind Shipley were several Milwaukee Road colleagues including Bill Shearer, Ed Hamm, and Mike Cain. They were among the first to make it safely off coach 4441. "We all crawled out of our coach. It was hard to see very much," recalled Shearer. "The mail express and baggage cars, which were between us and the locomotive, were piled up every which way. We crawled along the pile like monkeys, wondering how anyone could be alive."[6]

Soaked through their clothes but safe on dry land, it took a few moments for the men to regain their senses. In the pitch dark, Shipley panned his flashlight to reveal a scene of utter devastation. Piles of twisted and shredded steel lay everywhere, including scattered train wheels and mounds of coal. The crushed and smoking carcass of locomotive 220 hissed in agony on its side, next to the angry river of mud.

Realizing that they were among the first survivors off the train, Shipley and Shearer grabbed Hamm and Cain in a huddle. Shouting over the noise of the water, they agreed that the latter pair should head for the Saugus station, about a mile down the track, to call Miles City for help. The two men quickly disappeared into the night, sprinting down the tracks.[7]

STICKING to his vow, Tom Lallas was awake at midnight when the crash happened. His wife Esther and their three children had long since bedded down in their coach seats. Dressed in her day clothes, Esther had closed her eyes and seemed to be asleep. The two boys, John and George, slept together in one seat. Anna, the eldest, had a seat to herself.[8]

As the train rumbled toward Custer Creek, Tom quietly slipped into the aisle and made his way to the men's lounge, which also doubled as a smoking room, in the front of the car. He wanted a cigarette. The lights had been turned down in the car, and except for the click-clack, click-clack of the train, all was quiet. Joining a few other night owls in the lounge, he sat down and lit up. Then, without warning, all hell broke loose.

"The first I knew it was as if we were going through air," said Thorston Thoreson, still awake after watching the storm from his window earlier. "There was a terrible bump. I didn't know what happened. The water started pouring in. People screamed and fought to get out."[9]

The front end of the car, including the men's lounge where Tom Lallas was sitting, was crushed flat like a tin can onto the former grocer from Bellingham, fracturing his skull. Death was not instantaneous for Lallas. An autopsy revealed that he had in fact, after receiving the head injury, died from drowning. Many of those in the front end of the tourist coach who survived the initial impact lay trapped in the wreckage, seriously injured and dying.

Seated with her children toward the middle of the car, Esther Lallas was thrown violently against the wall and knocked unconscious. Her three children, though tossed around in their seats, were relatively unharmed except for John, who suffered a broken arm. Shaken, ten-year-old Anna reached over and opened the window shade slightly, hoping to see what had happened. She was shocked to see that the coach car appeared to be sitting in the rapids of a river. Anna screamed, dropping the shade. John and George could see the fear in her eyes.

As cold water began to pour into the tourist coach, passengers scrambled to stay out of the muddy swirl, some standing on top of their seats. Within seconds, the inside of the car became one with the river as powerful currents of silty water coursed through the aisle and among the seats. "Break the windows! Break the windows!" shouted frantic passengers. It was so dark inside the car that some passengers lit matches to try to find their way out. Meanwhile, the rising waters buffeted the motionless body of Esther Lallas, slumped over in her seat. The terrified children screamed for help. A man waded over and lifted seven-year-old George up to the luggage rack above the seats. Curling up in the cramped space, he held his straw hat tightly across his bare legs to stay warm.[10]

The car began to pitch and shake as it settled into the raging river and filled with muddy sludge. The sealed windows were no match for the force of the water and began to break, making a terrifying noise. Esther was now swallowing water and beginning to choke. Eight-year-old John and his older sister, Anna, struggled to keep their mother's head above the swirling water that pulled on them with increasing force. They furiously clung to her, grabbing her shirt and her black hair. "I tried to hold her, but the water was too strong," Anna later explained.[11]

A sudden rush of current sucked their mother out of their arms. The image of Esther being swept out of the car and into the darkness would haunt the children for the rest of their lives. It all happened so fast. Screaming for their mother, Anna and the two boys sobbed and howled for help.

When the train derailed, Paul Gehrig and his family were asleep in their two berths in the Ipswich, which landed upright and jackknifed next to coach car 420, coming to a rest near the middle of the raging Custer Creek. Another passenger on the Ipswich, identified only as F. Woltz, had been asleep in his berth when his window exploded, raining shards of broken glass on his face and bunk sheets, immediately followed by water gushing in. Woltz's first thought was that the train had crashed into a ditch. He threw his clothes on and tried to climb through the window opening, stopping short at the sight of the dark waters. "The current in the stream," he recounted, "was awful and we dared not see how deep the creek was at that time for fear we might be taken by the stream."[12]

Nineteen-year-old Catherine Hahn, traveling with her parents, had turned off the lights in their Ipswich berth at about ten that night. She and her parents awoke to violent jolts and then a shuddering sound as the sleeper plowed through the bridge and its concrete piers. "We're not on rails!" Katherine screamed. Out the window they could see water roaring by the car. Her father, sleeping in an upper bunk, jumped down in his pajamas and yelled, "Get dressed right now!" The Ipswich's porter ran by their berth, shouting, "People, this is a terrible wreck."[13] Expecting panic, the Hahn family was surprised by how calm many other people seemed.

In the darkness of their two sleeper sections, the Gehrigs' world turned upside down. Two of the Gehrig children, Paul Jr. and his younger brother, Jack, were awakened by a series of bumps, then an odd sensation of flying through the air, before a final terrific crash sent everyone tumbling out of their berths. The sound of glass shattering, people screaming, and the roar of angry river had the Gehrig children and Paul Sr. on their feet. Chunks of coal and soot rained down on them through a massive hole torn in the metal roof of the car.[14]

The Ipswich had plunged through the disintegrating bridge and landed hard on top of the decapitated bridge pier 4, which broke the sleeper across its midsection. Water poured through its cracked body and broken windows. Dressed in his pajamas, Paul rushed to check on his family. He found his wife, Marcella, unconscious, a crumpled bunk pinning her head against the berth's wall. Paul called to his eldest son, Lee, for help, and together they were able to free her. Marcella immediately regained consciousness but remained dazed and disoriented.

As the Ipswich rapidly filled with water, Paul and Lee looked for an escape. The front end of the Ipswich was crumpled and angled downward, almost completely submerged. The rear door was of no use either since it would open directly into the raging waters of Custer Creek. Paul and Lee concluded that they needed to get up onto the roof, which was split open, but the crack was not enough to safely get people through. That left the window. Breaking the glass on the west side of the car, the Gehrigs peered out and could hear shouts and screams from the passengers next door in car 420. Paul seized the fishnet storage hammock below the window, which he had used earlier in the evening to hold his book and shaving kit, tearing it off the wall and calling for Lee to help him make it into a rope. Tying the makeshift line around his waist, Lee climbed out the window, careful not to cut himself on the large shards that remained. It was a treacherous maneuver. Pounded by the raging waters of Custer Creek, the car pitched and rolled in the darkness. One slip would send him to his death.[15]

The sixth passenger car, the tourist sleeper Choteau, was stranded over the torrent of water near the bridge's twisted first pier, dangling precariously on the remains of the shattered bridge. Trapped inside were the Hanscom twins and the Clancy ladies, along with about twenty other passengers. The Choteau's rear coupler still held fast to the tourist sleeper behind it. As *Olympian* passenger Raymond Noftaker recounted, "It was too quick to get scared. All I knew was it happened, and then there were people with almost nothing on crawling from wreckage. Some of the bodies were swept downstream."[16]

Like most of the passengers aboard the *Olympian,* Don and Dean Hanscom had changed into their pajamas and were quietly reading in their bunks when a terrific jolt stunned both young men. Don was flung across the berth and knocked unconscious. Dean, lying in the forward lower bunk, slammed against the wall, hitting it hard. The once tidy berth was thrown into disarray by the sudden stop, with clothes, bedding, books, luggage, and other personal effects scattered around in a jumbled mess.

Before Dean could regain his senses, the entire outside wall of their berth heaved inward under the immense pressure of the the raging waters outside the car. The wall buckled, then cracked wide open under the windows, flooding the Choteau with a river of mud that sucked him out of his bunk. As the force blasted him toward the other side of the car, Dean caught one last terrifying glimpse of his twin brother being swallowed by the surging water.

Dean was hurled all the way across the aisle and pinned against the windows on the opposite side of the car. The windows held momentarily, then exploded outward, ejecting him into the dark, cold waters of Custer Creek. He fought the currents, gasping for breath and fighting to keep his head above the water. As the son of a seafaring father and having grown up in Seattle, Hanscom was familiar with ocean currents. He had learned that if caught in a riptide, to go with the flow. He stopped battling and let the currents take him. The creek was filled with debris, including clumps of sod, tree stumps, and an assortment of wood pieces. There were stars in the black sky, along with flashes of lightning in the distant mountains. Dean Hanscom did not know it at the time, but he had already been carried into the Yellowstone River, only a few hundred yards downstream of the Custer Creek bridge.

The Yellowstone was moving rapidly that night, but it remained relatively shallow. As Dean floated away from the crash scene, Custer Creek's angry roar receded, replaced by the smooth ripples of the Yellowstone. He used his legs to redirect himself to the shoreline. After some distance, he was able to feel his feet bouncing off the bottom of the riverbed. He crawled onto a sandbar and collapsed. Shivering uncontrollably, Dean lay on his back and caught his breath. Where was Don?

It was nothing short of a miracle that Dean Hanscom survived the violent accident and subsequent swamping of the Choteau. He was one of the few. Inside their berths, other unsuspecting passengers had smashed into the car's front end due to the sudden stop on the bridge.

Most of the passengers trapped in the Choteau died of their injuries or drowned. Margie Clancy suffered multiple internal injuries in the violent first moments of the crash. Subsequent autopsies for Kate and Nell Clancy revealed that both suffered serious fractures and internal injuries from the initial impact. Some, including Kate Clancy and porter Robert Nolan, were eventually washed out of the car's broken windows and carried into the Yellowstone. Within twenty-four hours of the accident, the Choteau was almost universally referred to as the "car of death" by reporters.

Anticipating the Olympian's arrival in Miles City, Florence Maguire had made a fateful decision to leave her seat in coach car 420 and walk back two cars to the ladies' lounge in the Choteau so she could "doll up a bit" and get ready to greet her family. After applying her makeup and adjusting her hat, Florence was suddenly thrown against the front wall of the lounge. She lay on the floor, stunned but conscious, thanks to a large couch that had cushioned her impact. Racked by a wave of nausea, Florence rolled over to vomit. Broken glass littering the linoleum floor beneath her made a crunching sound as she moved. The overhead lights blinked several times but stayed on. As she struggled to sit up, she noticed blood all over her hands where small chunks of glass had embedded. For what seemed like the longest time, she stared at them, trying to comprehend what had happened and how seriously she was hurt.[17]

Florence could see, but her hearing and situational awareness were muted. The car continued to rock and sway, which struck her as odd. It felt to Florence as though the train were still moving, but she knew it had stopped. A series of sharp screams followed by wailing startled her into jumping to her feet. All her senses roaring back, she realized that water was causing the car to sway.

Staggering to the lounge door, Florence turned the handle, but the door would not open. She could hear people screaming and yelling on the other side. She pounded on the door with both hands and yelled for help as loud as she could. No response. Unknown to her, the impact of the crash had twisted the steel frame of the Choteau, jamming the door shut.

As she pounded on the door, Florence realized she was standing ankle-deep in cold, muddy water that was rushing in from under the lounge door and starting to pour in from a large crack under the window. "There I was, trapped, like a rat in a hole, being put deeper and deeper into the water," she later recalled. Pushing back against the panic surging through her body, a steely determination took over. "I am not going to die here in this train car," she told herself. She looked back at the windows, knowing they were the only way out.[18]

Luckily for Florence, instead of the sealed windows used in the air-conditioned cars, the ladies' and men's lounges had two single-sash windows that could be opened by sliding up.

Gritting her teeth and screaming, Florence forced one open just wide enough to squeeze her small frame through. The roar of the rushing river water immediately filled the small cavity of the ladies' lounge, drowning out all other sounds and soaking Florence in the process. Her new rayon dress now stuck to her body like shrink wrap. Standing on the wash bowl, she hung onto the towel rack to prevent herself from being engulfed. Mustering all the courage she could find, Florence stuck her head and shoulders out the window. Waves of water slapped the side of the Choteau, rocking it crazily. Florence had learned to swim as a child but feared that attempting to brave the current would mean certain death. Over the roar of the river, she heard muffled shouting from the roof of the Choteau. Twisting her body around the small window opening, she started to climb up toward the voices. Now standing on the window's edge, she pressed her body against the side of the car as hard as she could, then reached up and grabbed the lip line that ran the length of the roof. Stretched across the exterior of the car, she took a moment to catch her breath. She later described the water licking at her legs as "sweeping, boiling, sucking down the submerged cars, bounding with waves forming." As she decided on her next move, the Choteau pitched slightly farther toward the opposite side, allowing her to crawl onto the roof.[19]

With the car rocking underneath her, Florence sat in stunned silence. As she later described, "Everything was dark. The night [was] hideous with lurid flashes of lightning illuminating in streaks, the deep purple and the black of night. There was a feeling of wildness about it." The lightning flashes gave her momentary glimpses of the wrecked train to the west and the immense amount of water that surrounded her. She could see other passengers trying to extricate themselves from the swamped cars, and still more struggling in the rapids, holding onto pieces of the wreckage to stay alive. "I could not see for any distance, but could discern that there were other people, some standing on ledges and places of safety." It appeared to her that the car was sitting in a lake of boiling water. She also realized that she was utterly alone on the roof. Worse, she was cut off from the rest of the train cars piled like toys on the west side of the river.[20]

Her only option was to turn around and follow the rounded train car rooftops that led back to land on the east side. She could see people waving to her and shouting, but the deafening roar of the water made it impossible to hear. Defying gusts of wind, and now starting to feel cold from her wet clothes, Florence began to crawl. When she was about halfway across the roof of the Choteau, the back of the car started to sink into the muddy water, pulling the head of the next attached car, tourist sleeper C, down into the water as well. The heavy steel couplings that bound the cars together screeched loudly.

Frightened by the sound and the teetering car, Florence started crawling faster: "Through the roaring of the wind, I could hear people trapped below me in the car, tapping on the ceiling of the car which was practically submerged in the raging torrent of water." She could also hear people tapping on the windows. "No doors could be opened," however, as she observed the water "flowing, surging, making a moaning sound, rushing swiftly, curling itself about the piled-up cars." Tragically, she realized, "I couldn't do anything to help them. I knew they were being slowly submerged in the water, like I was a few moments before."

By the time she reached the back end of the Choteau, she could see that the rear of the car had sunk in the water about halfway up the vestibule door. The lights on both cars were still on, which provided some visibility as she climbed down the ladder. The vestibule was partially torn off, and the platform that connected the cars was now underwater. As she clung to the ladder, the pitching and yawing of the car intensified as the fast-moving water battered its side, spraying mud and silt like a firehose. With a loud metal-on-metal shudder, the car dropped several feet deeper into the torrent. The dark, swirling water was now up to Florence's knees, and she could feel its powerful pull. Terrified, feeling alone and helpless, she froze. She wrapped her arms around the ladder and closed her eyes.[21]

MEANWHILE, like the Choteau, tourist sleeper C was in peril. Its occupants literally teetered between life and death. Its front end, still coupled to the doomed Choteau, hung over the raging waters of Custer Creek. Its back half, tethered to the dining car, clung to the track on the east bridge abutment.

Prior to the crash, Louis Williams was still hard at work, more than twenty-four hours after leaving Chicago. Passenger shoes and boots, left in heaps outside the berths, needed to be cleaned and shined. Lounge and lavatory floors needed mopping. Fresh towels had to be hung. Sinks required cleaning. Most importantly, Williams knew several passengers planned to depart the train in Miles City, requiring his assistance in escorting them to the car door and carrying luggage.[22]

Without warning, he felt a momentary flying sensation before the force slammed him into the front wall of the men's lounge. After a series of terrific jolts, the car came screeching to an abrupt stop, leaving Williams in a stunned heap. The car lights blinked several times. Following an initial wave of dizziness, he felt a searing pain in his left side but ignored it, knowing that something terrible had happened to the train. "When we got that bump, I knew mighty well something was wrong," he remembered.[23]

His immediate impulse was to check on his passengers. The car was quiet for a moment before the screaming began. As he made his way up the aisle to the front of the car, several passengers poked their heads out of their berths to ask what happened. Williams promised he would find out.

Not until he reached the ladies' lounge at the front of the car did he realize he was walking downhill. Puzzled, he may have wondered whether hitting his head had given him vertigo. At that moment, he began to hear the noise outside the car. The roar became louder as he entered the front vestibule. "I could hear the water and knew we must be in a river or a washout," he later explained. He could see the back end of the Choteau, but it was pitched down at an odd angle. Williams realized at that instant that the weight of the other cars were pulling his into the river. Wheeling around, he immediately knocked on the first set of berths on opposite sides of the aisle. "Everybody get up. We need to get out!" Williams shouted.[24]

As Evelyn Bratrud, a passenger on his sleeper car, recounted, "I was asleep in my berth, and he came running through the car. I wasn't afraid until I raised the curtain beside my berth and saw water rushing beneath my window." An accountant from Minneapolis on her way to Tacoma, Bratrud later praised Williams as calm and professional, focused on the safety of his passengers, not his own life.[25]

Hurrying back through the car, Williams urged his passengers to get dressed as quickly as possible and to exit to the rear of the car, into the dining car directly behind his assigned tourist sleeper. As he walked up and down the aisle, herding passengers out, the car started to lurch forward and pitch down, first by ten degrees, then twenty. Barefoot passengers, dressed in pajamas, nightgowns, or whatever clothes they could throw on, began struggling to climb up the tilted aisle. "Leave your luggage behind!" Williams shouted. "I will get it after you leave."

J. R. Knight from Evanston, Illinois, was just getting ready to bed down in his berth when the accident happened. "My first warning of the wreck was a trifle of a jolt," he explained. At Williams's urging, Knight was ready to go in minutes. "When I left the coach, water was running in the top vestibule. I ran through the car and got a dizzy feeling—you know the kind you get when you are running on a slanting surface. Boy, I felt dizzy."[26]

Thinking quickly, Williams entered several empty berths and ripped off the storage netting underneath each window. He quickly strung lengths of the mesh together to create a rope railing to help escaping passengers navigate the increasingly steep climb to the rear of the car. In constant motion, Williams pulled up those who were not strong enough to climb out themselves. Over and over, he reentered the car, looking in every berth for survivors. Each time he exited, his powerful arms were full of luggage. In the span of about eight minutes, all twenty-two passengers on his sleeper made it out safely.

The rushing water in Custer Creek had begun to hollow out the earthworks and the riprap protecting the east bridge abutment. Concerned that the diner car could also be in jeopardy, members of the train crew uncoupled the car from Williams's now empty sleeper, protecting not only the diner but also the two Pullman sleepers and the parlor car behind it. Many passengers and crew members stood on the relatively undamaged east-side abutment, watching in shock as the scene unfolded in front of them.

"We got out of our car onto the stone bridge abutment on the east side of the river," described Knight. "There were about 36 of us on our side of the creek. There wasn't any panic or anything like that. We just sat and watched. Kind of dumb." He thought the volume of water looked larger than Lake Michigan and recalled that it "made so much noise as it rushed over the cars that we had to shout at each other."[27]

The front end of sleeper C now pitched downward into the water at a thirty-degree angle. Williams knew that it would soon drop in the river. He made one last trip down the aisle to the front of the car to the ladies' lounge and knocked hard on the door, shouting to be heard over the roar of the water. He pushed open the door to be sure no one was left inside. The lounge was empty. About to climb back up the aisle for the last time, Williams thought he heard a faint cry for help. He searched around the front end of the car, looking inside the tall lockers. He heard the faint cry again, and that is when he realized the voice was coming from outside of the train. Through the vestibule window, Louis Williams could see a young woman hanging onto the back end of the Choteau. It was Florence Maguire.

The last four cars of the Olympian had come to a sharp halt just short of the bridge and Custer Creek that night. The train's sudden stop caused many injuries among the passengers in the two Pullman sleeper cars, but none were serious. "Every one of us was banged against the head of our berths," reported Mrs. A. E. Lawler, who was in the Pullman sleeper behind the diner car with her two daughters. "Our bags in the berth were thrown clear to the end of the car. We all screamed to beat the band at first, and then things calmed down."[28]

John Stahlberg, in the same Pullman as Lawler, felt a series of severe jolts while lying in his berth. Stahlberg initially thought that the train might have hit a horse. "I didn't even get up at first," he described. But, hearing other passengers stirring, he did the same. "It was so dark, we couldn't see much."[29]

Warren Jones had been asleep in his Pullman berth when the wreck happened. With his feet toward the engine in his bunk, Jones first became aware that something was wrong when he realized the train was no longer moving. Then, the strong scent of prairie sage pervaded the car, as if someone had just opened all the doors and windows on the train. His younger cousin, John Baxter, in an upper berth, remained asleep. Passengers in their nightclothes had begun to scramble into the aisle of the Pullman, fumbling in the dark, looking for their shoes, which had been thrown forward to the front of the car due to the sudden stop. Fortunately, Jones had tucked his into the hammock net beside his bunk.[30]

Eager to find out what was happening, Jones pulled up the window curtain in his berth. He was shocked at what he saw: "My first thought was we were in the middle of a lake." Pressing his face against the glass, all Jones could see was water "to the limit of my vision in all directions and high on the roadbed." More curious than panicked, Jones shook young Baxter awake to tell his brother they were going to be late reaching Harlowton. The ten-year-old sputtered a profanity in response and promptly went back to sleep. Jones quickly dressed and exited the berth to investigate.[31]

Jones walked forward and entered the dining car, which was empty of staff and passengers, but fully lit. He noticed the tables were neatly set, adorned with crisp white linens, ready for the first breakfast call. It wasn't until he reached the front end of the diner that he began to hear the frightening roar of the waters of Custer Creek. A small group of train personnel had gathered at the front vestibule, including the dining car's chief steward. Jones joined them in watching the awful predicament of tourist sleeper C pitched steeply into the water.

In another Pullman berth was eighty-year-old Amanda Growdon, who practically slept through the entire incident. After visiting her son in Pittsburgh, she was traveling home to Kettle Falls, Washington. Initially awakened by the sharp jolt of the train stopping hard, Growdon slid into her pillows in her Pullman berth. "A porter came along and asked me if I was all right. I said I was fine. He asked me again and then I asked him what was the matter with him as I had already told him I was all right. He told me there was 'a car off the track up ahead,' and that I should go back asleep. And I went back asleep."[32]

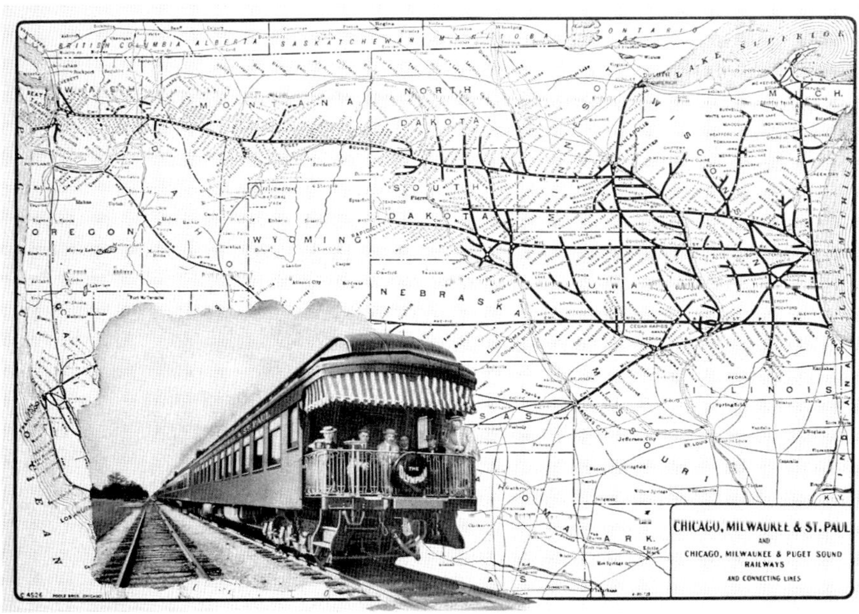

In 1912, not long after the *Olympian* began its regular service from Chicago to the West Coast, the Chicago, Milwaukee & St. Paul Railway produced a promotional booklet touting the beautiful vistas passengers could expect to see. A map showing the train's route featured the *Olympian*'s distinctive observation car. F852 .C55, Library of Congress

The illustrations on this 1938 *Olympian* trail guide invoked the mythic American West. The Milwaukee Road marketed the line as an ideal way to experience the region's iconic scenery. Milwaukee Road Collection, Milwaukee Public Library Archives

An *Olympian* cruises through the Bitterroot Mountains in this 1929 photograph. Milwaukee Road Collection, Milwaukee Public Library Archives

A group of women enjoy the fine fare in an *Olympian* dining car, ca. 1920. Milwaukee Road Collection, Milwaukee Public Library Archives

Two dining car waiters serve four o'clock tea to passengers in the *Olympian*'s observation car in this promotional photograph from the era of the Custer Creek crash. Milwaukee Road Collection, Milwaukee Public Library Archives

Several well-dressed men relax in an *Olympian* smoking car in this photograph from the 1930s. Milwaukee Road Collection, Milwaukee Public Library Archives

This 1938 photograph showcases part of the Milwaukee Road's massive railyard in its namesake city. Milwaukee Road Collection, Milwaukee Public Library Archives

The Milwaukee Road often added an open-air observation car to the back of the *Olympian* during the summer months to allow passengers to take in the views on the route to the Pacific. These passengers took in the view near Eagle's Nest Tunnel in Montana Canyon, outside of Ringling, in 1939. Milwaukee Road News Bureau, PAc 80–63.10, MTHS Photograph Archives

Remarkably, locomotive 220, which pulled the *Olympian* on the day of the crash, was later restored and put back into use. This photograph of the engine dates to the 1940s or 1950s. Robert Graham, photographer. Ian Campbell Wilson collection.

A crowd assembles on the platform at the Milwaukee Road station in Miles City in this scene from around 1920. L. A. Huffman, photographer. 981-993, MTHS Photograph Archives

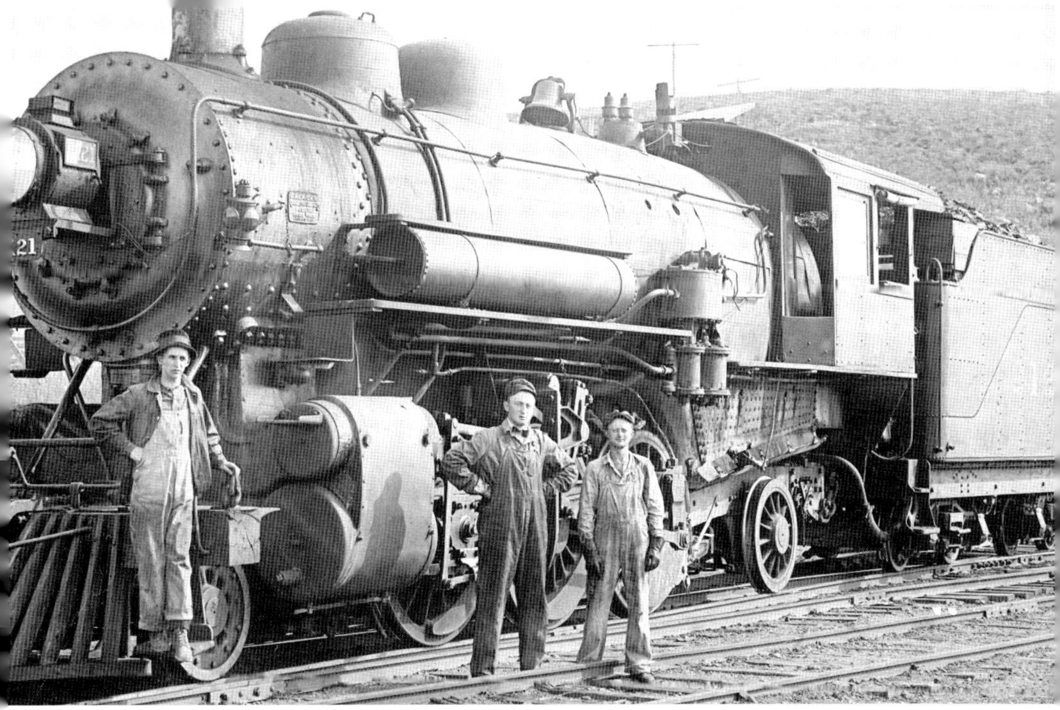

Three railroad workers, including fireman Henry Shipley, at far right, stand near a locomotive in Marmarth, North Dakota, in 1911. PAc 2011–58 B2F06.1, MTHS Photograph Archives

Milwaukee Road engineer Frank Merrifield, ca. 1935. PAc 2011–58 B2F36 WhiteEnv.1, MTHS Photograph Archives

The Gehrig family poses for a photograph—taken by Paul Gehrig's niece, Helen—outside their home for a photo on June 18, 1938, the day they boarded the *Olympian* in Minneapolis headed to California for a vacation. Gehrig and his oldest son, Lee, played a key role in saving the lives of sixty passengers on the *Olympian*. Back row (from left): Paul Jr., Lee, Paul, Marcella, Maureen, and Jack. Front row: Barbara. Courtesy of the Gehrig family

The Lallas family boarded the *Olympian* in Chicago en route to their home in Bellingham, Washington, having spent two months travelling in Greece, as seen in this photograph from their journey. Front row: Esther Lallas (left) and Tom Lallas (second from right). The three Lallas children stand behind their parents: Anna (left), John (saluting), and George. Courtesy of the Lallas family

A licensed nurse, Florence Hand Maguire was rescued off the roof of an *Olympian* sleeper car just before it plunged into Custer Creek. After being taken to the Miles City hospital, she returned to the scene of the accident hoping to aid other victims of the disaster. Courtesy of the Hand-Maguire family

George Hand, a Milwaukee Road policeman and Florence Maguire's father, stands at center in this photograph taken near the makeshift cabin he stayed in while helping with the cleanup efforts at the crash site. Courtesy of the Hand-Maguire family

At dawn on Sunday, June 19, 1938, the wreckage of the *Olympian* No. 15 remained in the still-raging waters of Custer Creek. The broken sleeper car Ipswich is in the foreground. The back end of the locomotive's tender is pitched into the air. Warren B. Jones, photographer. Courtesy of the Jones family

Passengers unhurt in the accident stand next to the diner car to observe as other cars are engulfed by the raging waters of Custer Creek at dawn on the morning of the crash.
Warren B. Jones, photographer. Courtesy of the Jones family

This wide view of the crash site shows the recovery efforts taking place on both sides of the bridge while capturing the extent of the damage. Courtesy of the Lallas family

A child plays in the receding waters of Custer Creek amid the cleanup effort that took place following the crash. Courtesy of the Hand family

A Milwaukee Road crane car pulls a piece of the wreckage down the tracks. Courtesy of the Lallas family

Crowds gathered along Custer Creek to help with the cleanup and search for survivors. The top of the sleeper Choteau, the "car of death," can be seen to the left of the demolished bridge pier. Courtesy of the Lallas family

RAILWAY EXPRESS
AGENCY

An unidentified family posed for this photograph in front of the demolished remains of the *Olympian*'s locomotive, mail express car, and baggage car, the latter of which split in two when it landed on top of the locomotive. Courtesy of the Lallas family

This aerial view of the wreckage appeared in *Illustrated Current News* out of New Haven, Connecticut, bearing the headline "Scattered Wreckage of Crack Train." Courtesy of the Lallas family

As this recent photograph of the rebuilt bridge shows, Custer Creek is a dry wash for most of the year, a stark contrast to the raging torrent that caused the *Olympian* disaster. Ian Campbell Wilson, photographer

Today, only this simple sign indicating the creek's name can be found at the site of the accident. Ian Campbell Wilson, photographer

CHAPTER 21

Hamm and Cain

Saugus, Montana, Sunday, June 19, 1938

Following a wild drive home from the dance, it had taken some time for Dan Haughian Jr. to settle down for bed. With the wind and rain moving away from his Saugus ranch, a smattering of stars began to appear in the inky night sky. Cowboy boots off, lying in bed and ready to blow out the kerosene lamp, Haughian thought he could hear the voices of men talking in the distance.

He must have been startled. Who could it be? It was rare to see strangers wandering by his ranch during the day, never mind at night. Dressed and outside in a flash, Haughian could clearly hear the voices from the direction of the mainline Milwaukee Road tracks that ran about a hundred yards west of the ranch house.

Haughian moved as quickly as the muddy slog allowed. In the darkness, he could now make out a flashlight flickering and bouncing as two men hustled south along the tracks. Haughian called out to the men to identify themselves: they were Ed Hamm and Mike Cain, the two flaggers from the *Olympian.*

The two breathless Milwaukee Road employees sputtered that there had been a train wreck. Many people had been hurt and killed, they reported. The wreck was about a mile back, at the bridge. Haughian knew that they were talking about Custer Creek. The duo explained that they had been directed to run to the Saugus station to call the dispatcher in

Miles City for help. Dan pointed toward the station, letting them know it was about two hundred yards farther down the track. Hamm and Cain thanked him and rushed off.

News of the nearby wreck surely shocked Haughian. Given that only treeless prairie separated his ranch from the bridge, lights from the *Olympian* cars left on the track might have been visible from where he stood, even a mile away. With not a moment to lose, Haughian ran back to the ranch house to wake Francis and Kathleen. Soon, the engine of his pickup truck roared to life as he headed to the accident scene. Since the dirt and clay roads were in bad shape due to the rains, they would have to use rough farm paths to get to Custer Creek. The headlights of the truck danced wildly in the night as it wheeled through the rolling fields next to the mainline track.

Back at the train, Henry Shipley and Bill Shearer had turned their attention to the screams for help coming from trapped and injured passengers in their coach car 4441. Using his flashlight, Shipley led the evacuation of many of the surviving passengers. Even though the car was situated close to the west bank, the darkness and swirling waters made rescue efforts challenging. Most of the shocked passengers remained calm in the chaos, but there were scenes of panic and gut-wrenching loss too. "We saw a woman jump out of a window she smashed," Shearer recounted. "She floated down against the pile of wreckage and I think she must have been drowned. Her husband yelled to us to help her, but it was of no use. It was bad going."[1]

Carrying children in their arms, and hoisting injured adults onto their backs, Shipley and Shearer ferried many passengers onto the embankment. Passengers Thorston Thoreson and Ellis Lund, both Minnesotans, did the same. Looking outside in the darkness after the crash, Thoreson saw that "the water was running swiftly over on the west bank of the creek and was about two or three feet deep." Lund and Thoreson made their way out through a broken window and, standing waist-deep in the fast-moving water, pulled and carried numerous other passengers to safety. Thoreson recalled that many passengers got to the creek bank through "a process of stumbling and sloshing through that frightening darkness. We were wet clean through."[2]

Maneuvering carefully in the darkness around heaps of train debris and jagged metal, Shipley and the other men returned repeatedly inside coach 4441 to rescue survivors. They had to be especially careful evacuating several seriously injured passengers from the front end of the coach car, which had been crushed in the wreck. Shipley saw a fair number of dead bodies and, for the moment, left them where they lay to concentrate on the living. As a veteran locomotive engineer, Shearer was a colleague and friend of Frank Merrifield. He later said that as he crawled across the demolished locomotive during the rescue efforts, he "knew the boys in the engine must be dead." Indeed, Merrifield and McCoy never stood a chance. The metal cab of the locomotive became their tomb.[3]

Satisfied that all survivors were off coach 4441 and receiving proper care from other crew and passengers, Shipley turned his attention to the plight of those in the other two cars that had jackknifed against each other in Custer Creek. Farthest out in the raging waters and pinned between the demolished remains of two bridge piers, tourist sleeper Ipswich was in the most perilous spot, but swift currents were also battering coach car 420. Shipley could see passengers breaking the windows and some scaling the sides, attempting to get onto the roofs.

Among them was Lee Gehrig, who, with his father Paul's help, had fastened a makeshift rope around his waist and crawled carefully through a broken window. The darkness, the constant heaving and rocking, and the slickness of the car's wet metal side made Lee's efforts treacherous. After multiple unsuccessful attempts to hoist himself up, he finally succeeded and crawled on his stomach to the center of the roof to catch his breath.

Next, Paul Gehrig and other survivors tied the mesh rope around each passenger in turn—starting with the injured ones, including Marcella Gehrig—and, one by one, hoisted them up. All the Gehrig children and about fifteen other passengers escaped. Joining them was conductor Chris McGee. When the *Olympian* crashed, McGee had been walking up the aisle of the Ipswich making his rounds. Only after Gehrig and the other men finished searching every corner of the Ipswich for survivors did he allow himself to be pulled up onto the roof, even though the injuries he had sustained would keep him hospitalized for days afterwards. Once outside, he realized that the survivors' predicament was more serious than he first believed. Their safety was not yet assured.[4]

From the rooftop, Gehrig could see that his group was on the farthest passenger car out in the swollen creek. It had been torn apart and partially submerged and was now being buffeted by the swift-moving water. Between the Ipswich and safety on the west bank lay the two tourist coaches, the baggage car, and the tender. The position of the tender, however, stood as the largest obstacle.

During the wreck, the *Olympian*'s baggage car had burrowed under the tender's rear wheels, thrusting its back end high into the air, which now amounted to a wall facing the survivors on the Ipswich. Not only did they need to cross atop two coach cars in the darkness, they would then have to either scale the upright tender or find a way around it to reach the shore. "The river . . . was running fast past this car," Gehrig recounted. "I could feel the current washing at the [Ipswich] we were standing on, but there was water on one side of us and the tender on the other, blocking our way off."[5]

Jackknifed next to them was coach car 420, where Paul Gehrig's niece, Helen, had been seated. Its front end had been sheared off in the crash, killing Tom Lallas and several other passengers, and its rear end had been partially driven underneath the Ipswich. Gehrig could see passengers emerging onto the roof of car 420. He called out for news of his niece. Word came back that she was alive but had suffered a broken ankle and leg. Very thankful for the good news, Paul braced himself on the unsteady roof of the Ipswich and jumped onto the roof of car 420 to lend a hand in evacuating Helen.

The violence of the wreck had sent coach seats flying inside car 420, leaving Helen trapped under a tangle of seats, suitcases, and other people. Unable to move, she remained conscious and screamed for help. Several men arrived to rescue her, struggling to stay calm as muddy water poured into the car. Their forceful tugging freed her from the wreck, but her leg was severely fractured. Passengers carried her to a broken window, where her uncle Paul and others lifted her onto the roof with other survivors.[6]

Also in car 420, paralyzed with fright and utterly alone, Anna Lallas and her two brothers saw a flashlight beam bouncing off the water in the flooded aisle. The light became brighter as several figures waded toward them while others climbed into their seats through a broken window. One of their rescuers was Paul Gehrig. Reassuring the Lallas children that they were now safe, Gehrig and the other men tied the makeshift ropes around Anna and John. They lifted George down from the luggage rack, where he had been quietly watching the chaos. To Anna, it sounded like they had landed near a waterfall. Rescuers shouted over the noise, while passengers stood shivering, waiting to be lifted through broken windows onto the roof.[7]

Within thirty minutes of the accident, there were at least fifty men, women, and children huddled on the roofs of the Ipswich and coach car 420. They comforted and steadied each other, as the water splashed them with muddy slime and rushed around the partially submerged cars. "The car top was nearly under water and slanting . . . the people had a hard time staying on it," recalled Paul Gehrig. He knew they had limited time to get everyone off the car roofs to safety on the west side. It seemed daunting. They needed a plan.[8]

Jim Griffith, a Milwaukee Road fuel supervisor deadheading on the *Olympian,* had been among those assisting in the search for survivors on the Ipswich. Wading waist-deep to check each berth, Griffith reached the rear door and vestibule. He could see the mangled remains of the bridge and the sleeper car Choteau dangling on spindly steel rails over the water. He also caught sight of a pair of white legs splashing frantically in the water. It was Axel "Bill" Olson, a fellow employee, up to his neck in the current, hanging onto a grab bar on the front of the Choteau. The Tacoma-based Olson had been asleep in his comfortable upper bunk in the car's middle section at the time of the accident. He was stunned to find himself sprawled on the floor of his berth, covered in broken glass after the window exploded in the impact: "The next thing I was out in the aisle and the water was up to my chest and still coming in."[9]

Wading through the slurry of mud, Olson headed for the front end of the Choteau, but found himself trapped. Unable to get past the vestibule, he figured he was a dead man. Miraculously, however, the car shifted in the water, tearing away the vestibule and providing an opening. As he described the scene, "It was so dark you couldn't see anything—just hear things—the water and people's voices." Olson knew he needed to get off the car, so he hung onto a grab iron and lowered himself into the frigid water. "The water was so fast it tore my pajamas off in minutes."[10]

The creek was still rising after the accident, pushed into waves by gusts of wind. The waters now reached up to just below track level on the bridge. Griffith yelled to Olson, "Hang on, Bill, maybe we can get you." He, Gehrig, and some other crew members quickly made a rope out of bed sheets and threw it to Olson, who was able to tie the sheets around his waist. As they started to pull, his foot got caught in the coupling. After a minute struggling to free himself, Olson signaled to pull again. As they did, the doomed Choteau lurched once more, submerging its back end. Griffith and the porters pulled the lucky dining car inspector across the river rapids to the rear door of the Ipswich in the nick of time.[11]

On the undamaged east-side abutment, a group of passengers and crew members stood stunned and speechless, watching the final minutes of the two tourist sleepers. The cars dangled perilously from a few lengths of steel rail on the remains of the bridge, while being pounded mercilessly by waves of water. The doomed, jackknifed cars formed a "V" pointing toward the current; as the rear end of the Choteau sank into the dark water, it pulled down the front end of sleeper C.

When it became decoupled from the cars behind it, the brake lines on sleeper C severed, clamping the brakes against its wheels. They now screeched loudly as the car slowly slid into Custer Creek. Everyone worried about Louis Williams. Without regard for his own safety, and against the advice of his colleagues, he had gone back into his car again to do one final search for passengers and to carry out another armful of luggage. He had been gone for several minutes. While he was inside, the car continued its death creep toward the edge of the bridge. Its front end was now pitched down at a forty-five-degree angle, making it almost impossible to navigate the center aisle.

Deep inside the car, Williams had barely turned the lever on the rear vestibule door when the force of the water slammed it open, immediately flooding the front third of the car, causing it to lurch farther into the swirling water. Holding on to what remained of the vestibule and shouting above the roaring river, Williams urged Florence Maguire to take his hand. She turned to him and could see his outstretched arm. Despite her reluctance to let go of the ladder to which she'd been clinging, she grabbed his hand, and Williams quickly pulled her into the flooding sleeper.[12]

Now in waist-deep water, Williams pushed Florence to the main aisle and told her to grab the hammock rope serving as a guideline up and out of the car. He stood behind her, supporting her, as they both scaled the aisle, foot by foot. The pitch was now so steep that Williams and Maguire had to crawl the final length of the aisle on their hands and knees. When the pair made it near the rear door, other crew members watching the rescue taking place grabbed the end of the rope and helped pull them to safety. The crowd of passengers erupted into applause as the two emerged from the back of the car. A few women threw dry blankets around Florence as she was led to the side of the tracks.[13]

Minutes after Williams and Maguire emerged from the sleeper car, a loud snapping sound startled the pajama-clad crowd hovering on the bridge abutment. The two cars still on the track and the demolished bridge finally had surrendered to the water's forces. The front end of the Choteau plunged into the roiling river, slamming against the concrete pier, its windows exploding. Passengers trapped inside sank with the car. It took only seconds for the Choteau to almost completely disappear in Custer Creek, with just a small portion of its roof remaining above water.

Minutes after the plunge of the Choteau, the back wheels of sleeper car C were losing their grip on the bridge as its clamped brakes emitted "a chorus of terrified screams," before the car let out a final loud groan and "toppled into the water." As Evelyn Bratrud recalled, watching the car she had been sleeping in moments before, it "made a horrible noise as it settled." The empty sleeper rolled once before wedging itself into a sandbar about one hundred yards downstream in the creek. Warren Jones watched the entire scene from the diner car: "I could see it clearly, water to the top of the windows, car lights on, shining dimly through the water, a very eerie sight!" Isadore Orenstein, a passenger on a Pullman sleeper at the end of the train, observed, "The most pitiful thing about it, we couldn't do anything to help those down in the river. The water was roaring just like Niagara Falls around the coaches."[14]

Pinned underwater against a sheared-off bridge pier, the Choteau had found its final resting place. Except for Dean Hanscom, Florence Maguire, and Bill Olson, none of its other passengers had been able to escape. They were trapped in a flooding capsule that would become a watery grave. The victims included Kate, Nell, and Margie Clancy of Bloomington, Illinois. "Its lights remained on all night as the car stood on the bottom," noted Belle McGalliard, traveling with her ten-year-old daughter, Mary Jane, in a Pullman sleeper at the rear of the train. "It was a ghastly reminder of other cars whose lights were snuffed out along with the lives of many passengers." Many of the survivors, including Warren Jones, remained haunted by the eerie underwater glow of the Choteau that night.[15]

CHAPTER 22

Ladder of Life

Sunday, June 19, 1938

Mike Cain and Ed Hamm finally made it to the small Saugus station around one in the morning. Using the siding block phone, Hamm immediately called Miles City dispatcher Neil Grogan, confirming that the *Olympian* had been wrecked and requesting "help of all kinds immediately." Grogan swung into action, ordering his telegrapher to notify all the major Milwaukee Road division offices from Tacoma to Chicago of the crash. He also ordered all train traffic detoured away from the west-side section from the Tusler Bridge near Kinsey to the Calypso Bridge just south of Terry. Milwaukee Road trains would need permission from the Northern Pacific to temporarily use their tracks on the east side of the river until further notice.

Ten minutes later, Grogan called the Holy Rosary Hospital in Miles City. With eighty-five beds, Holy Rosary was the town's main medical facility. Reaching the night administrator, Grogan warned that there would be many injured passengers needing immediate care. He also requested that a team of three doctors and five nurses travel to the crash site as soon as possible. A special hospital train was being assembled in the Miles City train yard to carry equipment and medical personnel directly to the scene.[1]

Reaching the site of the accident that night proved challenging. The primary paved roads in the area were all on the east side of the Yellowstone River. The roads on the west side were secondary roads—crude dirt roads at best, tractor and cattle paths at worst. The rainstorms had washed out many of these and transformed others into impassable gumbo. An article in the *Billings Gazette* the following day attempted to describe the challenge rescue crews faced trying to get to the *Olympian*. "The Yellowstone River, now at muddy high-water stage, runs between the Milwaukee tracks and U.S. Highway 10 and access to the wreckage was therefore cut off from that side," the newspaper reported. "No boats operate on the river, leaving the only means of access to the stricken train and its cargo of humanity by way of the railroad tracks from Miles City or by country road over circuitous routes through the foothills and across flooded upland coulees to the water-soaked meadows at the mouth of Custer Creek."[2]

Accessing the wreck site by rail was by far the easiest and fastest for rescue teams, except for one major issue: there were no "hot" steam locomotives immediately available in Miles City that night. Without a fire creating enough pressure to move its wheels, a steam locomotive could not move at all. It typically took between eight and ten hours to get a locomotive hot enough to be put into service. Grogan and the Miles City yardmaster needed to improvise.

Word soon came back from the locomotive roundhouse that an engine could be available for pulling the hospital train in about three hours. An experienced railman, Grogan knew that would be exceptionally fast under normal circumstances, but people would die if they could not move more quickly. Meanwhile, George and Rose Hand and their twin sons, Bill and Clarence, awaited Florence's arrival at the Miles City station. They joined other families gathered in small groups on the platform. Saturday's rainstorms had cooled the air a bit, but the night air remained sticky. With no trains chugging in the railyard, the trilling of crickets rang out.[3]

George Hand normally worked the night shift but had taken time off to help prepare for the upcoming wedding. He knew everyone at the railyard, including Neil Grogan, and had gotten word that the *Olympian* was running about twenty minutes behind schedule. But as the minutes ticked away on the master clock and the expected time of arrival came and went, there was still no sign of the *Olympian*.

The documentary record is silent on how the waiting families first learned about the wreck. Since the dispatcher's office window opened directly onto the platform, the Hands and others likely heard of the situation moments after Grogan received the call from Hamm and Cain. The news spread quickly at the station, and family members responded with shock, cries of anguish, and disbelief. The Hands, panicked about Florence's safety, left immediately and raced in their car to Saugus.[4]

At the crash site, the stunned and exhausted survivors of the wrecked *Olympian* waited in the darkness for help. "We saw a lot of bodies around, but we couldn't pull any on the tracks as we wanted to save all the persons we could," one passenger recalled. "It was an awful night." Suddenly, they saw the headlights of a truck bouncing toward them. Dan Haughian Jr. and Francis Motherhead drove as close to the west bridge abutment as they could, until the truck was mired in mud. Grabbing the wooden ladder from the bed, they headed up the tracks with their flashlights cutting through the darkness. The acrid smell of oil and burning coal mixed with the scent of prairie sage in the air. Water roared in the creek ahead.[5]

Haughian and Motherhead arrived at a scene of shocking destruction. The locomotive, tender, and mail and baggage cars were piled up like pick-up sticks on the west bank of the creek. A large debris field of twisted metal, train wheels, glass, large chunks of concrete, an assortment of luggage, hats, shoes, and hundreds of pieces of mail littered the area. Dozens of people stood atop the roofs of train cars in the middle of a raging Custer Creek. About twenty survivors sat near the creek embankment, many of them covered in blankets. Several small campfires warmed the shivering passengers. Not far from the huddled group lay a dozen bodies, lined side by side. Several were covered by white sheets soaked with blood. It was a grim sight.[6]

The two cowboys were heartily welcomed and directed to Henry Shipley, who had taken charge of the surviving passengers. Completely disheveled and covered in mud, Shipley offered both men a firm handshake and shared with them his plan to get the sixty passengers off the flooded cars and to safety on the west side. He could not believe his good fortune when Haughian showed him the ladder they had brought with them.

Shipley quickly led them past the carcass of the smoldering locomotive crumpled beside the river, back to the mainline tracks, and down a small hill to the front end of the tender, where tons of coal chunks littered the west-side bridge abutment. Shouting to be heard, Shipley explained that the back end of the tender, sticking up in the air, had created an impassable barrier to the passengers stranded on the roofs of the train cars. Scampering up and across the front and top of the tender, they shimmied up its backside, slipping on and cursing a greasy film of coal dust and water that covered its surface. Peering over the top rear corner of the tender, Shipley and Haughian lowered the ladder to a group of men standing on the roof of coach 4441, which now included Paul and Lee Gehrig. "It was not a strong ladder," recalled Paul Gehrig. "We had to place it on its edge along the slanting side of the engine tender. The coach car top was partially underwater, and the constant swaying and heaving of the car made stabilizing the ladder a real challenge." The darkness did not help, either. Shipley yelled down requesting that several men attempt the climb first, as they would then be needed to help the passengers off the slippery tender onto the ground.[7]

While the ladder was being secured, Paul Gehrig turned his attention to finding a safe way to get the surviving passengers, scattered across the different cars, onto the roof of coach car 4441. Many were too fearful to stand up on the swaying cars. The children, including Anna, John, and George Lallas, were terrified. Convinced the cars were stable enough to cross, Gehrig directed a group of men to form a human chain, passing each passenger off to the next man in line. One by one, they emptied the rooftops of the sleeper Ipswich and coach car 420 until all sixty passengers were gathered by the ladder on car 4441, awaiting their turn to crawl to safety. The prospect of climbing the rocking, tilted ladder was even more daunting than crossing over the car rooftops. The Gehrigs and other men made a rope railing out of the berth hammocks and strung it up beside the ladder and across the tender to help guide passengers in the darkness.[8]

Men accompanied the children up the ladder, while passengers with injuries, like Marcella and Helen Gehrig, were carefully hoisted up using the improvised ropes. One woman fainted while climbing the ladder, slipping between the wrecked cars and dragging down another woman who was holding her hand. Paul Gehrig and others quickly retrieved both women and resumed the orderly evacuation. It took about thirty minutes for all the passengers to make it safely onto land.

"It was so dark, we couldn't see much," reported Mabel Boone, a passenger on the Ipswich. "The cars ahead of the sleeper I was in just kind of hung there in an awful pile. To get to the bank, we had to climb over the tops of some cars ahead of us. There on the banks we stood bewildered. Some were dressed in blankets trying to keep warm. We didn't realize yet how lucky we were."[9]

Paul Gehrig and his son, Lee, were among the last to scale the ladder and tender to safety. As Lee edged off the tender, he heard splashing in the water. Aiming his flashlight toward the sound, he saw a small girl sitting alone in a pool of muddy water. It was seven-year-old Janet Pfleghaar from Cologne, Minnesota, Paul Gehrig's hometown. Janet and her older sister Marilyn were on their way to Montana for the summer when the *Olympian* wrecked. Holding onto his father's hand, Lee was able to reach out to Janet and pull her to safety. Spotting another woman struggling to stay afloat in the murky waters, the Gehrigs and others dragged her to the embankment near the tracks and pulled her onto land. Other surviving passengers flocked to her and Janet with dry blankets and comforting words. Janet's eight-year-old sister, Marilyn, was listed as missing after the accident. Her body was found five days later in the Yellowstone River. Janet would be hospitalized with head injuries but would recover.[10]

Milwaukee Road men in Miles City rushed to the railyards in response to Grogan's alarm, looking to help in any way they could. George Flynn was one of many who answered the call that night. The twenty-eight-year-old Flynn was a rookie, working as a file clerk and stenographer for the Trans-Missouri Division offices. Ordered by an early morning phone call to report immediately, Flynn was dressed and out the door in minutes.

The four blocks between Flynn's home and the railyards bustled with an unusual amount of activity for a Sunday morning. Extra yard crews called in were already assembling work trains and equipment to shuttle to the scene of the wreck. Flynn found the dispatcher and yardmaster's offices filled with people listening to briefings and taking orders. He overheard outgoing calls about the availability of heavy equipment for clearing debris at the scene, including rail-mounted wrecking cranes, commonly known as hooks, capable of lifting one hundred tons or more. There was "an aura of desperation as well as foreboding" on the faces of the railroad employees. It had begun to sink in that this wreck was a major disaster, the worst passenger accident in the Milwaukee Road's history. The young Flynn was put to work answering the phone in the division offices. It would soon be ringing off the hook. By dawn, the national news media was on the story, and Flynn spoke that day with reporters from *Time*, *Life*, and *Look* magazines, among many others. Everyone wanted detailed information about the crash, which he did not have. He described feeling "more than thankful when passenger service and public-relations people took over the task."[11]

Knowing that delays could cost lives, Grogan and other railyard officials hurriedly discussed options for getting rescue teams and equipment to the crash site in Saugus. There were two viable options by rail. First, they could employ gasoline-powered speeders, like the one used by Lou Goplen on his section patrols. Each could only transport six to eight people along with some light equipment, but they could travel thirty miles per hour on the track, meaning it would take about an hour to travel the twenty-seven miles to the scene.

The only "hot" locomotive in Miles City that night was a switcher locomotive, the small, snub-nosed equivalent of a tugboat, used for muscling freight and passenger cars around a railyard, an essential duty called "switching." Clunky and slow, it could be loaded up with equipment and another six or eight men. The "yard goat," however, was not designed for open rail running, and it could take up to ninety minutes to get to Custer Creek. With no other options, Grogan cleared the path for the speeder and the yard goat to be dispatched to the accident scene. Just after two in the morning, about ninety minutes after the accident, the first, hastily organized rescue teams were on their way to Saugus.

The hospital, meanwhile, called in all available personnel and prepared to receive fifty or more injured passengers. Staff prepared three operating rooms. Nurses in the hospital's training program were called in to assist with the expected flood of patients.

The rescue effort required establishing a supply chain between Holy Rosary and the Miles City station to ferry crucial medical supplies and equipment to the special hospital train being assembled in the yard. Dispatcher Grogan urged the hospital to have its doctors and nurses ready to go at the station by half past two o'clock. Officials commandeered employees' cars and trucks to shuttle mountains of supplies, including bandages, splints, linens, stretchers, oxygen, and pain-killing drugs, along with a team of doctors and nurses. They gathered flashlights by the bushel, along with a vast assortment of clean sheets, pillows, and blankets. Later in the morning, the same trucks and cars would be used to ferry the injured from the station to the hospital.

Given what was known about the scale of the wreck, coroners from Custer and Prairie counties were alerted and urged to get to the station as quickly as possible and prepare their facilities to receive the dead. Hearses in the 1930s often doubled as community ambulances, and calls went out to local funeral homes requesting assistance. Calls also went out to several local priests and ministers, asking that they ride with the hospital train to the scene to offer spiritual care.

As they waited at the crash site, the surviving passengers and crew continued to locate and save additional victims. Hours after the crash, Henry Shipley was still on the scene searching for survivors, participating in passenger rescues, and tending to the injured. As he sat down on the west bank for a moment to catch his breath, he thought he heard some moaning in the water. Shipley aimed his flashlight at the spot and glimpsed a woman's golden blond hair. Shipley, who had emigrated to America from Norway, would later say, "I saw that blond hair out there, and knew it was a Swede, and I needed to rescue her." He alerted a group of men to the passenger in distress, and they quickly made a rope of bedsheets, which he tied around his waist before diving into the cold waters, swimming hard against the currents to reach her.[12]

Slipping in and out of consciousness, nineteen-year-old Evelyn Janssen had been in the water for several hours. On her way to visit her uncle, Al Bunker, in Miles City, Evelyn had been gently awakened by the porter on tourist coach 420, letting her know that the train would soon be arriving at her stop. Evelyn's father, Edward Janssen, worked for the Illinois Central Railroad in Freeport, Illinois, and had secured a free employee pass for her to ride the *Olympian* from Chicago to Montana. She had rented a pillow on the train to help her get some sleep on the coach. Fully awake and waiting in her seat, she got up to give the pillow to a young mother and her child across the aisle from her.

At that moment, the crash catapulted Evelyn through the car window and into the "awfully cold" water of Custer Creek. She recalled that one minute she was in a warm, comfortable car, and the next, she was "out in the country," having no idea how she ended up in the raging creek waters. In a bit of good fortune that saved her life, a corner of the coat she was wearing snagged on a piece of twisted metal from the bridge, preventing the teenager from being washed away and drowned. Unable to swim, Evelyn was terrified of the water. The muddy waves thrashed her and pushed her underwater twice before she was able to grip some metal dangling from the ruined trestle.

Evelyn was barely alive by the time Henry Shipley reached her in the creek. She would not regain consciousness until later that morning in the hospital train. She had a clear memory of the crash but no recollection of her rescue. "I guess I'm the luckiest girl in this world," she said. "Won't Daddy be glad when he knows I'm alright."[13]

Immediately after the wreck, a Milwaukee Road flagman identified in press accounts only as Preston, who had been seated at the very tail end of the *Olympian*, jumped unharmed off the rear platform of the observation car. He ran northeast on the tracks toward Terry, setting flares to notify oncoming trains of the accident up ahead. Hustling along in the darkness, he carried a lantern and a flashlight to use as additional signaling devices. Satisfied he was far enough from the crash site to provide sufficient warning for any rail traffic, he stopped and stood guard on the track.

It was dark and quiet where Preston stood. The calming undulation of the nearby Yellowstone River had replaced the roar at Custer Creek. Still in shock, he might have felt very alone far away from the chaos of the wreckage. Suddenly, he heard something moving through the tall grasses near the river—perhaps a deer. The crunching sound grew louder. Preston nervously clicked on his flashlight and started panning the area. A ghostly white figure limped into the light, naked except for shredded pajamas. Preston soon realized it was a young man. Shivering uncontrollably, the pale, skinny stranger blurted out that he was on the *Olympian* and had been washed down the river. It was Dean Hanscom.

CHAPTER 23

First Doctor

Crash Site, Sunday, June 19, 1938

Word of the accident did not reach Lou Goplen's section house until about three in the morning, when telephone service was restored between Terry and Calypso. Walter Plath, the operator on duty in Terry, briefed Goplen on the wreck and asked that he meet Terry section man George Hickman at the Calypso Bridge to pick up I. J. Bridistine, a medical doctor, and take him and two nurses to the accident scene as quickly as possible.[1]

Goplen tore out of his house into the darkness, pulling on his clothes and jacket. He powered up his gas speeder and turned it northeast toward Terry, about six miles away, accelerating as fast as it could go. At the bridge, Goplen saw the small headlamp of Hickman's speeder, which carried several people. Black medical bag in hand, Bridistine jumped into Goplen's track car with two nurses. Stanley Guy, the Prairie County coroner, had also hitched a ride.

Racing to the crash scene, Goplen stopped momentarily in Calypso to pick up his co-worker Eastwood. As the group approached Custer Creek, they could see the back lights of the *Olympian* parlor car parked on the east side of the bridge. Heart racing, Goplen braked the small track car to a stop at about four o'clock. He and his group arrived just minutes before the bright headlamp of the steam locomotive pulling the special hospital train from Miles City cut through the early morning light from the opposite side of the bridge.[2]

Bridistine and the nurses were quickly escorted to the crowd of bedraggled passengers standing quietly on the east bridge abutment. The doctor must have gasped as he saw the submerged Choteau, its lights still on, being thrashed against a demolished bridge pier. A shocked Louis Goplen joined him on the bridge; he had never seen Custer Creek with more than a few feet of water, even during the rainy season. All stood speechless at the sight of the demolished bridge and the "cars heaped in a crazy jumble" on the west-side abutment.[3]

For what seemed like hours after the accident, the passengers and crew on the east side of Custer Creek listened to the cries and screams for help coming from the pile of cars that lay in the surging water. Warren Jones, standing quietly among his fellow travelers and feeling upset at being unable to help, could make out people crawling across the rooftops trying to rescue others. Flashlight beams shone through the darkness. The "roaring flood" silenced all attempts at communication, recalled Jones: "We were survivors, indeed, but also just spectators viewing a tragedy on an unreachable stage 100 feet away." Similarly, as Estelle Drew, an Alaska-bound passenger who had been in a Pullman sleeper at the rear of the train, remembered, "We waited until dawn, before we caught the full significance of the terrible disaster." She added, "It was appalling to think that down there in the murky waters were human beings who had succumbed to drowning, caught like animals in a cage and unable to escape."[4]

Crew members directed Bridistine and the nurses to the dining car, one of the undamaged cars still on the track. Injured passengers had assembled inside, some of them sitting at tables with bandaged heads and eyes, and handmade slings supporting hurt or broken limbs. A few were lying on the floor, tended to by other passengers. Everyone was quiet. The doctor immediately set to work, with *Olympian* crew members providing fresh towels, sheets, and hot water.

One of the injured was Dean Hanscom. Beaten up after his near drowning in the Yellowstone, the college student had also suffered some deep cuts in his hands and arms from flying through a window on the Choteau. Swaddled in blankets on the floor of the diner car, Hanscom kept asking about his brother Don. Had anyone seen him? Had he been rescued? No one had an answer. Another passenger, Florence Maguire, had less serious injuries: bumps, bruises, and small cuts on her hands due to broken glass. Like Hanscom, she was also hypothermic from her time in the water.

Bridistine was concerned enough about Hanscom's condition that he requested an immediate evacuation to Terry and then on to the Holy Rosary Hospital in Miles City. Hearing this conversation, Florence Maguire spoke up and insisted she be taken as well, but not for her own sake. She informed Bridistine that she was a registered nurse and wanted to get to the hospital so she could change into her uniform and return to the crash scene to help injured passengers on the east side of the creek. A group of passengers and crew members carried Hanscom to the track car. Florence Maguire got in as well, along with several others who wished to leave the scene.[5]

Soon, Bridistine and the others inside the diner car heard that a plume of dark smoke from a locomotive could be seen coming toward the crash site from the direction of Miles City, on the other side of Custer Creek. More than three hours after the wreck of the *Olympian*, the special hospital train made it to Custer Creek, carrying doctors and nurses and loaded with railroad men eager to help.

Later, one of the first rescuers on the scene tried to recount what he saw as he waded into the murky waters to look for survivors:

> There are no words descriptive enough to reveal the tangle of steel, leather and wood that once was a coach interior. Baggage, clothes, pillows, bedding, hats and purses were one solid mass of sodden and tangled material. Mud and particles of bushes that had washed in through the open and broken windows and wrenched off doors, silted the interior as the waters receded. And through the tangled mass in the smoker one pale and ghastly face thrust up, twisted in the agony of slow and horrible death. A few feet away, an arm, with fingers clenched and corded, stuck up in mute evidence of the impact that reduced the coach to shambles.[6]

Maurice Odquist, who had survived the wreck in a Pullman sleeper at the back of the train, captured the moment with his camera. Odquist's early morning photos of the accident gained national attention when *Life* magazine published them in early July under the splashy headline, "A Survivor Photographs the Worst American Train Wreck Since 1887."[7]

With multiple cars to carry the injured, the hospital train brimmed with blankets, drugs, bandages, and splints, as well as stimulants, oxygen, and carbon dioxide for resuscitating passengers. Father Merrill, a Miles City priest, and Custer County coroner Ralph Bray and his assistant Louis Durante also rode the hospital train to the scene. Survivors immediately directed two of the doctors to the three partially submerged passenger cars on the west side of the bridge to administer aid to trapped passengers. Henry Shipley, Paul Gehrig, Bill Shearer, Jim Griffith, and others showed the doctors the way and helped them safely access the cars. Four bodies were discovered in the crushed front end of coach car 420, including that of Thomas Lallas. Because the tender blocked safe access to the three water-logged cars floating near the west bridge abutment, rescuers could not retrieve the bodies until later in the day.

The number of injured and the extent of their injuries quickly overwhelmed the doctors and nurses, likewise the coroner. Bray and Durante would stay at the crash scene for thirty-six hours, until noon Monday, organizing the dead and shipping bodies to morgues in Terry and Miles City, including a makeshift morgue in the Miles City High School gymnasium.

By the time the hospital train arrived, the opportunity to administer aid to the most grievously injured had long since passed. Of the forty-nine passengers and crew that were killed in the accident, an estimated one third died immediately from massive trauma. Another third suffered serious injuries and then drowned either while trapped in their car, as in the Choteau, or when washed into the waters of Custer Creek and the Yellowstone River. Most of the remaining passengers who died likely survived the initial crash, but suffered injuries that could not be treated in time. Massive bleeding and vascular trauma can quickly lead to shock, unconsciousness, and death. Some of these passengers may have died within thirty minutes to an hour, with a few others hanging on longer.[8]

Hypothermia posed an additional threat. Many of the surviving passengers and crew on the two forward coaches and on the sleeper Ipswich had to wade through cold water to get to safety. In the middle of summer, it is not unusual for river water temperatures in Montana to hover between fifty and sixty degrees. A combination of frigid water and cool nighttime air would have accelerated hypothermic effects such as numbness, loss of dexterity, and mental confusion in less than fifteen minutes. Loss of consciousness can happen in an hour or less.

The small number of Milwaukee Road employees who arrived before the hospital train assisted in rescue attempts and provided care and comfort to the many passengers suffering from injuries or from shock and hypothermia. Many *Olympian* crew members and passengers also volunteered to help at the scene. Nineteen-year-old Katherine Hahn, who had escaped from coach car 420 with her parents, comforted and rubbed the legs of a small child suffering from hypothermia while waiting to board the hospital train.[9]

Passengers with the most serious injuries were carried onto the hospital train first and placed in military-style cots hanging from the ceiling of several of the World War I–era cars that had been assembled in the Miles City railyard. The special train was on the scene for less than an hour before it reversed direction and headed back to the station full of *Olympian* passengers. Katherine Hahn vividly recalled the old kerosene lamps swaying from the ceiling as the train chugged away. Maureen Gehrig, just seven years old, never forgot the sight of the bodies wrapped in white sheets laying in the aisle of the hospital train. Like other survivors, she tried to avoid looking at these silent forms during the slow ride back to Miles City.[10]

Distressed passengers and crew on the east side of Custer Creek had to wait even longer for assistance. At about eight in the morning, a locomotive dispatched by the Milwaukee Road arrived to evacuate passengers and crew from the four *Olympian* cars stranded on the track. The exhausted passengers and crew, joined by Bridistine and his assisting nurses, were towed in the undamaged cars back to Terry and then south to Miles City using the tracks of the Northern Pacific Railway on the east side of the Yellowstone River. It was a morose return trip. They reached the Miles City station at about eleven on Sunday morning.[11]

A large crowd had gathered at the station to greet the dazed and exhausted survivors. "We were treated to our first meal since the night before," recalled Warren Jones. "We were queried by doctors as to possible injuries and able to contact family members by telegraph." Ambulances and hearses transported a few injured passengers to the Holy Rosary Hospital.[12]

The evacuation of passengers, crew, and cars from the east side opened the track corridor for the arrival of work crews and heavy equipment, including a one-hundred-ton derrick mounted on a flatbed railcar dispatched from Mobridge. Recovery teams waited anxiously for its arrival so they could gain access to the bodies still trapped in the Choteau. Still pinned next to a demolished bridge pier in the slowly receding waters, the front end of the car had plowed six feet into the silty streambed of Custer Creek. When rescuers accessed the inside through broken windows, they discovered that many of the passengers had been thrown during the crash into the front of the car, now the most difficult part to safely access.

By nine on Sunday morning, more than eight hours after the wreck, the Milwaukee Road had assembled a sizable force to assist at Custer Creek, with estimates varying between 100 and 175 men. Crews made it a priority to clear the large and dangerous debris field on the west side of the bridge to hasten rescue and recovery efforts. Safely accessing the three cars still submerged in the creek bed required moving the tender and the crushed baggage car. By noon on Sunday, there were two one-hundred-ton derricks working the accident scene, one on each side of the wreck.

The hospital train made multiple trips on Sunday morning to the west side of Custer Creek, ferrying railroad workers, doctors, nurses, and medical supplies to the crash site and then returning with *Olympian* passengers and the recovered dead. Ultimately, sixty-eight *Olympian* passengers were transported to the Holy Rosary Hospital for care on Sunday. About half—those suffering from cuts, bruises, and bumps—were treated and released within hours. By Sunday night, six passengers remained in serious condition with broken bones, severe cuts, and internal injuries. One man reportedly had had his back broken in the crash. An attending nurse indicated that many passengers suffered from shock and "many were so badly bruised and battered we have been unable to get a complete check of their injuries, other than to make them as comfortable as possible."[13]

As the day progressed, bodies wrapped in white sheets became the primary cargo on the trains shuttling back from Saugus. Doctors and nurses from Holy Rosary remained on the crash scene until late Monday night. Watching the rescue teams work frantically, they stayed until they held no more hope of finding any additional survivors.

CHAPTER 24

War Zones

Sunday, June 19, 1938

> White-patched people in misfit clothing walked the streets, broken arms in splints and slings, heads wrapped with gauze. Black eyes and bruises were everywhere.
>
> —*Great Falls Tribune*[1]

Instead of chiming church bells, wailing ambulance sirens greeted residents of Miles City on Sunday morning. Local minister Reverend Paul Jones rushed down to the station to offer his assistance after an early morning call from railroad officials. Shortly after he arrived, at about half past five, the hospital train returning from the scene of the wreck pulled up to the platform carrying about forty *Olympian* passengers, many of them injured. A crowd of railroad workers and locals loaded those in need of medical attention onto ambulances and hearses bound for Holy Rosary Hospital. Uninjured passengers were herded into the depot's large waiting room where Milwaukee Road employees offered water, hot coffee, and breakfast rolls. Railroad officials and clerks stood by with clipboards to register the names of survivors.[2]

In Chicago, the lights in the corporate offices of the Milwaukee Road burned bright. A telegraph bearing news of the *Olympian* wreck arrived early that morning. Awakened at home, the company's chief public relations officer, Frank J. Newell, hustled downtown to take charge of the situation. Educated, jovial, and as prone to quoting Shakespeare as he was popular with the rank and file, the forty-five-year-old Newell was the perfect man to lead in a disaster situation. An experienced railroad man who started his career with the Great Northern at age sixteen, Newell had been managing public relations for the Milwaukee Road for almost two decades. Newell knew the inner workings of the press corps and had good relationships with reporters with just about every major news outlet in America.[3]

By the time he walked into the corporate offices where "the official family were collected in a sorrowful group," Newell had mapped out a plan of action for the company. First, they needed to issue a press statement before the wire services opened at dawn. Newell knew how important it was to get ahead of the news. Second, management had to set the tone for its thirty thousand employees across its system. Employees, like the public, would be stunned by the news of the accident and should feel like the Milwaukee Road's leadership had their back.[4]

As staff members hauled out and dusted off maps so that they could pinpoint Saugus and the wreck location, Newell and his team prepared a statement that addressed the specifics of the situation. It also helped frame coverage of the accident in a way that cast a good light on the company. The statement emphasized that the bridge was a permanent structure of concrete and steel. It also highlighted the unprecedented nature of the local rains, the fact that there was no water on the track at the time, that the engineer did not drive through the cloudburst, and that a trackwalker had recently checked the bridge. Most importantly, it touted the company's excellent safety record, noting that it had not lost a paying passenger in twenty years.[5]

Newell's media strategy was spot on, as the wire services, hungry for all details of the crash, blasted the company's talking points across North America. Newell also had the statement telegraphed to every major radio station in the country so that their audiences could hear it verbatim. A man of great energy, Newell took to the phones early Sunday morning and called outlets across the country. "I knew the territory and the consist of the train and the floor plan of the cars and all the other factors," he later remarked. His goal was to expertly answer every question possible without delay.[6]

Even while Newell and his team managed the media, the full course of the tragic events had not yet played out. It would take time to retrieve bodies from the battered train and those that had been flushed down the Yellowstone River. Accounting for all the estimated 190 passengers and crew aboard the *Olympian* when it crashed was a painstakingly slow process. Newell later said that he thought the Custer Creek accident would have only merited a single day in the press if not for the difficulty of recovering and identifying all the victims.[7]

Milwaukee Road officials knew that the day's headlines would spark hundreds of calls from panicked families across the nation. The company needed a full accounting of every *Olympian* passenger and crew member as soon as possible. Members of its corporate team soon flew out to Montana. The company also mobilized a team to support its employees in Miles City working to verify and record the status of passengers, whether alive, dead, or missing.[8]

This essential task proved daunting for the Milwaukee Road. The man in charge of the passenger list, Chris McGee, the *Olympian*'s conductor, was injured in the crash and on his way to the hospital. Vital information about who exactly was on board when the accident happened, including ticket stubs and reservations slips, was lost in the crash. McGee had tucked the records into the small, leather satchel tethered to his side by a shoulder strap, but the bag had disappeared into the waters of Custer Creek, never to be seen again.

The loss of McGee's records turned the process of reconciling the passenger and crew list on the doomed *Olympian* into chaos. Sleeper cars required reservations, but passengers traveling by coach in the tourist cars could board or depart the train at any station. In one such example of the confusion, Leonard Kulesa of Ismay, Montana, had purchased a coach ticket for the *Olympian* that night but missed the train as it came through town. Nonetheless, the company chased its tail for days trying to determine his status. Another passenger, Mrs. Kenneth Romney, had booked tickets for the *Olympian,* wishing to visit friends in Livingston, Montana. In Chicago, however, she changed her itinerary to travel on the

Northern Pacific for the remainder of her journey. The Milwaukee Road initially had Mrs. Romney listed as "missing" before discovering her alive and well in Livingston.[9]

As Frank Newell and the Milwaukee Road management team anticipated, newswire services spread word of the wreck across the continent. Stories about the Custer Creek disaster, including graphic images of the *Olympian* wreck, dominated the front page of almost every major American and Canadian newspaper the day after the accident. The *Chicago Tribune* headlined "34 DEAD IN OLYMPIAN WRECK, Chicago Train Plunges into Montana Creek" in its Monday edition. The *Minneapolis Star* dedicated its entire front page to the crash, which included five large photographs of the wreck and the screaming headline, "37 BODIES RECOVERED, One Body Found 50 miles Down Creek from Scene of Milwaukee Road Wreck." The *Green Bay Press Gazette* featured a front-page story about the *Olympian* wreck, including a story about Frank Merrifield indicating that the veteran engineer started his career working out of Green Bay.

Newspapers in Montana splashed news and photographs of the wreck across their front pages too, including the *Billings Gazette,* which headlined "WRECK KILLS OVER 30, 65 Hurt as Olympian Plunges Into Creek East of Miles City." The *Seattle Times,* representing the destination city of the *Olympian,* published a Monday extra dedicated to crash details with the headline, "40 Killed and Many Missing in Montana Rail Wreck" and a graphic story titled "How Wrecked Coaches Piled Up in Raging Custer Creek." Supplied with updates by Milwaukee Road officials, just about every newspaper published a daily list of the dead and missing, which grew in number for days after the crash.

News of the wreck also quickly spread around the world. Almost two thousand miles from Miles City, the *Montreal Daily Star* featured a large photo of the wreck on its front page with the title, "Where Two Score Persons Died When Train Crashed Through Bridge." The day after the disaster, the *Regina Leader-Post* of Saskatchewan marked the wreck on its front page with the headline, "40 KILLED in WRECK, Sudden Flood Sweeps Away Trestle Bridge and Crack Train Plunges into Swollen Creek Water." A day after the accident, an auto dealer in Miles City received a call about the accident from a woman living in South Africa. The caller, Mrs. William Foard, was the sister of injured and hospitalized *Olympian* conductor Chris McGee.[10]

Incoming calls swamped the Western Union office and local telephone agencies in Miles City. Having heard about the wreck, Helen Woodcock, a Western Union clerk, stopped by the downtown office on Sunday morning to "see if there was any excitement." She was pulled into a whirlwind. Woodcock worked almost twenty-four hours straight, managing hundreds of calls and communications for employees, families, and the media. She recalled that demands from the media kept the midnight oil burning at the office: "They wrote, and wrote, and wrote and wrote."[11]

By Sunday afternoon, dozens of injured survivors—released from the hospital—wandered Miles City's downtown. World War I veterans watching the hospital trains arrive from the crash site said it reminded them of the war-battered towns they saw in Europe. Word of the accident had traveled fastest in Miles City, home to many of the employees onboard. Expecting her husband's return in the middle of the night, Marie Merrifield was instead widowed at age thirty-four, left to care for four young children, including two-month-old Phyllis Marie. Hausmer McCoy left behind his wife and two daughters, Betty Lou and Ardella. Charlie James's family would learn Sunday morning that he had died in the wreck. The company sent couriers to the homes of Fred Woolsey and Ed Arnold, both residents of Miles City, to let them know that their wives were missing after the accident. A division engineer, Ernie Johnson, was called in early Sunday morning to work the accident scene, at which point he realized that his wife had been on the *Olympian*. When he found out, he screamed, "My God, my wife's on that train!" Sadly, she did not survive the wreck.[12]

The close-knit Greek community in Bellingham, Washington, was thunderstruck at the news about Tom and Esther Lallas. The railroad company confirmed by telegram late Sunday that Tom had died in the accident and Esther was listed as missing. Jim Thomas, Esther's brother, was greatly relieved to learn that Anna, John, and George had survived with minor injuries and were safe in the hospital. He immediately arranged to make the one-thousand-mile drive to Miles City and take custody of the Lallas children.

Dean Jewell Hanscom received a telegram on Sunday at his home in Bronxville, New York, indicating that both Donald and Dean were missing following the *Olympian* crash. In a state of shock, he and his wife, accompanied by their daughter, Janet, arranged to fly from New York City to Montana later that day. Zac Hanscom, the twins' uncle from Seattle who had been planning to host them that summer, made his own plans to fly from Seattle to meet his brother and the family in Miles City. Just before boarding the plane, the Hanscoms received word that Dean was alive and in a hospital. Donald was still listed as missing. The *Seattle Times* story that ran on Monday included a photo of the Hanscom boys at Dartmouth College.

The Milwaukee Road sent word to Phillip Clancy in Bloomington, Illinois, on Sunday that they had not yet found his daughter, Margie, or his two sisters. Knowing that he would want to travel to Miles City as soon as possible, the company offered him a seat on a special train leaving from Chicago on Sunday. Phillip quickly packed a suitcase and headed to Union Station. The news of the crash and the fate of the Clancy women stunned the community of Bloomington. The *Pantagraph,* the town's major newspaper, followed the rescue and recovery events closely for the following week. The crash also made front-page news in Minneapolis, where the *Olympian* had stopped the morning before it derailed and where the Gehrig family was well known in the community.

Meanwhile, there was no sleep for the Hand family on Sunday. After leaving the Miles City station at about half past one in the morning, they spent the night traveling between Miles City, Terry, and Saugus in search of Florence. As dawn broke, they still did not know her fate. With many of the dirt roads washed out and impassable on the west side of the Yellowstone River, it took some time for the Hands to find a safe route to the scene of the accident. At about six o'clock, they finally got near enough to the west bank of the creek to park their car and visit the crash site by foot.

What they found offered little reassurance to the Hands. The water in the creek had begun to recede, but it still roared like an angry river. A blend of morning mist, smoke, and steam shrouded the demolished locomotive and tender. One newspaper reporter observed "a dozen bright red boxes of valentine candies, with ripped ribbons fluttering in the wind . . . a blaze of color in the midst of a smoking debris field of ripped metal, wheels and train parts that were scattered around the engine and tender."[13]

The family noticed small groups of what appeared to be *Olympian* passengers standing by as crew members and workmen waded into the slurry in search of other possible survivors. They immediately inquired about their daughter, but no one could say for sure whether she had survived the wreck. Knowing Florence had booked a reservation on a coach car, the Hands became especially unnerved at the sight of the five mangled coach cars and sleepers lying in the water. Someone told them that the hospital train had already returned to Miles City carrying forty passengers, many with severe injuries.[14]

So distraught was George Hand that he waded directly into Custer Creek, to get to where the Choteau lay submerged in the murky waters. Concerned for his safety, railroad workers pulled the Milwaukee Road policeman back ashore. Finding no sign of Florence among the piled-up cars near the west bridge abutment, a soaking wet George Hand returned to his family to discuss finding a safe way over to the east bridge abutment, where a large crowd of passengers and train personnel had gathered. The water in the creek remained treacherously high.[15]

Rose and the two boys, Clarence and Bill, decided they would return to Miles City to see if Florence had been on the hospital train. George stayed at the scene and convinced a local farmer familiar with the back roads in the area to take him to the east side. One can imagine the agony endured by the Hands until mid-morning on Sunday when Rose Hand discovered Florence alive.

As the family later learned, Florence wanted to return to the station to assist other *Olympian* passengers after receiving treatment for the minor injuries she had sustained in the crash. She was also eager to return to Custer Creek to personally thank porter Louis Williams for saving her life. The joyous reunion between Florence, her mother, and her two brothers took place at the Miles City station. Informed that her father had stayed at the scene, Florence insisted that they all drive back to Saugus to give him the good news.[16]

Returning once again to Saugus and the smoldering ruins of the *Olympian*, Florence leaped out of the family car in search of her father. "Daddy,

daddy, where are you?" she repeatedly called. With no sign of him among the workers on the west side, Florence looked across the demolished bridge and caught the eyes of her father on the other side. With tears in his eyes and jumping with joy, her father became "almost crazy when he saw me," recalled Florence. Their voices drowned out by the roaring creek, they waved madly back and forth at one another. Father and daughter were finally reunited later that day.[17]

A thousand miles east in Milwaukee, Florence's husband, Bernard, was with friends when news of the wreck arrived. Sick with worry, he hailed a cab for the downtown Milwaukee Union Depot to get as much firsthand information about the accident as he could. Waiting in the station for word of his wife's well-being, Bernard would later tell Florence that "my heart beat until I thought it would be busted."[18]

Bernard experienced hours of stress and worry before he found out that Florence had survived. At about nine in the evening on Sunday, he received a Western Union telegram from her reading, "Am Fine. Don't Worry. Letter Following. Lost Everything Not Hurt." About a half hour later, Bernard received another telegram from George Hand: "Florence Home Safe." Even after the reassurance, it took another hour for his knees to stop shaking. Florence's sister, Irene, and her fiancé, Byron Roberts, who had been vacationing in Roundup, Montana, for the weekend, rushed back to Miles City by car when they heard news of the *Olympian* wreck.[19]

Three hundred miles northwest of Saugus, Jim McIntosh woke up early on Sunday and checked on his wheat fields before driving to the small, wood-clad train station in Geraldine. The streets of the tidy, small wheat farming community in central Montana were quiet except for the usual throng of churchgoers. McIntosh and his wife, Grace, had reason to be joyful: their son, Bill, was expected on the morning train. A branch line of the Milwaukee Road connecting Harlowton with Great Falls ran through Geraldine.

Obsessed with planes and flying as a boy, Bill was chasing his aviator dream as a student at the Parks Air College in East St. Louis, Missouri. In fact, the twenty-year-old had excitedly called his parents to inform them that he had just passed his exams and secured a commercial pilot's license.

He had not been back home to Geraldine to see his parents since he left for school in the fall of 1936, and planned to visit for two weeks before returning to Missouri for flight training.

The lanky farmer did not learn about the crash until he walked into the cottage-sized station. News of the crash was all over the radio that morning, but Jim and Grace, focused on their son's arrival, had not turned it on. With no specific information about Bill, and only knowing that many had died in the wreck, a stunned McIntosh drove quickly home to tell Grace the news. The distraught couple and their twelve-year-old daughter, Margaret, quickly packed bags and headed for Miles City, a three-hundred-mile drive. They arrived Sunday evening, joining many other anxious families waiting for news of loved ones.[20]

In addition to concerned family members, sightseers and gawkers by the hundreds descended on Custer Creek, lining the muddy, deeply rutted roads that led to the scene. Some onlookers even tried to drive across the streambed, as the water levels had dropped significantly since the night before, with the predictable result of getting stuck in the muck. Those without the means or impulsiveness to drive to the site instead walked many miles to see the wreck, while others arrived on horseback.

To aid the search for survivors in the submerged cars, Dan Haughian Jr. loaned his water pumps to rescuers. He then ferried news photographers and cameramen on horseback to get a close-up look at the wrecked cars lying in the muddy creek bed. Charlie Belden, a dude rancher from Wyoming, flew his red monoplane to the area, offering rides for the media and others. As H. R. Kester of the *Miles City Star* described the scene from the air that day, "It was as though some great force had set about to scramble effectively the train and create every possible hazard for its load of humanity, and at the same time select a spot where aid was almost entirely impossible."[21]

Reverend Paul Jones, the Miles City minister who was at the station at dawn to meet the hospital train, traveled out to Custer Creek Sunday afternoon but was not able to get closer than about a quarter mile away. Literally hundreds of cars "in an awful mess" lined the roads south and west of the site, hastily parked by both people wanting to help and the simply curious. At last arriving at the scene, Jones could see rescuers on top of the wrecked cars trying to save passengers. As he described, "The survivors were covered in mud and debris, and all wore a funereal expression."[22]

Jones approached a despondent man, standing on the running board of his car, who introduced himself as Milton Leer from Billings. Leer told Jones that his wife, Gladys, and their fifteen-month-old baby were missing. He had gone to the Billings train station early Sunday morning to pick them up. They never came, nor did the *Olympian*. While waiting at the station, Leer had bumped into his close friend, Leroy Bailey. Bailey was waiting for the arrival of his family as well. He was expecting his wife and two young daughters, Juanita, age six, and Joyce, age four, to arrive in the early morning hours after an extended visit with family in Hettinger, North Dakota.

Once they heard about the crash, the men drove the 145 miles east to Miles City together as fast as they could. It would be the worst day of their lives. Upon arrival, they were informed that their wives and children had perished at Custer Creek earlier in the morning. Bailey and Leer later joined the desolate line of friends and relatives waiting for hours at the Miles City morgue to identify the bodies of their loved ones. Still missing was Leer's baby, Lavonne. Rescuers could not locate her body and believed she had washed down the Yellowstone River. Some later saw Milton Leer wandering aimlessly in the streets of Miles City, sobbing, "Oh God, they're gone—my wife and kid. There doesn't seem anything to live for now."[23]

Dorothy Zimmerman, a newlywed living in Billings, had been excited for a visit from her newly engaged younger sister, Marie, who had boarded the *Olympian* in her hometown of Aberdeen, South Dakota. Instead, it would be a day of deep sadness for the Zimmerman family, as Marie, a full-time student who had just celebrated her nineteenth birthday, was killed in the wreck. Marie's fiancé, Jay Kervin, alerted to the accident by Dorothy and seeing the horrific news reports, drove four hundred miles directly to the crash site at Custer Creek. Kervin was at the scene when rescuers removed his fiancée's broken body from the twisted wreckage.[24]

The accident set off a chain reaction of tragedy for another family. Twenty-four-year-old nurse Lucille Stumley of Volga, South Dakota, survived the initial crash but died late Sunday evening. "She's like others here," remarked a nurse attending to Stumley. "They're so badly hurt, we don't know what's wrong." Lucille had suffered multiple serious fractures in the crash, and ultimately died when gas gangrene, a highly lethal infection of deep soft tissue, set in. Compounding the loss, eight-year-old Robert Stumley died in a freak accident while traveling from California with his family to attend Lucille's funeral. Experiencing engine trouble, the family stopped at a gas station in Casper, Wyoming. A gas leak in the engine compartment started a fire that ignited the young boy's clothes. Robert later died of his burns. The horrors of the *Olympian* crash came to extend far beyond the banks of Custer Creek and the halls of the Holy Rosary Hospital.[25]

CHAPTER 25

Desolation

Under other circumstances, Monday, June 20, 1938, would have been a spectacularly beautiful Montana day. With abundant sunshine and clear blue skies, the warmth of early summer called for swimming or fishing in a river or napping on a shaded porch. In Miles City, however, the scene was far from idyllic. The unassuming cow town, now overrun with outsiders, had earned the unwelcome attention of a nation. Reporters prowled the streets looking for interviews and information, making everyone uncomfortable. The city morgue, meanwhile, had run out of space. The local high school offered to temporarily store bodies in its gymnasium.

The "aura of desperation and foreboding" that George Flynn saw on the faces of railroad employees Sunday had spread across the community by Monday. The initial shock of the wreck had begun to wear off, replaced by the community's realization that they were now host to a major disaster. "The whole town wore an air of tragedy during the day as people who had viewed the wreckage returned and told their friends about it," remarked Reverend Paul Jones.[1]

In Saugus, daybreak revealed a throng of workmen and rescuers still hard at work. Despite the floodlights brought to the scene late Sunday, the darkness complicated rescue attempts and added to the gloom. For rescue crews, an endless night had followed an impossibly long day. They had set up a temporary camp at the scene to allow them to continue their efforts around the clock. Men barked orders and shouted across the creek, with the two heavy derricks and cranes towering overhead. Dan Haughian Jr.'s water pumps chugged, and derrick engines throttled up as they hoisted wrecked cars and train debris into the air like tinker toys. The constant arrival and departure of trains continued; fresh crews and supplies flowed in, while bodies wrapped in white sheets streamed back to Miles City.

The sole good news on Monday was that the floodwaters had receded remarkably fast. By noon, less than a foot of muddy water ran through the creek bed, down from an estimated twenty feet at the time of the accident. Deep gouges on each bank marked the high water line.

Gail Brown of Helena happened to be visiting friends in Miles City when the *Olympian* wreck occurred. Curious to see the crash site firsthand, she and her friends ventured to Saugus on Monday. She witnessed a scene of "utter desolation" when she got there. "Somehow the crumpled cars and cracked bridge abutments brought the idea that they had been there a long time. Sand and silt covered the ragged ends of steel, and a blistering sun had dried out parts of the wreck. Near us stretchers, each covered with a white sheet, were piled six or seven feet high," Brown recounted.[2]

Brown and the large crowd of onlookers watched as rescuers carefully pulled the battered body of baggageman Charlie James from the pulverized remains of the baggage car. A rescuer indicated he found James's coat, in the pocket of which was his railroad watch. The hands had stopped at precisely 12:35 A.M. "The baggage car was a shambles," recalled Brown. "Yet, as rescue workers pried bent steel, tiny chickens, part of a shipment, cheeped above the low hum of conversation." More chicks were rescued during the day, including "a little black fellow with bright eyes." Some bystanders crawled under the twisted wreck of the mail express car to rescue the chick. They reported that "his gait was somewhat wobbly, but [his] voice was loud and shrill." A rescuer summoned a few young boys nearby and gave them the chicks, saying, "You kids better take these chickens. No use leaving them here. They'll only die too."[3]

Brown noticed piles of clothes and shoes near the west bridge abutment and saw shabbily dressed men—survivors of the wreck—carefully looking them over in search of their personal items. Small planes constantly droned overhead. Brown and her friends took off their shoes and stockings and walked through the muddy water to the other side of the bridge. By that time, the water in the creek had receded to a trickle. "It was an eerie sensation," she noted, "to walk across a place where a wall of water 22 feet high had broken a train as though it had been cardboard."[4]

She stood beside a woman who was taking in the scene and asked her if she was a survivor. The woman told Brown no, but that her husband had been in the wreck. He was injured, suffering a serious head gash from being thrown through a sleeper car partition. Nonetheless, "he was one of the lucky ones."

Back in Miles City later in the day, Brown and her friends came across a woman sitting alone on a bench on Main Street. It was Florence Post, the mother of twenty-eight-year-old Dixon Post, killed in the wreck. Obviously in shock, Post told them she and her son had been on their way to Seattle for a vacation. "That night he [Dixon] decided to sit in the daycoach [car 420]. I was in a sleeper [Ipswich]. When the impact came, I thought the train had been struck by lightning. I was thrown ahead against the end of my berth. My son was in the daycoach. When I think what he must have suffered . . ." She trailed off, and said no more, clenching her hands tightly in her lap. Dixon Post died of multiple fractures and internal injuries in the accident.[5]

At Holy Rosary Hospital, Marcella Gehrig lay recovering from a severe concussion. She would remain in the hospital for a week, but her three daughters had avoided serious injury and were released Monday. Paul and Marcella's niece, Helen, spent six weeks in the hospital to allow her badly broken ankle to set and heal. With their summer trip to California canceled, Paul and the boys stayed in a Miles City hotel while they waited for their family members to recover.[6]

By Monday night, about twenty eight passengers and crew members, including conductor Chris McGee and porter Louis Williams, remained in the hospital. Two were still in critical condition. Dean Hanscom spent several nights in the Holy Rosary Hospital, recovering from his lacerations. Tuesday's newspapers still listed his twin brother Donald as missing. Rescuers believed he had died and was still "imprisoned" beneath the murky waters.[7]

The doomed Choteau still lay submerged in Custer Creek on Monday. Efforts to recover the bodies inside were among the most difficult of the entire operation. Having sucked the Choteau into its mucky bed, the creek seemed unwilling to let it go. Initial attempts to lift the car using the derrick were foiled. The tons of silt, mud, and debris that had filled the car through its broken windows made it nearly impossible to move. Several times the car slipped off the blocks set by rescue crews and sank again into the creek. Rescuers worried that if they lifted the sleeper too fast, the bottom of the car could crack open, and spill the bodies inside downriver.[8]

Late Monday morning, the floodwaters had receded enough to grant rescuers access to the car through its windows. A chilling sight greeted the sweaty men toiling in the heat. The bodies of several Choteau passengers sat in their seats by the broken windows. Using heavy wood planks as makeshift ramps through the shattered windows, workers pulled the first corpses from the car around noon. Cutting through the roof with acetylene torches, they recovered seven more that day.

A large crowd of onlookers lined the banks of the creek, including relatives of possible victims on the Choteau. "Mud splattered sheets, taken from sleeper [cars] that were not submerged in the creek, were folded over the victims before they were placed on the stretchers," reported the *Billings Gazette*. Rescuers then had to wade through the murky, knee-deep waters of Custer Creek, carrying the stretchers up the slippery west-side embankment where train cars waited to take the dead back to Miles City.[9]

The body of forty-two-year-old Valerie May Conway from Omaha, Nebraska, was among those pulled from the Choteau on Monday. An employee of the Union Pacific Railroad, Conway had suffered multiple fractures in the crash and drowned, like many others trapped in the sleeper car. Workers also carefully lifted the lifeless body of John Dana of Seattle from the car, angling the stretcher so it could pass through the shattered windows. On his way home, the fifty-three-year-old salesman had been on a business trip for his employer, the Cooperative Egg Poultry Association. Bill Range and his wife Carrie had also been aboard the Choteau. Bill worked as an officer with the Salvation Army, and the couple was traveling from their home in Atlanta to attend a national conference on social work in Seattle. Identification of their bodies fell to their adult children, who hurried to Miles City following the accident.[10]

Recovery efforts for the Choteau's passengers continued into Tuesday. Additional commercial water pumps were brought to the scene to clear the muck and debris that had swamped the car up to its windows. Tuesday night, rescuers pulled three more bodies out of the car. One of them was later identified as Donald Hanscom. The two others were eighteen-year-old Margie Clancy and her aunt Nell. Phillip Clancy anxiously watched the operation at Custer Creek, but soon became so overcome by the scene—and the ninety-degree heat—that he suffered a heart attack. The sixty-four-year-old was rushed to the Holy Rosary Hospital, where his condition stabilized.[11]

By Wednesday, June 22, crews found no new bodies at the crash site despite their around-the-clock efforts, but the grim search of the Choteau, known as the "car of death," would not officially be completed until Thursday evening. Rescuers could not locate the body of Kate Clancy, dealing a crushing blow to her family, who desperately wanted to bring closure to the painful event. As of Thursday night, five days after the accident, she was still listed as "missing."

Although search efforts continued into the week, hope of any additional survivors at the crash scene had faded by late Sunday afternoon. Officials working at the site continued to insist that the word "rescue" be used to describe their efforts when talking to the public or to news reporters. By early Monday morning, about twenty-four hours after the crash, officials started to refer to their work as "recovery" efforts. By day's end, reported the *Miles City Star*, "the morgue at Miles City was a scene of intolerable sadness Monday as relatives and friends passed through the rows of sheet-draped dead looking for bodies of loved ones."[12]

Even before rescuers could safely gain access to the sunken Choteau, railroad officials knew that the current had swept some passengers into the Yellowstone River. Several survivors, including *Olympian* crew members, had witnessed people being swept away in the fast-moving waters. Late Sunday, four bodies were found near Terry, about sixteen miles downriver. One was identified as Mrs. Fred Woolsey, who just days earlier had attended her daughter Mary Louise's graduation from Macalester College in St. Paul. Woolsey and the three other souls were carefully laid on the shore of the river to await transportation to Miles City.[13]

The sheriff of Prairie County had searchlights strung across bridges at Terry, Fallon, Glendive, and Sidney to aid nighttime recovery efforts on the muddy waters of the Yellowstone. People volunteered as "day watchers" on the bridges, keeping an eye out for any bodies floating downstream. River recovery efforts continued all week long in the sweltering weather. Searchers, including Duane and Lee Parks, scoured the river from Saugus to its confluence with the Missouri some 124 miles to the northeast. Upon finding a body, they looked for the nearest home so they could call it into Miles City.[14]

An additional corpse appeared Sunday evening in the murky waters near Glendive, about fifty miles downstream from the wreck site. A local farmer reported it to the Montana Highway Patrol. Two more were fished out of the Yellowstone on Monday near Fallon, about forty miles downstream. Another, discovered late Tuesday afternoon, had nearly floated to North Dakota. The grim discovery came near Sidney, over one hundred miles from the crash site in Saugus. The passenger, later identified as P. F. Schultz, an off-duty Milwaukee Road engineer based in Tacoma, had been riding as a passenger on the Choteau. The discovery of Schultz's body initially confused Milwaukee Road officials, since their records indicated there were two male passengers with the name Schultz from Tacoma on the doomed Choteau. In eerily similar circumstances to P. F. Schultz, Henry Schultz had also been washed down the Yellowstone River, but was not found until early September 1938 near Sidney.[15]

It took several days for the bodies of Sarah and Margaret Olson to be recovered and identified. The elderly sisters had boarded the westbound *Olympian* in Aberdeen, South Dakota, and were returning to Seattle following a two-month vacation visiting their brother in Sioux City, Iowa. The Olsons were well known and adored in their community for their work in the arts. Margaret operated an acting studio at the Odd Fellows Temple in the city. Both were drowned after washing into the Yellowstone from the Choteau.[16]

Stanley Guy, the Custer County coroner, had a week like no other following the wreck of the *Olympian*. Guy arrived at the scene early Sunday morning on the hospital train and spent the next thirty-six hours without a break at the crash scene, doing his best to recover, organize, and identify the dead. Late Sunday, when the waters started to retreat in the creek, Guy crossed over to the Terry side of the bridge, where he oversaw efforts to care for the dead and to transport them to the Miles City morgue for identification. Shortly after the accident, calls for help went out to undertakers across Montana and to funeral homes as far away as North and South Dakota. Trained medical personnel were needed to assist in the task of identifying bodies. Truckloads of caskets were ordered.

At the Miles City morgue, George Flynn, the Milwaukee Road stenographer and file clerk, was pulled onto the team working with families to identify the dead. With his stenographic notebook in hand, he "followed the doctors, dentists around the mortuary as they examined the unidentified bodies to determine if they matched the known medical and dental records." Rings, watches, pocketbooks, and markings on bodies were also used as clues. Flynn noted that some of the victims who drowned at Custer Creek were in such good physical condition due to the frigid water temperatures, that "they seemed almost alive" while lying in the quiet darkness of the mortuary. Flynn saw the motionless body of Don Hanscom and later recalled how young he looked. Still, decomposition had rendered Don's face unrecognizable, compelling his father to identify his son by the rings on his fingers and a scar on his back. The Hanscom family spent the week in Miles City, making funeral arrangements for Donald while waiting for Dean to recover enough to travel. They finally left by plane for Seattle on Monday, June 27, and buried nineteen-year-old Donald two days later.[17]

Flynn also recalled that rescuers brought a sealed coffin into the mortuary. The coroner recommended that Flynn not open the polished wooden box, since the body inside had washed down the creek into the river. Exposed to the sun for too long before he or she was recovered, it had rapidly decomposed, making identification difficult if not impossible. All told, Flynn spent three full days in the Miles City morgue dealing with the *Olympian* dead. He was finally relieved of this duty on Thursday, June 23, recalling that it had been a "grueling, emotional and nightmarish experience."[18]

For days after the accident, seventeen-year-old Randy Perkins remained on the list of missing passengers. Time had stopped for his father, Milo Perkins, informed by telegram that no one had seen Randy following the crash. Still in high school, Randy had boarded the *Olym-*

pian in Chicago on his way to a summer job in Avery, Idaho. In 1938, Milo Perkins, who had made a fortune manufacturing burlap bags in Texas, was knee-deep in a new career working as a high-level bureaucrat in the U.S. Department of Agriculture in Washington, D.C. Unable to leave Washington, Perkins arranged for a federal official, Paul Banfield, to fly to Miles City to get more information about Randy [19]

Train officials could not confirm that Perkins had a reservation on the Choteau for the trip from Chicago to Tacoma. Yet while Randy's luggage had been found, there was no sign of him. Banfield found his way to the morgue. Doctors had him view the body of a young unidentified man, but he could not be sure it was Randy. For two days, Banfield insisted to medical personnel and the Perkins family that the young man lying in the morgue was not Randy. Increasingly distraught and eager for any news about the fate of his eldest son, Milo Perkins asked that a family friend go to Miles City to help make the determination. On Wednesday, June 22, the Perkins family received confirmation that Randy had died. Like many other passengers on the Choteau, he had received serious injuries in the initial impact of the crash, but ultimately drowned in the sleeper car when it flooded and sank to the bottom of Custer Creek.[20]

Milo and Theron Perkins had their son's body shipped back to Chicago for burial. Less than five years later, the Perkinses suffered through another family tragedy when Randy's younger brother George, who had secured a commission as a naval aviator for the Marine Corps, was killed on May 20, 1943, while practicing dive bombing tactics at a training base in Jacksonville, Florida.[21]

At Holy Rosary Hospital, physicians set eight-year-old John Lallas's broken arm and tended to Anna and George's minor cuts, bumps, and bruises. George remembers Anna screaming and sobbing when she first learned that her parents had died in the accident. She cried out for her mother. "I tried to hold her, but the water was too strong," she said. "A lot of water rushed into the car and she was carried away into the darkness." Anna never saw her father after the crash: "I don't know what we are going to do now, with mama and papa both gone," she lamented.[22]

Jim Thomas had driven one thousand miles from Bellingham to Miles City. Two friends, Frank Holmes and Louis George, accompanied him.

The trio barely escaped injury while driving near Missoula, Montana, when Jim's light blue Plymouth sedan lost its brakes, wheeled off the highway, and ran over five fence posts before coming to a stop. Nobody was hurt, but the vehicle was destroyed. They rented a car to make it the rest of the way. Meanwhile, Miles City restaurant owner Peter Lucas learned about the three orphaned Lallas children, and immediately contacted the hospital, offering his home on Orr Street as a place for the youngsters to stay until their family arrived from Washington.[23]

Upon reaching Miles City on Wednesday evening, Jim Thomas arranged to take the children, along with their parents' bodies, back to Bellingham on another Milwaukee Road–flagged *Olympian*, leaving early Friday morning. Jim Thomas was deeply moved by the generous support of Miles City residents and of the Lucas family in particular. Their kindness, he declared, would "never be forgotten."[24]

On Tuesday June 21, Ned Clancy, Margie's brother and Phillip's son, flew by plane with his cousin Edward Raycraft to attend to his ailing father and assist in the recovery of his aunts' and sister's remains. Immediately after arriving, Ned and Edward were asked to identify two bodies at the Graves Funeral Home mortuary. Having been submerged in the murky waters for more than thirty-six hours, the corpses were bloated and difficult to recognize. With the assistance of dental records, jewelry, and clothing, Ned positively identified his aunt Nell and his sister Margie.[25]

Raycraft flew back to Bloomington to help set up funeral arrangements, leaving Ned and Phillip to continue to search for Kate's body. The Clancy family was deeply discouraged. "Railroad officials who are directing operations say that it may be tomorrow, or it may be a month, or perhaps a year before they recover her body," Raycraft explained to the local paper back home. "You see the Yellowstone is full of caves and brush. It could be that the body was washed out of the car and may have become lodged some place. Time will tell." There were no bodies discovered at the scene of the wreck on Wednesday.[26]

On Thursday, June 23, Kate and ten other passengers remained missing. Scouring the Yellowstone River more than fifty miles downstream, rescuers discovered several bodies the following night, including two women. They brought the remains to Miles City for identification. At around midnight Friday, June 24, Phil Clancy, still recovering from his heart attack earlier in the week, identified one of the deceased as his sister.

WHILE the search for bodies in the twisted waterways of the Yellowstone River continued and construction crews dynamited the wreckage of the Custer Creek bridge, funerals and burials had already begun in Miles City. On Wednesday, the First Methodist Church held back-to-back services for Frank Merrifield and Hausmer McCoy. Both were standing room only. Just two days earlier, Milwaukee Road employee Gus Waldo drew the unenviable task of crawling into the locomotive with a torch to free the burned, mangled bodies of Merrifield and McCoy. Waldo was the only person small enough to squeeze inside the crushed cab. Merrifield apparently was still gripping the throttle when Waldo reached him. He would later recount "never before or since having been so repelled."[27]

Merrifield's pallbearers included Henry Shipley and Bill Shearer, among other trainmen. Shearer eulogized Merrifield, his friend and fellow engineer, as "one of the best men to handle a locomotive." Just before the funeral, Shearer, who spent hours helping rescue passengers in the aftermath of the *Olympian* disaster, learned he had fractured several ribs in the crash. Dozens of flower arrangements encircled Merrifield's casket, spilling out across the altar of the otherwise drab church. With the Reverend George Reid presiding, the pews, packed with somber faces, joined in singing hymns in remembrance of the veteran engineer, including "Jesus, Savior, Pilot Me" and "This Old Rugged Cross." Many family members traveled to Miles City to support Marie and her four young children at the funeral, including his sister Leta Golden and three brothers, Edgar, Bert, and John Merrifield. "Nearer, My God, to Thee" played as the mourners exited the church.[28]

Some unfamiliar faces joined those assembled at Merrifield's funeral, including a mysterious woman with a child in tow. She did not leave the crowd wondering for long. Having traveled from Marmarth, North Dakota, she informed them that she was married to Frank Merrifield and that the child was his. The locomotive engineer's long-held secret was exposed. This spectacular revelation devastated Marie and roiled the community. Meanwhile, Della McCoy, his partner Hausmer's wife, had her husband's body brought to Des Moines, Iowa, to be buried in the place where they first met, fell in love, and married some twenty years earlier.[29]

On the same day as the services for Merrifield and McCoy, a double funeral to celebrate the lives of two local women, Mrs. Fred Woolsey and Mrs. Ed Arnold, took place at the First Presbyterian Church in Miles City. Around the same time, a large crowd mourned veteran Milwaukee Road baggageman Charlie James, whose service was held at the Miles City Order of Elks Lodge, of which he was a loyal member. Along with his widow, Vera, James's sister and three of his four brothers attended. They buried him in the Miles City cemetery.[30]

On Sunday, June 26, a full week after the *Olympian* wreck, what was thought to be the last body recovered from the Yellowstone River was identified as sixty-three-year-old Sarah Bard of Seattle. Since the middle of the week, there had been confusion among Milwaukee Road officials as to whether Bard had been on the train. She had been visiting her son, Captain Elliott Bard, in Quantico, Virginia, where he was stationed. Elliot had planned to drive his mother back to Seattle, but his vacation was canceled due to a military-ordered relocation. Having received no word from her in days, another son, Burt Bard, contacted the Milwaukee Road, who put her on the list of missing. Burt Bard flew to Miles City on Wednesday, June 22, hoping to find his mother. Sadly, mother and son would reunite in a cold morgue, surrounded by doctors and representatives from the Custer County Coroner's office.[31]

Of the estimated 190 passengers and crew members on the *Olympian*, the accident killed forty-nine persons and injured at least seventy-five. Even weeks after the crash, three persons listed as dead had not yet been recovered. The missing included Robert Nolan, the Choteau porter; Henry Schultz of Tacoma; and fifteen-month-old Lavonne Lou Leer of Billings. Also added to the final death count was Sharlot Daniels of Deer Lodge, Montana. Daniels, injured in the crash, succumbed to septicemia and died on July 2, 1938, at Holy Rosary Hospital.[32]

Months afterward, in September 1938, the body of Henry Schultz, age seventy-seven, was discovered in the Yellowstone River about one hundred miles downstream from the accident site, near Sidney, Montana. Stories circulated around Miles City for years after the accident that a body pulled from the Mississippi River in New Orleans was that of porter Robert Nolan. The rumor was never substantiated, and Nolan was never found. Neither was little Lavonne Leer. In the end, they were the only two *Olympian* victims never located.

Miles City may have resembled a war zone in the week following the wreck of the *Olympian,* but the community's response was one of pure compassion. Residents rallied around the many hurt and traumatized passengers and embraced the families who started pouring into their community the morning after the crash.

Many downtown merchants normally closed on Sundays opened their stores for survivors and relatives. Since the accident happened in the middle of the night, passengers arrived in Miles City dressed in pajamas and either barefoot or wearing only socks. Their shoes, along with their other belongings, went missing in the wreckage. Working with local churches, the Miles City Salvation Army sprang into action and collected clothing for the survivors. Community volunteers showed up at the hospital and at the station to retrieve victims' wet, muddy clothing and then returned them within hours in neat bundles, cleaned and ironed. Among those who received fresh clothes and shoes was Evelyn Janssen, the young woman with the golden hair rescued from the raging creek by Henry Shipley. Janssen was hospitalized for a day with a severely swollen leg and cuts all over her body. The navy blue and red crepe dress she wore when the wreck happened was ruined, shrunk to miniskirt length. "I would have been embarrassed if I hadn't been so out of it," she later remarked.[33]

Young Catherine Hahn recalled a man offering her father fifty dollars in cash to help with her family. Her father declined, saying, "No thank you, my family's safe and we're very thankful. Give this to someone else." Alvin Wright, a young *Olympian* passenger on his way to Butte, made good use of himself in the hours following the accident. Wright was on one of the Pullman sleepers in the rear of the train and unharmed in the wreck. According to other passengers, he helped people find their luggage on the train. He even made coffee for the passengers as they waited to be towed back to Miles City.[34]

Staff at the Miles City post office spent the better part of a week trying to dry out sixty sacks of "water-soaked, silt-grimed" mail and packages scattered about the debris field near the Custer Creek bridge. The employees took over a room in the post office and carefully placed the packages and letters in piles, working for days to identify their owners.[35]

Locating and returning passenger luggage in the aftermath of the wreck was enormously challenging, given the destruction of the baggage car and the subsequent littering of suitcases, clothes, and personal effects at the crash scene. The Milwaukee Road's office on Main Street became the repository for all such items. It was a scene of "endless activity" for several days after the accident, locals recalled.[36]

Milwaukee Road employees in Miles City and from across Montana volunteered to provide all manner of assistance to *Olympian* survivors and their relatives. They opened their homes, providing shelter, clothing, and food. They also helped family members separated at the accident scene find one another in the confusion that followed. A few employees loaned out their cars to survivors so they could pick up arriving family at the airport. At the station, the company set up special teams to assist those who wanted to continue their journey west and for those who wished to return home.

The *Billings Gazette* editorialized on the outpouring of kindness and support in Miles City: "From all sides has come praise for Milwaukee railway employees and members of the company's women's auxiliary at Miles City for their services in extending aid and comfort to survivors. The people of Miles City also wholeheartedly assisted in every way possible."[37]

At the scene of the accident, Saugus locals also helped in whatever way they could. Returning from the family's Little Sheep Mountain ranch, Susan Haughian joined Dan Jr., Kathleen, and Francis Motherhead in supplying food and fresh water to rescue teams. For Dan Jr., pulling his water pumps from his fields would have been unthinkable just a day earlier, but removing silt and water from the submerged cars proved more urgent than irrigating his crops.[38]

Despite all that had happened the night before, the Milwaukee Road was a railroad company with a duty to deliver its passengers to their destination. Even as rescuers worked frantically in Custer Creek and personnel attended to the survivors and families in Miles City, the company worked to cobble together another *Olympian* to continue the journey, combining the four undamaged cars from the back of the original train with other available cars in the railyard.

The remade westbound *Olympian* No. 15 pulled out of the Miles City station late Sunday evening, resembling but irrevocably different from the No. 15 that had last stopped in Mildred the night before. Those aboard had likewise been forever altered.

CHAPTER 26

Aftermath

> The disaster at Custer Creek will never be forgotten. It will remind us from time to time of the utter futility of man's works standing against the fury of nature at her worst.
>
> —*Billings Gazette*[1]

Efforts to find the cause of the *Olympian* accident started immediately. The Montana State Railroad Commission and Public Service Commission launched an investigation the day after the wreck, as did the federal Interstate Commerce Commission (ICC), then the principal regulatory agency on railroad matters. As luck would have it, two ICC inspectors, F. F. Engles and A. C. Murphy, happened to be visiting Montana at the time of the accident and were ordered to the scene.[2]

On Tuesday, June 21, Prairie County coroner Stanley Guy called for a coroner's jury to probe the cause of the crash. A legal tradition dating to medieval England, a coroner's jury typically reviews evidence from an event or disaster but cannot issue indictments like a grand jury. Since the accident took place in Prairie County, Guy himself led the inquiry. County officials selected nine prominent residents from Terry who had been at the scene of the wreck and were witnesses to the death and destruction at Custer Creek to serve on the jury.

The same day, Guy gaveled open the inquest at the Graves Funeral Home in Miles City at three in the afternoon. Exhausted, he had arrived directly from the crash scene. Prairie County attorney W. R. Flachsenhar and Sheriff R. P. Lane joined Stanley in overseeing the inquiry. The nine members of the jury were instructed to inquire into and render a verdict as to the cause of death for engineer Frank Merrifield, his partner Hausmer McCoy, and the other victims who had been recovered as of early Sunday morning. The jury heard details from six witnesses, a process that took most of the afternoon.[3]

Jim Griffith, the fuel supervisor who was on the Ipswich, was the first witness called. Griffith, who had been operating out of Miles City for decades with the Milwaukee Road, indicated that the water level in Custer Creek was about three feet below the track when the *Olympian* crossed the bridge at about 12:35 A.M. Sunday morning. After the crash, the waters continued to rise, coming within a foot of the track on the bridge. Griffith testified that this was the highest level of water he had ever seen in the creek since the Milwaukee Road started operating in the area in 1908.[4]

Section foreman Lou Goplen testified that he was under standing orders to patrol the section when there was water in Custer Creek. Contrary to the early news reports that placed Goplen at the bridge just before the *Olympian* crossed, Goplen told the jury that his last check of the bridge took place at about 10:20 P.M. on Saturday, more than two hours before the crash. Goplen saw about four feet of water running under the bridge at the time, an insignificant amount. In fact, it was so negligible that Goplen did not bother to mention it to Miles City dispatcher Dave Hagerty when he called to check in at 10:55 P.M. Goplen's account was validated by a freight engineer named Davis, whose train was the last to cross the bridge before the *Olympian*. Davis reported that when his train crossed the bridge at about 10:15 P.M., headed west to Miles City, he saw about three or four feet of running water in Custer Creek.[5]

Early Tuesday evening, coroner jury foreman H. W. Turnbull announced that the crash of *Olympian* No. 15 was an accident, caused by flooding at Custer Creek. Turnbull indicated that the victims of the wreck "came to their deaths in Prairie County, Montana between the hours of 12 midnight June 18, and 1 A.M. of the morning of June 19, 1938, and that their deaths were caused by the derailment of train No. 15 of the Milwaukee railroad at Custer Creek bridge, Prairie County, Montana, during floodwaters in Custer Creek."[6]

Despite this conclusion, which blamed the weather rather than the Milwaukee Road, the company was horrified by the *Olympian* accident at Custer Creek. It had been twenty years since a passenger had died on a Milwaukee Road train. Only days after the crash, attorneys were already estimating that the railroad could be on the hook for $750,000 of damages (over $15 million today) if the wreck was deemed preventable. Some newspapers were quick to accuse the company of negligence and not properly maintaining its rail infrastructure due to cost-cutting during its 1935 bankruptcy—its second such filing in less than ten years. The major newspaper in its hometown, the *Chicago Tribune,* suggested as much in an editorial published two days after the tragedy: "We have no wish to prejudge the findings of those who will investigate the Custer Creek catastrophe, but certainly the question whether the financial problems of the company had anything to do with the accident should be investigated with utmost thoroughness."[7]

The suggestion that the company's financial plight had led to inadequate bridge inspections and lax maintenance stung the company. In response, H. A. Scandrett, acting chief trustee of the Milwaukee Road during its bankruptcy, had the company publicly release the complete history of bridge AA-438, which included details of years of inspections and maintenance efforts. Frank Newell also drafted a testy response to the *Chicago Tribune* on behalf of Scandrett that was published in full the next day. It insisted that throughout the Depression, the company focused on passenger safety: "The management, confronted with the necessity of either failing to pay interest on its debts or skimp its maintenance to a point which might have resulted in unsafe operating conditions, chose unhesitatingly the former course."[8]

Led by Newell's public relations team, Scandrett and the Milwaukee Road brass stayed consistent in their messaging from the moment they were first made aware of the wreck. In a telegram issued to all its employees on Sunday, Scandrett stated, "The accident resulted from a condition that developed without warning and was not due to any shortcoming in the operating organization." He ended the note with a call to employees to be upbeat and positive: "It would be easy to become discouraged in the face of the disaster, but that is not the way of the good fighter who makes of adversity a spur to greater effort, and that is exactly what we will do. I know the spirit of the Milwaukee Road. It is to 'Carry On.'"[9]

Beginning on the awful morning after the accident, Frank Newell's goal had been to "calm the hysteria" of the news media and to get the *Olympian* story off the front pages. Fate would have it otherwise. Six days after the Custer Creek tragedy, another westbound *Olympian* was involved in an early morning head-on collision with a Civilian Conservation Corps train in Ingomar, Montana, about eighty-five rail miles southwest of Miles City. One person was killed and thirteen were injured, including the engineers and firemen from both trains. Both steam locomotives were "badly smashed." The head-on collision was met with disbelief by the company. A veteran Milwaukee Road engineer with a spotless record had ignored a dispatcher's order, resulting in the crash. "Throughout the week, we had gone about with our heads bowed in sorrow," remarked Newell. "On Saturday, our sorrow was changed to anger even hatred." He added, "Although there are 30,000 of us, it took but one man to put us 'back of the eight ball.'"[10]

Newell and the Milwaukee Road suffered another broadside in early July when *Life* magazine published "A Survivor Photographs the Worst American Train Wreck Since 1887," featuring the sensational photographs of the accident taken by passenger Maurice V. Odquist. It was a shock to the Milwaukee Road that he had sold his images to *Life.* The accompanying story incensed the company, which insisted it was full of errors and inaccuracies. Seething, the Milwaukee Road considered contacting Odquist's employer, presumably to have him reprimanded or even fired.[11]

Only a few short weeks later, to the great relief of the company, news coverage of the *Olympian* wreck had all but disappeared. A satisfied Frank Newell had reason to be pleased with the overall management of the news, noting, "We have seen nearly 300 editorials and, with the exception of three, all have expressed understanding and sympathy."[12]

The ICC investigated the *Olympian* accident for about six weeks following the wreck. In early August 1938, members of the ICC traveled from Washington, D.C., to Miles City to conduct a public hearing. They heard from many experts, including railroad officials and witnesses who were both aboard the train and on the ground that night. The federal investigators focused on two specific areas: the design and construction of the bridge and the local weather. Crew members and other investigators testified that there was no indication that Frank Merrifield applied the air brakes on the *Olympian* at any time before the crash, a sign that Merrifield and McCoy had no warning of the disaster to come.

The ICC took a substantial amount of expert testimony from division-level Milwaukee Road engineers and inspectors responsible for bridge construction and maintenance in eastern Montana. It seemed clear that, despite the financial challenges facing the company at the time, the railroad had not cut corners on critical right-of-way maintenance issues, including bridges and trestles. In fact, engineers had inspected the Custer Creek bridge just six months prior to the accident and found the core of the bridge and its piers sound. Previous actions further demonstrated the railroad's diligence. Following an inspection in 1935, the Milwaukee Road had substantially reinforced riprap around the Custer Creek bridge piers. Additional strengthening of the bridge occurred in 1937 based on annual engineering reports.

The Milwaukee Road's assistant chief engineer testified that, in his opinion, the bridge was intact at the time of the *Olympian* No. 15 crossing, but piers two and three had been undermined by the speed and strength of the water cascading down the hills of Saugus. As the 440-ton locomotive and tender began to cross the bridge, several piers shifted, pitching the tremendous weight of the locomotive to the right and triggering a series of events that caused the entire bridge to collapse and derail the train. Providing evidence of the power of the water, investigators found huge chunks of the riprap meant to protect the piers, weighing hundreds of pounds, washed a considerable distance downstream.

The ICC also heard from other key witnesses on the train that night, including fuel supervisor Griffith, flagman Preston, and the conductor, Chris McGee. Section men Goplen and Eastwood were called to testify, as were dispatchers Hagerty and Grogan. Hagerty noted that he had never issued an order regarding the Custer Creek bridge in the ten years he had been a dispatcher in Miles City. The ICC also heard testimony from a few locals, including Dan Haughian's brother Henry, who detailed the series of violent cloudbursts that took place that Saturday evening near the family's Little Sheep Mountain ranch.[13]

Almost all the news accounts that followed the accident referred to the series of violent cloudbursts that occurred on the west side of the Yellowstone River in and around the Little and Big Sheep Mountain ranges and close to the Haughian's ranch. The cloudbursts stalled over the area, dropping as much as seven inches of water within two hours on the southwestern slopes of the mountains and near the headwaters of Custer Creek. The downpour quickly filled and overwhelmed every stream, creek, wash, coulee, and depression in the area. The water had only one place to go: down, to the Yellowstone River. Bridge AA-438 in Saugus and the Milwaukee Road's mainline track stood in the way.

John T. ("Jack") Sleavin, an insurance adjuster from Spokane, Washington, spent several days exploring the Custer Creek watershed area in the month following the accident. He determined that the cloudburst was so intense that a new creek was carved, adding more water to an already flooded Custer Creek. "I find names of all kinds attached to the feeders to Custer Creek, but none for what looks like a new one brought about by the unprecedented flow of water which swept down like a powerful avalanche down Custer Creek on that fateful morning," reported Sleavin.[14]

Milwaukee Road management waited nervously for the ICC's conclusion on the root cause of the Custer Creek crash. Their attorneys knew that in fatal train accidents the law held a "prima facie presumption of negligence on the part of the carrier." The burden of proof lay on the railroad to prove that they had taken every possible precaution against an accident. "Courts may hold that railroads must anticipate high water, or cloudbursts as in this case," stated a prominent personal injury attorney in Minneapolis.[15]

On August 9, 1938, the ICC released the results of its investigation, absolving the Milwaukee Road of any direct responsibility or legal liability associated with the accident. The ICC concluded that the Custer Creek bridge was "adequate as to design for the traffic it was required to support." The crash of the *Olympian,* it determined, was accidental, caused "by the undermining of the piers of the bridge, due to a cloudburst."[16]

Despite being off the hook in terms of criminal liability for the crash, the Milwaukee Road worked with the families of employees who were hurt or killed in the accident, providing a modest financial payout for each. Given the legal cover provided by the ICC's ruling, the company had no obligation to passengers affected by the crash, but it attempted to make amends anyway. The Lallas family was promised $30,000 from the Milwaukee Road, $10,000 for each of the three orphaned children. According to the family, they only received $10,000, still a source of bitterness to the Lallases more than eighty years later.[17]

While the ICC investigation was underway, the company was quick to carry on the business of railroading after the accident. In addition to assembling another *Olympian*-flagged train within a day to carry the fifty-five unhurt passengers the rest of the way to Tacoma, construction crews worked around the clock to reopen the mainline track on the west side of the river. In less than a week, they erected a temporary timber bridge across Custer Creek just to the north of the mangled remains of bridge AA-438. Freight and passenger trains once again rolled through Saugus and past the Haughian's ranch. At night, floodlights shone for weeks at the accident scene, an eerie reminder for the trains passing by on both sides of the river.[18]

Work started simultaneously on a permanent replacement for bridge AA-438. A special flatcar-mounted crane brought in from Mobridge started driving the piles for the new bridge. When it was completed in the fall of 1938, crews dynamited the temporary timber bridge.[19]

Within a week after the accident, the pieces of the wrecked locomotive were shipped back to the West Valley shops in Milwaukee on flatbed cars. It was rebuilt and put back into service in less than a year and continued pulling trains until it was retired in the 1950s.[20]

In 1950, the centennial of the company's founding, the Milwaukee Road operated and managed a vast national rail system of about 10,556 miles of track. Around that time, the company began to scrap its large inventory of steam locomotives, finally making an overdue transition to diesel engines. The change proved devastating to Miles City. Its last working steam locomotives were gone by 1954. That same year, the twenty-four-stall steam engine roundhouse was torn down along with many other buildings and facilities in the railyard. The Milwaukee Road's division offices in Miles City were closed in 1959. Five years later, the company's storied transcontinental passenger trains, including the *Olympian* and the *Columbian,* passed into history.[21]

The Milwaukee Road's last steam locomotive was retired in 1957. The legendary railroad company then began a long, slow decline as passenger service dried up and revenue from freight—once the company's bread and butter—declined due to transportation alternatives like trucking. By the early 1970s, operations and traffic were so feeble on the Milwaukee system that it was referred to as a "transportation slum," particularly on the rails west of Miles City to Puget Sound. In 1972, the company halted electric-powered operations on the Coast Division in Washington State, and in 1974, did the same on the famous all-electric route from Harlowton, Montana, to Avery, Idaho, home of its Rocky Mountain Division. Teetering on the financial edge once again, the Milwaukee Road declared bankruptcy for a final time in 1977, and by April 1980, its tracks across Montana were quiet. Despite strenuous efforts to keep operations moving, the Milwaukee Road had no choice but to abandon 7,500 miles of track in February 1980, most of it west of Miles City. It was the largest rail line abandonment in U.S. history. By the time the Milwaukee Road fully disappeared from Miles City in the spring of 1982, it was down to thirty five local employees, a far cry from the one thousand residents that once worked for the railroad.[22]

The management of the Milwaukee Road remained fiercely and stubbornly independent to the end. For well over one hundred years of operations, it actively resisted mergers and situations that could force a takeover of the company and its rail assets. But on February 19, 1985, the Milwaukee Road came to its own terminus. After years of legal wrangling and financial somersaults, the company ceased to exist as a standalone business, becoming a subsidiary of the Soo Line Corporation. The ink was barely dry on the final legal papers when the Soo Line snuffed out all remnants of the once-famous orange and black brand that blazed America's railroads for over a century.[23]

After the accident, news stories celebrated the two deadheading Milwaukee Road employees, Ed Hamm and Mike Cain, as heroes. Coverage hailed as heroic their breathless run to Saugus in the dead of night to spread word of the tragedy. Milwaukee Road management and employees, however, viewed their efforts differently. The fact that neither Hamm nor Cain returned to the accident scene that night to assist with rescue efforts led to deep criticism of their actions inside the company. The critique of Hamm and Cain suggests that, despite the disciplined presentation of company unity following the accident, management likely did some serious soul searching and internal review in the weeks and months that followed.[24]

Chris McGee, the conductor on the ill-fated *Olympian* who was injured in the crash, spent several days recovering in the Holy Rosary Hospital. He soon returned to work and was eventually appointed as senior passenger conductor for the Milwaukee Road's Trans-Missouri Division in Miles City, the top ranking for a man in his position. McGee wore his conductor's cap for the last time in the fall of 1954, ending a remarkable fifty-four-year career working the rails. His last ride before retirement was on the sister train to the *Olympian,* the flagship *Hiawatha.*[25]

Neal Grogan, the dispatcher on duty in Miles City when the Olympian crashed into Custer Creek, continued his career with the Milwaukee Road. In the summer of 1947, he moved to Washington State after appointment as chief dispatcher of the Coast Division, based in Tacoma. In April 1952, Dave Hagerty ended a fifty-year career dispatching for the Milwaukee Road and other railroad companies. At a banquet to honor him at the Cross Roads Inn in Miles City, his friends and colleagues presented him with a brand-new fishing rod and tackle. He did not run for political office again, satisfied with his two terms as a Montana state representative in the 1930s. Frank Newell, the company's public relations master, ended his forty-year run with the Milwaukee Road in the summer of 1958. The "flowing fountain of railroad yarns" decided to "take up whittling" instead, ending an era and a colorful career.[26]

Once a thriving small community of homesteaders, Mildred today is nearly a ghost town. The railroad tracks that the speedy *Olympian* ran on remain, but they are used exclusively by freight trains. The passenger era that spawned the community in 1908 has been relegated to the history books. Mildred's water tower, one of the first structures built in the town and an important visual marker for passing engineers such as Frank Merrifield, was torn down in the 1950s along with the coal dock.

Mildred had about five hundred residents in 1920, but persistent drought, the Great Depression, and the decline of the railroads converged to debilitate the community. The rerouting of U.S. Highway 12 was also a major blow, stranding a gaggle of struggling communities including Mildred, Westmore, and Ismay. In the early 1950s, the high school closed, followed by the shuttering of its grade school in 1974. By 2021, the town's population was listed as just two residents—marked informally by a small metal number two hung on a hook, nailed to a tree by the road.

Epilogue

The Merrifields

Stunned by the revelation at Frank's funeral that he had been unfaithful to her and fathered a child with another woman, Marie's moods alternated between rage and depression. Her painful upbringing as an orphan surfaced again, as she felt abandoned by someone she dared to love. The walls of their small home on North Center Avenue became claustrophobic. Her colorful garden of dahlias suffered from neglect in the summer of 1938. The months following the wreck of the *Olympian* were exceedingly difficult for the Merrifield children as well.

Frank's younger brother Bert stayed in Miles City after the funeral out of concern for Marie's well-being. Of all the Merrifield siblings, Bert had the best relationship with Marie and sought to console her and the children as best as he could. Bert eventually convinced the distraught widow of four that she and her children should relocate and start anew in Los Angeles near him and his mother, Addie. The family patriarch, George Merrifield, tragically, had died of a heart attack a few years earlier after his car was struck by a train at a railroad crossing.[1]

Marie agreed, and within six months of the accident, she and her four children made the move. With the money that the Milwaukee Road provided her as a death benefit, Marie bought a large house in the West Adams district of south Los Angeles, just blocks away from Bert and Addie Merrifield. Working in real estate, Bert also convinced Marie to invest some of her money into a six-unit apartment building in the neighborhood as an income property. To make ends meet, Marie also took a job working night shifts at a nearby dye factory.[2]

To her children, it seemed like their mother worked all the time. To save money, Marie also refused to hire anyone to assist with the upkeep of the apartment building. She put her kids to work cleaning apartments when tenants moved out. Frank, Audrey, Leatrice, and even the toddler, Phyllis Marie, often spent weekends painting rooms, sweeping sidewalks, and mowing lawns.

As the Merrifield family settled into their new life in California, Bert was a constant presence. His real estate office was walking distance from Marie's house, and he often joined the family for lunch and helped Marie do yard work. Bert was married, and had two of his own children, but Marie and her children became his extended family. Bert was always present for birthdays, Valentine's Day, and Christmas, with gifts in hand and hugs for all. In many ways, Bert became the father to Marie's children, and a loving, dedicated friend to Marie. "I always remember my uncle [Bert] wearing a suit, nice shirt, a gray hat, glasses and a loving smile," recalled Phyllis Marie.[3]

In the 1950s, Marie's health began to decline. As an adult, she developed a heart condition and needed to take nitroglycerin pills on occasion. Her doctors told her to slow down, but she stubbornly refused their advice and kept working. On August 23, 1954, Marie Mary Hunter Merrifield died quietly in her Los Angeles home at age fifty-one, surrounded by her four children and Bert Merrifield. True to the end, Bert insisted that Marie receive a proper memorial service and that she was buried in an elegant place. Her body rests in the Forest Lawn Memorial Park in Glendale, California, a few rows away from the likes of Walt Disney and Samuel Goldwyn.[4]

Clancy Women

Weary and heartsick, Phil and Ned Clancy were eager to return to Bloomington with the bodies of their family members. But while officials in Montana approved the request for Margie's remains to be shipped home, they refused permission to send Nell and Kate back to Bloomington, citing the poor condition of their bodies. The state ordered that the two sisters be buried in Miles City. Stunned by the ruling, the Clancys began the process of arranging funeral services for Kate and Nell in Miles City while continuing to negotiate with officials. Their efforts succeeded. By late Saturday, they had secured a special permit allowing them to ship Kate and Nell Clancy back to Bloomington the next day.

Margie's body arrived by train in Bloomington at about two in the afternoon on Sunday, June 26. The bodies of her aunts arrived on Monday. Tuesday, June 28, 1938, was a day of deep mourning in the Clancys' hometown. Bloomington's first "triple funeral" in many years, the service for the three women at St. Patrick's Church was also the largest in recent memory, with over one thousand people in attendance according to the *Pantagraph,* the local newspaper. While three black hearses stood parked outside, pallbearers set the caskets in line down the aisle of the church, with Kate first, followed by Nell and Margie. Among the mourners were several nuns and teachers from Trinity High School and Rosary College, where Margie had just completed her freshman year. The Dean of Rosary College, Sister Cyrill Gill, also traveled to Bloomington for the funeral and to pay her respects to the Clancy family.[5]

A teacher who helped students with special needs, particularly those with visual impairments, Nell Clancy left behind a meaningful legacy in the community. "As a man lives so shall he die," remarked the Reverend Father Martin Spalding, who gave the sermon to the packed audience at St. Patrick's. "But in the case of these three good women who spent their lives giving and acquiring knowledge, imparting hope and good cheer, kindliness and love, these same words are a promise of eternal life."[6]

But even the funeral and burial did not bring an end to the Clancy tragedy. In a macabre discovery, Montana officials realized that Nell's body had been misidentified at the morgue in Miles City in the chaotic days after the accident. The body just buried as Nell was in fact that of someone else. Horrified, the Clancy family arranged to have the unidentified woman exhumed from the freshly dug grave. It fell to Ned Clancy to accompany the stranger's body back to Miles City and return with his Aunt Nell.[7]

Henry Shipley and Evelyn Janssen

Henry Shipley spent hours the night of the accident leading passenger rescues and tending to the injured and frightened. Focused on saving lives, Shipley ignored his own injuries until the hospital train and the teams of rescuers arrived at dawn. It was only when he sat down and was tended to by a nurse that he realized he hurt all over. Shipley rode the hospital train back to Miles City on Sunday morning and was hospitalized for several days. His injuries were not serious, but he had bumps, bruises, and cuts everywhere.

In the days following the accident, J. T. Gillick, the Milwaukee Road's operating vice president, traveled to Miles City to oversee recovery operations. He tracked down Shipley and offered him a cash reward for his rescue efforts and courage. When Shipley refused to take the payment, Gillick promised him, "As long as the Milwaukee Road has a railroad, you shall have a job." To formalize the offer, Gillick put a letter in Shipley's personnel file attesting to the commitment.[8]

Shipley formed a special relationship with Evelyn Janssen, the young woman with the golden hair whom he rescued from the raging waters of Custer Creek. When Janssen was released from the hospital, she stayed for three weeks with Henry and his wife Ida in Miles City before returning to her home in Freeport, Illinois. After learning that Shipley was an avid hunter, Janssen arranged to have an elk skin jacket made for him in appreciation for saving her life. Shipley and Janssen corresponded for over thirty years, and she even traveled to Miles City in 1969 to visit him. She lost touch with him after the last visit. Henry Shipley retired from the Milwaukee Road in 1953, at age sixty-five. The wiry Norwegian passed away at age ninety in June 1978. He is buried in Hamilton, Montana.

Evelyn Janssen married Bob Dunaway in 1939, a union that would last sixty-two years, until Bob's death in 2001. She and Bob had two children. "It took years before I realized how lucky I really was," she later mused. "I'm a survivor."[9]

Dean Hanscom

It is not known whether Dean Hanscom stayed in Seattle for the summer after the burial of his twin brother, Donald, or if he returned to Bronxville, New York, with his parents and sister, Janet. Dean did, however, resume his studies at Dartmouth College in the fall. He lived in the Kappa Sigma fraternity that both boys had pledged the previous year. Dean graduated from Dartmouth in 1940, with a degree in journalism. In the 1940 edition of the *Aegis,* Dartmouth's student yearbook, there was no mention of Donald's death, but he was listed on a page titled "Ex Members of the Class of 1940."

Warren Jones, another survivor of the Custer Creek disaster, was enrolled as a freshman at Dartmouth College in the fall of 1938. In a twist of fate, Jones and Dean Hanscom crossed paths on the campus at Dick's House, the college's infirmary. Jones had spent the better part of his first month at Dartmouth getting treatment for a stubborn bout of pneumonia. Knowing of his Montana roots, his doctor asked Jones if he had noticed the young man who had just exited the infirmary. The doctor informed him that it was Dean Hanscom, who was still being treated for injuries suffered in the crash. Apparently, Hanscom had a leg wound that continued to spit out small pieces of gravel from the Custer Creek riverbed. Jones vowed to look up Hanscom, but never did, which he regretted for the rest of his life.[10]

Dean Hanscom went on to receive his master's in journalism at Columbia University in 1941 before enlisting in the U.S. Navy at the outbreak of World War II. While in the service, Hanscom spent time on ships in the Pacific Theater, including seeing action during military operations at Okinawa, Leyte, and the occupation of Tokyo Bay. He was discharged as a lieutenant commander in November 1945.[11]

While serving in the navy, Hanscom married Marjory Eagan in 1943. They had three boys together, Steven, Douglas, and Mark. After the war, he worked for the Sears Roebuck Company as a buyer before taking a job at the Northwest Metal Products Company, where he became assistant sales manager. At the young age of forty five, Dean Hanscom died in Seattle on November 29, 1963, of coronary thrombosis, a few months shy of his twenty-first wedding anniversary. Dean and Donald Hanscom rest together in a family mausoleum at Acacia Memorial Park cemetery in Seattle, Washington.[12]

Louis Goplen

The wreck of the *Olympian* was especially devastating for trackwalker Lou Goplen. The crash happened on his watch, on his ten-mile stretch of track. Goplen and his partner Eastwood spent hours carefully inspecting his section of track that night. According to family, he took the accident personally and it haunted him for the rest of his days.

The media frenzy that followed the accident got the facts maddeningly wrong. The early news stories put Goplen on the bridge just before the train arrived and erroneously attributed to him a statement that Custer Creek was dry as a bone and had no running water in it. Adding insult to injury, the media repeated these bungled facts over and over again as early accounts spread like wildfire. There was no correcting the record. Despite the facts, the damage to Goplen's reputation had been done. Fortunately, the tight-knit community of Milwaukee Road railroad workers in Miles City knew the truth and respected Lou Goplen. Any person who visited the accident site in the day or two that followed understood that an epic weather event caused the derailment of the *Olympian* that night, not the inattention of a section chief. Investigations cleared the Milwaukee Road and Goplen of any blame.

Following the wreck, he worked the accident site for many days, never taking a break and not returning home until the end of the week. Dedicated to his colleagues, he preferred to stay with the work crews camped out by the track near Custer Creek. Goplen also oversaw the building of a new bridge over the creek, so the Milwaukee Road trains could run once again on the west side of the Yellowstone River.[13]

Goplen continued his trackwalker work for the Milwaukee Road for another thirty years: once a section man, always a section man. He was working in Hettinger, North Dakota, about seventy miles east of Marmarth, when he retired in 1969. He liked to tell people that his fifty-four-year career with the Milwaukee Road had him working at "every Milwaukee station between Mobridge and Miles City."

In retirement, Lou and Christine Goplen moved to Billings to be close to their children. Louis Edward Goplen died May 21, 1979, at the age of seventy-seven, having outlived his wife Christine by five years.[14]

George Lallas

George Lallas, the youngest of the Lallas children to survive the *Olympian* wreck, celebrated his ninetieth birthday in August 2020. Eighty-two years after the accident, he reflected, "To this day, I'm still asking the guy upstairs: 'Why? Why would you take parents away from three kids?'" He went on to say, with good humor, "Maybe one of these days, I'll be lucky to go up there, and He will give the answer."[15]

The three orphaned Lallas children returned to Bellingham, Washington, and joined the household of Gust and Mary Trames (Trambaklos). Gust Trames was Esther Lallas's brother, and the Trames had three children of their own. Gust owned the Royal Inn, a restaurant in Bellingham.

Anna, at age sixteen, insisted that she repay the Trames for caring for her and her brothers. While going to school, Anna held three jobs. She later became a public schoolteacher and, in 1947, married fellow teacher Gust Rakus, who taught foreign languages and worked real estate on the side to make ends meet. Anna and Gust had three children.[16]

After high school, John and George were determined to get out of Bellingham and see the world. John enlisted in the U.S. Army and was sent to Korea after America entered the war. There, he focused on logistics and securing supplies for the troops. George signed up with the U.S. Marines in 1948 and also went to Korea.

While fighting with the First Marine Division during the frigid winter of 1950, George found himself on a frozen, barren battlefield near the Chosin Reservoir. The winter cold was so severe—the temperature often stayed below zero degrees for days on end—that foxholes could not be dug by hand; dynamite and bulldozers were necessary to open the frozen tundra to protect the troops. During the Battle of Chosin Reservoir, George's unit was surrounded and overrun by Chinese troops. He found himself face-to-face with a Chinese soldier pointing a submachine gun at him as he tried to sink into a shallow foxhole. The soldier started firing. In that split second, according to George, his mother, Esther, appeared to him. Speaking in Greek, she calmly said, "No, George, your time hasn't come yet."

Later, George Lallas and his unit would be reported as "Missing in Action." When his family back in Bellingham was notified, George's older brother, John, home from his service in the army, was awakened that night by the apparition of his father, Thomas Lallas, telling him, "Don't worry, George is alright." In Korea, George survived his second near-death experience, avoiding capture by the enemy and marching out of the dangerous situation with his fellow soldiers in the freezing cold. The

First Marine Division suffered about ten thousand casualties during the Chosin Reservoir campaign, many of them due to the cold. George spent six months recovering from frostbite in an army hospital before returning home.[17]

Back in Bellingham, both John and George went to work for their uncle at the Royal Inn, which became a successful business. George and John used some of the settlement money that the Milwaukee Road awarded to the family to go into partnership with Gust. George married Alta Miller in 1959 and the couple had four children, three boys and a girl. Both Lallas boys stayed in the business for over thirty years, retiring in the mid-1980s. John died in 2007, and Anna (Lallas) Rakus died in 2017 at age eighty-nine.[18]

George Lallas died on September 25, 2022, at age ninety-two, in Bellingham, Washington. In his last years, George Lallas spent as much time as he could with his children, grandchildren, and great-grandchildren. He had a big backyard that kept him busy throughout the year. "If you want to let yourself get old, you will," said a ninety-one-year-old George. "But I don't want to get old." He still drove his car every day, and the local grocery store employees knew him by his first name. He was often the first customer to arrive when the doors opened each morning.[19]

Louis Williams

Recovering from his injuries in the Holy Rosary Hospital in Miles City, Louis Williams, the Pullman-trained porter on sleeper C, had a special visitor. Florence Hand Maguire, dressed in her white nurse's uniform, came to Williams's bedside to thank him for saving her life. She had looked for him when she returned to the crash site, but Williams had already been taken to the hospital. Deeply grateful for his actions, Florence told reporters, "That porter was one of the heroes of the wreck. He tore down the hammocks in the sleepers and made rope bridges and rope guides . . . that got everyone to safety."[20]

Indeed, Williams was hailed for his actions on the night of the *Olympian* disaster, but he agonized over the media attention following the accident. "I can't see why everyone is making a fuss because I carried out a few bags in the car and told passengers which door to leave from. I do that every time the train stops," Williams declared in a newspaper interview. "The passengers deserved all the credit. They believed me when I told them to move quickly and be careful." He went on to say, "I just did what any real porter does when the company had hard luck. Their hard luck is our hard luck too. All I want is for people to let me alone and get back on my run."[21]

Newspapers across the country gobbled up the story of the Black porter saving the lives of white passengers. The front-page headline in Alabama's *Cullman Banner* read, "Negro Pullman Porter Who Saved All Sleepers in His Coach, Acclaimed Number One Hero of The Occasion." The *Daily Herald* in Provo, Utah, used the headline, "Negro Hero Risks Life in Rescue." The headline in the *Pittsburgh Courier* exclaimed, "Pullman Porter Who Saved 22 Lives When Train Was Wrecked." The *Courier* article called Williams "heroic and valiant" in his efforts to save twenty-two "white" passengers. It included a page one photo of Williams and his wife Ruth alongside his brother Cleopas and his wife Dolores.[22]

The *Billings Gazette* praised Williams in an editorial about the tragedy:

> If it can be said that there is a bright side to the tragedy, it is in the accounts of the heroic acts of men and women who forgot their own harrowing experience in escaping death and turned immediately and willingly to the rescue of others. There is the story of the brave negro porter, Lewis Williams, who coolly directed many of his passengers to safety although he had been injured, to cite only one instance of the capacity of the human race to reveal its finer qualities in times of grave emergencies.[23]

The *Pantagraph* in Bloomington, Illinois, also published an editorial about Williams, titled "The Modest Porter." The paper summarized his courageous deeds after the *Olympian* crashed, observing: "In those precious minutes, Williams forgot himself and thought only of his passengers, most of them asleep in their berths. He roused them from their sleep, grabbed what pieces of handy luggage he could, rushed to the upper end of the car, which stood at a dangerous tilt, and got all his passengers outside the door and on the ground before the car slipped into the stream." While Williams "renounced the throne of a hero," the newspaper praised his courage and modesty.[24]

His injuries from the accident were not serious, but the doctors kept him in the hospital long enough that he was unable to continue to Tacoma with the reassembled *Olympian* that left on Sunday evening. Later in the week, he caught a ride home on an eastbound *Olympian* No. 16.

Back in Chicago, Williams became a reluctant local celebrity. Radio stations asked for interviews, including an invitation for an appearance on Robert Ripley's *Believe It or Not*. Hoping to avoid drawing any further attention to the disaster, management at the Milwaukee Road declined the opportunity on behalf of Williams. "We appreciate your offer," the company wrote, "but do not believe this accident, which already has so much publicity, should again be revived in the public mind by a dramatic radio program." The media magnate Paul Block promoted a special fund to raise money for a cash award to Williams, an initiative that the Milwaukee Road supported with its own donation. Some of the surviving *Olympian* passengers who Williams saved suggested that he be nominated as a "Carnegie Hero" for his courage and for saving so many lives, but this idea was quietly dropped in the aftermath of the crash.[25]

Relieved to exit the spotlight, Williams returned to his quiet, private life as a Pullman porter. According to the last records available, he was still working seventeen years later, at the age of forty-two. By that time, he and his family had moved out of Bronzeville and were living on West Maypole Avenue, in the Garfield Park area of Chicago. His home was within walking distance of the Milwaukee Road's service hub, the West Valley Yards.[26]

While the Milwaukee Road kept accurate records for white employees, its employment records for Black railroad workers were spotty at best. It is unclear how long after 1955 Williams continued his career as a porter. The hero of Custer Creek, Louis Clyde Williams, died in Chicago on July 26, 1978, at the age of sixty-five.

The Hand Family

With the Milwaukee Road needing every available employee to help at the crash site, George Hand worked the accident scene for a week after the *Olympian* accident. Like many workmen called in for duty that week, George never went home. He lived out of a makeshift campsite near Custer Creek and slept in a hastily built hut made of logs and canvas.

George Hand did, however, excuse himself from his crash site duties to attend his youngest daughter's wedding, which took place as planned on Wednesday, June 22. Married three days after the *Olympian* accident, Irene recalled that the stress of the crash had a big impact on the festivities. "We were just so happy that so many people survived and were alive," she recalled. Florence, still stitched up and black and blue from her near-death experience, was all smiles and deeply appreciative of the opportunity to be there for her sister.[27]

For years, Irene teased Florence about the loss of her wedding gift in the crash: "You never gave us a wedding present. It had all gone down the drain." They laughed at the joke. The newlyweds went off to Yellowstone National Park for their honeymoon. Despite being Montana residents, neither had yet been.[28]

Almost a year to the day after the *Olympian* accident, Florence gave birth to a daughter, Patricia. Three additional children would follow for the Maguires: a boy named Jimmy and twin girls Margaret and Kathleen. Florence gave up her nursing career to raise the children and run the household. Bernard continued to work for the Milwaukee Road, rising through the company ranks to ultimately lead the deployment of the railroad's refrigerated freight cars from Chicago to Tacoma. "He worked hard for the company," noted daughter Kathleen, "and his growing responsibilities often required rail trips to the West Coast checking on things." The Maguire family took advantage of the free travel passes offered by the Milwaukee Road, taking summer trips to see grandparents George and Rose in Miles City and going on vacations to the West Coast. Their son Jimmy worked for the railroad for a few years. Encouraged by their mother, Patricia and Margaret became nurses. Kathleen, whose middle name is Rose, after her grandmother, became a special education teacher in public schools in the Chicago area.[29]

In an interview after the accident, Florence recalled her harrowing escape from the doomed tourist sleeper Choteau. "Never, for as long as I live, will I forget that tapping on the window," she declared, remembering the passengers trapped alive in the car that soon sank in the turbulent waters of Custer Creek.[30]

"She didn't talk much at home about the Custer Creek accident," recalled Kathleen. "It was only when the family was together, usually around

Christmas time, when she would talk about how she escaped from the train car with the help of the porter." When asked about her mother's steely determination to survive on that dark night in June 1938, Kathleen listed two contributing attributes: her strong Catholic faith and her love for her husband, Bernard, whom she had married just four months before the accident.[31]

Florence's twin brothers Clarence and Bill had almost finished college at the outbreak of the Second World War. Interested in flying, both enlisted as pilots, Bill with the Navy Air Corps and Clarence with the Army Air Corps. Clarence deployed to Egypt, Bill to Alaska. One week after Bill's departure, the Hands received a telegram announcing that the plane he was piloting had been lost in a snowstorm. A search of the area was called off after six days, and the Hands were informed that their son Bill was declared "missing."

Two weeks later, the Hands received another telegram indicating that Clarence had been taken prisoner in Turkey when the plane he was in mistakenly landed on Turkish soil. After four months, Clarence was released in a prisoner exchange and was allowed to return home to Montana to recover before being restationed. The Hands hoped and prayed that perhaps Bill was taken prisoner as well and would return after the war. The conflict ended in 1945 with Bill still listed as missing and now presumed dead. It was tragic blow for the Hand family. "It was so hard living in that house knowing Bill was gone," remarked Rose.[32]

George Hand continued working for the Milwaukee Road until he hit the golden age of sixty-five and retired in 1954 with the rank of police captain. When he became captain in 1953, he was finally able to work days instead of nights, a relief to him and his family. After retirement, George put his considerable carpentry skills to work building desks for students at the local Sacred Heart Parish School and doing projects for the Sacred Heart Church, of which he and Rose were devoted members. Rose and George Hand found time every day to attend mass at the church on Montana Avenue in Miles City.

In their retirement years, the Hands traveled extensively, taking advantage of the free train passes offered by the Milwaukee Road to retired employees. An active hunter, George also kept the family freezer full of pheasants, deer, and antelope. After he noticed blood in his mouth following a coughing spasm, George was diagnosed with lung cancer in 1956 and spent two months in a Montana sanatorium recovering from surgery. Pneumonia eventually set in, requiring long rest periods in hospitals, during which his health declined. George Bernard Hand died on June 10, 1961. He is buried in the Calvary Cemetery in Miles City.[33]

Looking to stay busy after George's death, Rose agreed to cook for a religious conference at the Sacred Heart Church. The weekend stint cooking for the priests turned into a full-time job for the next eight years. Rose also took up oil painting and quilting in later years while remaining active with her church. Seeing her friends retire, she remarked, "I think I should retire too but as long as God gives me health, I will continue doing and enjoying my life." Rose Hand outlived her husband by more than twenty years, until her death in Miles City in August 1982 at the age of ninety-one.[34]

Later in life, when the children were out of the home and they had more time on their hands, Florence and Bernard Maguire traveled the world, visiting Ireland, England, and France multiple times. "Traveling really became a passion for them," Kathleen recalled. "My mother would encourage us to be active and 'get out and see the world.'" Florence's husband, Bernard, retired from the Milwaukee Road in 1976, ending a remarkable forty-seven-year career with the railroad. Sadly, he died from cancer a year later at age sixty-six. Florence—like her mother—lived for almost another quarter century after her husband's death. In 2001, she passed away in Milwaukee at age eighty-seven.[35]

Florence's younger sister, Irene, who had been living in Helena, Montana, died on July 13, 2021 at the age of 104.

The Haughians

The Haughian family will be forever tied to the June 1938 wreck of the *Olympian*. Soon after the accident, seeking to distance itself from the memory of the crash, the Milwaukee Road quietly erased the name "Saugus" from its train schedule and—in a nod to Susan Haughian, Montana's "favorite redhead" and matriarch of the area's most prominent family—replaced it with "Susan."

Officials from the Milwaukee Road also gave Dan Haughian Jr. the locomotive bell salvaged from the demolished engine in appreciation for the help that he had provided in the days and weeks following the accident. The bell, which the Haughian family still possesses, was used for years to inform all within earshot that another meal was ready at the ranch house.[36]

The company changed the name of the station, but the community kept it. The glory days of Saugus as a major horse and cattle shipping location had long since passed by 1938. The post office had been shuttered for thirteen years. The small public school closed soon thereafter. Even still, as the town struggled, the Haughians resolved to build upon their success in the area. An active social calendar finally paid off for Dan Haughian Jr. In 1944, while attending a dinner/dance in Terry, Dan took a spin with Mary Rose Kasten, a nineteen-year-old Miles City girl. It did not matter that he was two decades older than she; the laconic bachelor was smitten. Born in Ismay in June 1925, Mary Kasten was the daughter of a seamstress who owned her own dress shop. The Kastens later moved to Mildred, where Mary recalls using a crude cable car to cross O'Fallon Creek to get to school. In 1935, the Kastens moved to Miles City.

When they met at the Terry dance, Mary was securing her credentials as a schoolteacher. When they were dating, Dan admitted to Mary that the first thing that he thought of in the morning was his horse and then himself. They shared a good laugh over his priorities. Dan and Mary were married in 1945. Soon after the wedding, Dan was hard at work softening the rough edges of the former railroad bunkhouse on the banks of the Yellowstone River, adding rooms for Mary and a future family. In the Irish tradition, Dan and Mary Haughian had nine children.[37]

In addition to growing the family, the Haughians continued to expand their land holdings and livestock business in Prairie and Custer counties. In earlier days, as local homesteaders quit the land and moved elsewhere, the Haughians picked up the abandoned holdings for pennies on the dollar, gradually becoming one of the largest and most successful cattle ranching outfits in Montana. They continued to amass new land in the years after the Custer Creek disaster. As Susan's grandson, Dennis, noted of his grandmother, "Once she got her hands on an acre, she never let go." Susan Quinn Haughian outlived her husband Dan Sr. by over forty years, dying on August 16, 1972. She left forty-five grandchildren and twenty-four great-grandchildren to carry on the family legacy.[38]

The 1938 *Olympian* wreck became part of family lore. The Haughian children learned early on about the Custer Creek accident since it happened in their backyard. It was not until many years later that they learned the vital role their father, Dan Jr., played in saving lives that night. Dan's son Quinn Haughian received an article about the crash in the 1990s that revealed his father's rescue efforts. "We would have never known, if we hadn't read that," he remembered. "He never boasted about it. He didn't want any recognition. Nowadays, if you saved 30 or 40 people, you'd be a hero." The train wreck "was something that we grew up with," noted Donna Faber, daughter of Dan Jr. and Mary, who works today as an instructor at the community college in Miles City. "My dad never talked about much. He was not a chatter. He liked to talk about old times, especially with his brothers."[39]

Dan Haughian Jr. died on November 16, 1993, at the age of eighty-five. His bride, Mary, would carry the torch for the family until her death in March 2013. She was an inveterate history buff and wrote and coauthored several books on the history of Mildred, Ismay, and Prairie County.

When the Milwaukee Road dissolved, the Haughians bought the abandoned rail bed. They use it now as a ranch road for their cattle business. Even though the tracks on the west side of the river were abandoned in the 1970s, both the Calypso and Kinsey bridges still stand today, a testament to the excellence of the engineering and construction crews that built them over a century ago.

It is fitting that the land around Custer Creek is now owned by the Haughians. The family that was so connected to the wreck of the *Olympian* is now the caretaker of its memory. The tracks have long since disappeared, ripped up in the 1980s for scrap metal. The rebuilt Custer Creek bridge still stands, its wood ties and flooring looking weather-worn and tattered. Other than a small green metal sign with a few bullet holes that reads "Custer Creek," the spot offers no hint of the terror or the heroism that occurred there on that fateful night in 1938.

APPENDIX A

Milwaukee Road Names

1847 Incorporated as the Milwaukee & Waukesha Railroad.

1850 Rechartered as the Milwaukee & Mississippi Railroad.

1861 Renamed the Milwaukee & Prairie du Chien Railroad.

1867 After Alexander Mitchell engineers a merger with other railroad companies, the line becomes known as the Milwaukee & St. Paul Railroad.

1874 Name changed to Chicago, Milwaukee & St. Paul Railway (CMSP).

1909 Completion of the Puget Sound Extension to Tacoma, Washington. Part of the company rechartered as the Chicago, Milwaukee & Puget Sound Railroad.

1927 Emerging from bankruptcy, the company is reorganized as the Chicago, Milwaukee, St. Paul & Pacific Railroad and adopts the famous "Milwaukee Road" trademark.

1985 The Milwaukee Road goes out of business after being purchased by the Soo Line.

APPENDIX B

List of Persons Killed

Mary Elizabeth Arnold, age 82, Miles City, Montana

Gertrude J. Bailey, age 24, Billings, Montana

Juanita J. Bailey, age 6, Billings, Montana

Joyce E. Bailey, age 4, Billings, Montana

Sarah August Bard, age 63, Seattle, Washington

Valerie May Conway, age 12, Omaha, Nebraska

Fern L. Beer, age 20, Centerville, Iowa

Fannie S. Berry, age 50, Malute, Alabama

Nell G. Clancy, age 60, Bloomington, Illinois

Marjorie J. Clancy, age 18, Bloomington, Illinois

Katherine P. Clancy, age 72, Bloomington, Illinois

John N. Dana, age 53, Seattle, Washington

Sharlot O. Daniels, age 51, Deer Lodge, Montana

Dorothy M. Debeer, age 49, Sioux City, Iowa

Emma De Thier, age 67, Des Plaines, Illinois

Helen De Thier, age 34, Des Plaines, Illinois

Lillian K. Erickson, age 30, Mount Vernon, Washington

Josephine Frelick, age 56, Lemmon, South Dakota (formerly Miles City, Montana)

Fred E. Glenny, age 67, Everett, Washington

Donald J. Hanscom, age 19, New York, New York
Charles James, age 47, Miles City, Montana
Katherine H. Johnson, Miles City, Montana
Joyce C. M. Kaskie, age 14, Mitchell, South Dakota
Marth Ann Kittle, age 76, Three Forks, Montana
Thomas Lallas, age 42, Bellingham, Washington
Esther Lallas, age 32, Bellingham, Washington
Gladys C. Leer, age unknown, Billings, Montana
Lavonne Lou Leer, age 15 months, Billings, Montana
Hausmer McCoy, age 57, Miles City, Montana
William Tarves McIntosh, age 20, Montague, Montana
Frank C. Merrifield, age 58, Miles City, Montana
Alice Middleton, age 51, Tacoma, Washington
Robert Nolan, age unknown, Chicago, Illinois
Milton C. Norberg, age unknown, Aberdeen, South Dakota
Mrs. E. M. Odleton, age unknown, Tacoma, Washington
Sarah D. Olson, age 68, Seattle, Washington
Margaret Olson, age 67, Seattle, Washington
Milo Randolph Perkins Jr., age 17, Bethesda, Maryland
Marilyn Pfleghaar, age 8, Cologne, Minnesota
Dixon Post, age 28, Omaha, Nebraska
William H. Range, age 59, Atlanta, Georgia
Carrie Range, age 63, Atlanta, Georgia
Fred Raschke, age 54, St. Paul, Minnesota
Henry Schultz, age 77, Tacoma, Washington
Paul Frank Schultz, age 63, Ladd, Illinois
Lucille Clarice Stumley, age 24, Volga, South Dakota
Louise Woolsey, age 55, Miles City, Montana
Dorothy L. Yontz, age 34, Butte, Montana
Marie Zimmerman, age 19, Aberdeen, South Dakota

Notes

Epigraph

Chicago, Milwaukee & St. Paul Railway, "Olympian, Fit for the Gods," advertisement, 1912, Michael Sol Collection, https://www.milwaukeeroadarchives.com.

Chapter 1

1. Tracy Laqua, "100 Years of Family History," *Montana GLCI Newsletter* (Jul. 2012), https://www.nrcs.usda.gov/Internet/FSE_DOCUMENTS/nrcs144p2_050255.pdf.
2. Samuel Gordon, "Recollections of Old Milestown" (Miles City: n.p., 1918), https://milescity.com/history/books/room/part2; Mary Haughian et al., *Wheels Across Montana's Prairie* (Terry: Prairie County Historical Society, 1974), 5.
3. August Derleth, *The Milwaukee Road: Its First Hundred Years* (Iowa City: Univ. of Iowa Press, 2002), 179.
4. Bill Kiley, "Montana's Red-Headed Legend," *Range Magazine*, Spring 2006, 64–65.
5. "Saugus Train Wreck of '38 Etched in Man's Memory," *Miles City Star*, Jun. 19, 1998.
6. Jean Freese, "Wreck 50 Years Ago Went into Records," *Miles City Star*, Jun. 17, 1988.
7. "Saugus Train Wreck of '38 Etched in Man's Memory," *Miles City Star*, Jun. 19, 1998.
8. "Three Clancy Bodies on Way to Bloomington," *Pantagraph* (Bloomington, IL), Jun. 26, 1938.

Chapter 2

1. U.S. Department of Commerce, Bureau of the Census, 1860, 1870.
2. "The Last Link Has Been Closed," *Chicago Daily Tribune*, Jun. 15, 1938.
3. "The Crime Clock," *Chicago Daily Tribune*, Jun. 14, 1938.
4. "2 Roads Begin Fast Eastern Run Tomorrow," *Chicago Daily Tribune*, Jun. 14, 1938.
5. "Elgin Time from the Stars," *Chicago Daily Tribune*, Jun. 15, 1938; "The Last Link Has Been Closed," *Chicago Daily Tribune*, Jun. 15, 1938.
6. "Police Outdistanced," *Chicago Daily Tribune*, Jun. 16, 1938.
7. *Seattle Times*, Jun. 20, 1938.
8. New York Central System, "The *20th Century Limited*," Streamliner Schedules, Aug. 1938, http://www.streamlinerschedules.com/concourse/track5/century193809.html; Adam Burns, "20th Century Limited Train," American-Rails.com, https://www.american-rails.com/20th.html#gallery[pageGallery]/2/.
9. Glenvick-Gjonvik Archives, "Dollar Steamship Line History and Ephemera," https://www.gjenvick.com/OceanTravel/SteamshipLines/DollarSteamshipLine.html.
10. *Seattle Times*, Jun. 20, 1938.

11. Stanley Johnson, *The Milwaukee Road Olympian: A Ride to Remember* (Coeur d'Alene: Museum of North Idaho, 2001), 33.
12. *The Alton Railroad Company, Eastern Division, Timetable No. 5, Apr. 1933*, http://wx4.org/to/foam/maps/1_habegger/1933-04-30Alton_Eastern5-Jon%20Habegger.pdf.
13. *Cross-Roads of the Nation*, Chicago Union Station (1955), posted by Ryan Griffin-Stegink, May 23, 2012, https://www.metroplanning.org/multimedia/publication/570.
14. George Lallas, phone interview by author, Jun. 21, 2021.
15. U.S. Declaration of Intention, Tom Lallas, Jun. 11, 1913.
16. U.S. Declaration of Intention, Tom Lallas, Jun. 11, 1913.
17. "Art Howard, the Dean of Local Grocers," *Bellingham Business Journal*, Jan. 2005.
18. "Art Howard, the Dean of Local Grocers," *Bellingham Business Journal*, Jan. 2005.
19. Lallas interview, Jun. 21, 2021.
20. Lallas interview, Jun. 21, 2021.
21. "Art Howard, the Dean of Local Grocers," *Bellingham Business Journal*, Jan. 2005.

Chapter 3

1. Alex Bean, "The Incredible History and Cultural Legacy of the Bronzeville Neighborhood," *Chicago Detours*, Feb. 22, 2016, https://chicagodetours.com/bronzeville-neighborhood/; "The History of Bronzeville," *Chicago Studies*, https://chicagostudies.uchicago.edu/bronzeville/bronzeville-history-bronzeville.
2. 1880 and 1910 U.S. Federal Census records.
3. 1920 and 1930 U.S. Federal Census records.
4. "Porter Is Hero of Wreck," *Chicago Defender*, Jun. 25, 1938; Tilden School, yearbook (1936), https://www.classmates.com/siteui/yearbooks/77218?page=19.
5. Arthur C. McWatt, "'A Greater Victory': The Brotherhood of Sleeping Car Porters in St. Paul," *Minnesota History* 55, no. 5 (1997): 202–16.
6. Thomas C. Fleming, "Phil Randolph and the Pullman Porters," *San Francisco Sun-Reporter*, Jul. 22, 1998.
7. *Milwaukee Road Olympian Fares and Schedule, Jan.–Mar. 1940*, 41, http://streamlinermemories.info/Milw/Milw40TT.pdf.
8. *Milwaukee Road Olympian Fares and Schedule, Jan.–Mar. 1940*, 8.
9. "Instructions to Porters, Attendants and Bus Boys," The Pullman Company, Aug. 1, 1952, http://scsra.org/library/pullman-rulebook.html.

Chapter 4

1. Merrifield family, "Phyllis Marie Merrifield" (unpublished biography, 2016), provided by the Merrifield family; U.S. Department of Commerce, Bureau of the Census, 1880, 1890, 1900.
2. Frank Calvin Merrifield, Ancestry.com, https://www.ancestry.com/family-tree/person/tree/15897039/person/2044233959/facts.
3. Gordon, "Recollections of Old Milestown."
4. Steve McCarter, *Guide to the Milwaukee Road in Montana* (Helena: Montana Historical Society Press, 1992); Helen Carey Jones, *Custer County Area History: As We Recall* (Dallas, TX: Curtis Media Corp., 1990), 39.
5. Merrifield Family page, Ancestry.com.
6. Rose Hand, "History of My Life" (unpublished memoir, 1976), 3, provided by the Hand-Maguire family.
7. Hand, "History of My Life," 12–15.
8. Hand, "History of My Life," 23–29.
9. Irene Hand Roberts, interview by author, Sep. 19, 2019.

Chapter 5

1. "Olympian, Fit for the Gods."
2. "Olympian, Fit for the Gods."
3. "Olympian, Fit for the Gods."
4. George H. Drury, *Guide to North American Steam Locomotives* (Waukesha, WI: Kalmbach Books, 2015), 138–39; Bill Wilkerson, *Milwaukee F Class Locomotives* (Harlowton: Times Clarion, 1995), 2, 32.
5. Wilkerson, *Milwaukee F Class Locomotives*, 30.
6. "4-6-4 'Hudson' Locomotives in the USA," Steamlocomotive.com, https://www.steamlocomotive.com/locobase.php?country=USA&wheel=4-6-4.
7. "4-6-4 'Hudson' Locomotives in the USA."
8. "4-6-4 'Hudson' Locomotives in the USA."

Chapter 6

1. Derleth, *Milwaukee Road*, 227.
2. Johnson, *Milwaukee Road Olympian*, 48; "Instructions to Porters, Attendants and Bus Boys."
3. "Instructions to Porters, Attendants and Bus Boys."
4. "Instructions to Porters, Attendants and Bus Boys."
5. George Lallas, phone interview by author, Jun. 9, 2020.
6. Derleth, *Milwaukee Road*, 167; "The Buried Loot of the Newton Gang," *Lone Star Treasure*, http://www.lonestartreasure.com/buried-loot-newton-gang/.
7. Derleth, *Milwaukee Road*, 23; Jim Sands, *Brief History of the Milwaukee Road* (n.p., 1968), 4.
8. Derleth, *Milwaukee Road*, 34.
9. "Milwaukee Steam," *Milwaukee Road Magazine*, Oct. 1974, 8.
10. Derleth, *Milwaukee Road*, 61.
11. Derleth, *Milwaukee Road*, 91.
12. Walter Gilman Berg, *Buildings and Structures of American Railroads: A Reference Book for Railroad Managers, Superintendents, Master Mechanics, Engineers, Architects, and Students* (New York: John Wiley & Sons, 1893), 372.
13. Irene Hand Roberts, "Lifelong Learner, Irene Roberts—95-Year-Old Carroll Student Still Going Strong," *Helena Independent Record*, Dec. 2, 2012.
14. Roberts interview.
15. Roberts interview.

Chapter 7

1. Warren Jones, "The Wreck of the Milwaukee Road's Olympian," *Hoofprints*, Summer 2006, 3.
2. Joseph M. Sherlock, "Lionel Hiawatha O-Gauge Passenger Train," http://www.joesherlock.com/Hiawatha.html.
3. Sherlock, "Lionel Hiawatha O-Gauge Passenger Train."
4. "M.T.H. Electric Trains," Jun. 1, 2011, https://mthtrains.com/news/473.
5. Jim Scribbins, *The Hiawatha Story* (Minneapolis: Univ. of Minnesota Press, 1970), 40–51.
6. "Tells How Rio Got Its Name," *Portage (WI) Register Democrat*, Jan. 12, 1924.
7. *Chicago Tribune*, Oct. 29, 1886, 1; *Daily Alta California*, Oct. 29, 1886.
8. Ralph S. Podas, "A Point in Time on the Milwaukee Road: The Custer Creek Olympian Tragedy, Jun. 19, 1938," *Railroad History*, no. 166 (Spring 1992): 49.

Chapter 8

1. Laqua, "100 Years of Family History."
2. "Montana's Tallest Peaks by Mountain Range," Montana State Library, https://msl.mt.gov/geoinfo/geography/geography_facts/montanaxs_tallest_peaks_by_mountain_range.
3. Haughian et al., *Wheels Across Montana's Prairie*, 199–200.
4. Kiley, "Montana's Red-Headed Legend," 64.
5. Kiley, "Montana's Red-Headed Legend," 64. Years later, in April 1912, the SS *Parisian* would play a role in the search for survivors of the *Titanic*; it found none. See "Norway-Heritage, Hands Across the Sea," http://www.norwayheritage.com/p_ship.asp?sh=paris.
6. Haughian et al., *Wheels Across Montana's Prairie*, 201.
7. Haughian et al., *Wheels Across Montana's Prairie*, 201.
8. Haughian et al., *Wheels Across Montana's Prairie*, 203.
9. Haughian et al., *Wheels Across Montana's Prairie*, 203.
10. Haughian et al., *Wheels Across Montana's Prairie*, 201.
11. Great Northern Railway, *Montana, A Homeseeker's Guide* (By the Organization, 1900), 2.
12. Dan Fulton, "Failure on the Plains," *Agricultural History* 51, no. 1 (1977): 51–62; Amie Thompson, "Homestead Act Had a Huge Impact on Montana's History," *Great Falls Tribune*, Nov. 1, 2014; John Leakey, *The West That Was: From Texas to Montana* (Lincoln: Univ. of Nebraska Press, 1965), 183. See also K. Ross Toole, *Twentieth Century Montana: A State of Extremes* (Norman: Univ. of Oklahoma Press, 1983).
13. Haughian et al., *Wheels Across Montana's Prairie*, 203.
14. Michael Bugenstein, *Since the Days of the Buffalo: A History of Eastern Montana and the Kalfell Ranch* (Helena: Farcountry Press, 2013), 94.
15. Haughian et al., *Wheels Across Montana's Prairie*, 203.
16. Kiley, "Montana's Red-Headed Legend," 65.

Chapter 9

1. Wilkerson, *Milwaukee F Class Locomotives*, 20–21.
2. "179 Roads Fight I.C.C. Automatic Stoker Orders," *Chicago Daily Tribune*, Jun. 15, 1938.
3. Wilkerson, *Milwaukee F Class Locomotives*, 20.
4. U.S. Department of Commerce, Bureau of the Census, 1910, 1920.
5. Louis Goplen obituary, *Terry Tribune*, May 21, 1979.
6. Interstate Commerce Commission, *Investigation Inv.-2278*, Aug. 9, 1938, 5.
7. *Investigation Inv.-2278*.
8. Podas, "A Point in Time on the Milwaukee Road," 40; *Investigation Inv.-2278*, 3.
9. Ride the Hiawatha, "Section Gangs," https://www.ridethehiawatha.com/core/files/hiawatha/uploads/files/17_small_SECTIONGANGS.jpg, accessed Sep. 2019.
10. Walt Whitman, *Leaves of Grass* (Boston: James R. Osgood and Co., 1881–82), 359.
11. Drury, *Guide to North American Steam Locomotives*, 135.
12. Wilkerson, *Milwaukee F Class Locomotives*, 19.
13. Wilkerson, *Milwaukee F Class Locomotives*, 21; Bill Wilkerson, *Fifty Years of Olympians* (Harlowton: Times Clarion, 1996), 13.
14. The Milwaukee Road referred to their F6-type locomotives as Baltics, a name drawn from a European tank car with the same wheel arrangement. "4-6-4 'Hudson' Locomotives in the USA."
15. Drury, *Guide to North American Steam Locomotives*, 135.

Chapter 10

1. "Herder Killed by Lightning Near Choteau," *Great Falls Tribune*, Jun. 21, 1938.
2. Clark, Jul. 4, 1805, *The Journals of Lewis and Clark*, https://lewisandclarkjournals.unl.edu/item/lc.jrn.1805-07-04#lc.jrn.1805-07-04.02.
3. Kevin Conradt, "Weathering Montana: The Social Meanings of Extreme Environments in the Big Sky" (master's thesis, Montana State University, 2002), 20.
4. McWatt, "'A Greater Victory,'" 210. "Doubling back" referred to demands that porters take another trip before their layover was complete, or before they were rested.
5. McWatt, "'A Greater Victory,'" 210.
6. Johnson, *Milwaukee Road Olympian*, 80–81.
7. Bill Wilkerson, *Milwaukee S2 Class Locomotives* (Harlowton: *Times Clarion*, 1994), 20.
8. Mary R. Haughian, *Mildred Memories on the O'Fallon* (Terry: Prairie County Historical Society, 1979), 41.
9. Haughian, *Mildred Memories on the O'Fallon*, 41.
10. Haughian, *Mildred Memories on the O'Fallon*, 41.
11. Haughian, *Mildred Memories on the O'Fallon*, 36.
12. Derleth, *Milwaukee Road*, 187.
13. U.S. Department of Commerce, Bureau of the Census, 1950, "Number of Inhabitants, Montana," 26-10, https://www2.census.gov/library/publications/decennial/1950/population-volume-2/15276180v2p26ch1.pdf.
14. *O'Fallon Flashbacks* (Baker: O'Fallon Historical Society, 1975), 89–98.
15. U.S. Department of Commerce, Bureau of the Census, 1960, "Rail Transportation," *Historical Statistics of the United States*, 429, https://www2.census.gov/library/publications/1960/compendia/hist_stats_colonial-1957/hist_stats_colonial-1957-chQ.pdf; Merrifield Family page, Ancestry.com.
16. Bill Wilkerson, "Seniority and Enginemen: How It Worked on the Milwaukee Road's Musselshell District, 1907–1982," *Railroad History*, No. 187 (2002): 44–49.
17. Podas, "A Point in Time on the Milwaukee Road," 36.
18. Lorelei E. Merrifield, "Find a Grave," https://www.findagrave.com/memorial/140278462/lorelei-e-merrifield.
19. Merrifield biography, 1.
20. Merrifield biography, 1.
21. Merrifield biography, 9.
22. Merrifield biography, 9.
23. Merrifield biography, 10.

Chapter 11

1. Louis Gehrig, phone interview by author, Oct. 30, 2020.
2. W. B. Townsend, "The Ideal Freight Solicitor," *Railway Journal* 20 (1914): 6–7.
3. Gehrig interview.
4. Chicago, Milwaukee, St. Paul and Pacific Railroad Company, *Annual Report, 1937*, (Chicago: By the Organization, 1937), 66–67.
5. Chicago, Milwaukee, St. Paul and Pacific Railroad Company, *Annual Report, 1937*, 46–54.
6. Renewable Technologies, Inc., "Great Falls Coal Field: Historic Overview," Jun. 2009, 13–14, http://waughfamily.ca/Orr/GreatFallsCoalField_HistoricOverview.pdf, accessed Sep. 2019.
7. *Milwaukee Road Olympian Fares and Schedule, Jan.–Mar. 1940*.
8. Gehrig interview.
9. Podas, "A Point in Time on the Milwaukee Road," 34–56.

10. Podas, "A Point in Time on the Milwaukee Road," 38.
11. Johnson, *Milwaukee Road Olympian,* 17; Gehrig interview.
12. V. E. Rennix, "High Mileage Performance on the Milwaukee Road," Baldwin Locomotive Company, Apr.–Jul. 1934, https://www.milwaukeeroadarchives.com, accessed Sep. 2019; Wilkerson, *Milwaukee S2 Class Locomotives,* 16.
13. "Milwaukee Road Locomotives," *Railroad History,* No. 136 (1977): 28–124.
14. Wilkerson, *Milwaukee S2 Class Locomotives,* 25.

Chapter 12

1. A half century later, Mitchell's grandson, Captain Billy Mitchell, would also lead the way in a different mode of transportation, air travel.
2. Lance Nixon, "Cowtown on the Strip: Evarts, S.D. Helped Feed America's Appetite for Beef," *Pierre (SD) Capital Journal,* Sep. 13, 2013.
3. Don Baker, *Ghost Towns of the Montana Prairie* (Boulder: Fred Pruett Books, 1995), 55.
4. Baker, *Ghost Towns of the Montana Prairie,* 55, 56; Joseph A. Hartman and Allen J. Kihm, *The Marshall Lambert Symposium Contributions and Road Log* (Grand Forks, ND: Geology and Geological Engineering Faculty Publications, 1993), 70, http://archives.datapages.com/data/meta/ndgs/data/011/070/pdfs/070_firstpage.pdf.
5. Podas, "A Point in Time on the Milwaukee Road," 37.
6. Johnson, *Milwaukee Road Olympian,* 137.
7. Merrifield biography.

Chapter 13

1. Dartmouth College, "Life and Community," *History and Traditions,* https://admissions.dartmouth.edu/about/history-traditions.
2. Robert B. Graham, *The Dartmouth Story: A Narrative History of the College Buildings, People, and Legends* (Hanover, NH: Dartmouth Bookstore, 1990), 18. The 1978 movie *Animal House,* starring John Belushi, was based in part on experiences at Dartmouth fraternities.
3. Chicago, Milwaukee, St. Paul and Pacific Railroad Company, *June 1938 Olympian Schedule* (Chicago: By the Organization), 14.
4. Wilkerson, *Fifty Years of Olympians,* 6–13.
5. Johnson, *Milwaukee Road Olympian,* 101.
6. James D. Porterfield, *Dining by Rail: The History and Recipes of America's Golden Age of Railroad Cuisine* (London: St. Martin's Press, 1998), 119.
7. Jim Scribbins, *Milwaukee Road Remembered* (Minneapolis: Univ. of Minnesota Press, 1990), 98.
8. Porterfield, *Dining by Rail,* 116.
9. "Enlisted in the Navy," *West Valley (MN) Journal,* May 30, 1918.
10. "Dad, Where Do the Tracks Go," Milwaukee Road advertisement, 1944.
11. J. J. Oyen, *Watson Community Pioneers* (Watson, MN: Watson Voice, 1932), ch. 13, http://www.cityofwatson.com/chapter-13.

Chapter 14

1. "400 Sheep Are Drowned During Cloudburst at Ranch Near Hedgesville," *Great Falls Tribune,* Jun. 24, 1938.
2. Mark Hufstetler, "South Dakota's Railroads: An Historic Context," South Dakota

State Historic Preservation Office, Jul. 1998, https://history.sd.gov/preservation/docs/SDRailroad.pdf.

3. "History of Aberdeen," Aberdeen.com, https://www.aberdeensd.com/117/History-of-Aberdeen, accessed Sep. 2019.
4. Johnson, *Milwaukee Road Olympian*, 117.
5. "Former Montana Legislator, Dave Hagerty, Dies," *Santa Cruz Sentinel*, Jan. 5, 1961.
6. "District, County Relief Chiefs Held Meeting Wednesday," *Kalispell Daily Inter Lake*, Jan. 13, 1936.
7. William L. Gwyer, "Train Orders," Trains.com, May 1, 2006, https//www.trains.com/trn/train-basics/abcs-of-railroading/train-orders, accessed Sep. 2019.
8. Gwyer, "Train Orders."
9. Gwyer, "Train Orders."
10. Gwyer, "Train Orders."
11. Derleth, *Milwaukee Road*, 177.
12. Dale Martin, *Ties, Rails, and Telegraph Wires: Railroads and Communities in Montana and the West* (Helena: Montana Historical Society Press, 2018), 42.
13. "Rain Sends River Level Higher Again," *Great Falls Tribune*, Jun. 22, 1938.

Chapter 15

1. Robert Louis Stevenson, *Across the Plains* (New York: Charles Scribner's Sons, 1892), 42.
2. John Wesley Powell, "The Irrigable Lands of the Arid Region," *Century Magazine*, Mar. 1890, 775–76. See also Harvey Leifert, "Dividing Line: The Past, Present and Future of the 100th Meridian," *Earth Magazine*, Jan. 9, 2018, https://www.earthmagazine.org/article/dividing-line-past-present-and-future-100th-meridian.
3. Fred Carcy, "Early Railroads," *Blair History*, Blair Historic Preservation Alliance, https://blairhistory.com/archive/early-railroads/.
4. Derleth, *Milwaukee Road*, 136.
5. Derleth, *Milwaukee Road*, 158.
6. John A. Weeks III, "Mobridge," 2008, https://www.johnweeks.com/river_missouri/pages/sd_mo_12.html.
7. Baker, *Ghost Towns of the Montana Prairie*, 6.
8. Johnson, *Milwaukee Road Olympian*, 1.
9. Derleth, *Milwaukee Road*, 195.
10. Sands, *Brief History of the Milwaukee Road*, 12.
11. Wilkerson, *Milwaukee F Class Locomotives*, 24. Other Milwaukee Road misfortunes included the Newton Gang's spectacular rail robbery of $3 million in 1924, the largest robbery in the history of U.S. rail travel. A year later, the company had to spend a lot of money it didn't have to repair damage caused by a major earthquake in Barren, Montana. See Derleth, *Milwaukee Road*, 217, 222.
12. Derleth, *Milwaukee Road*, 232; Sands, *Brief History of the Milwaukee Road*, 13.

Chapter 16

1. Johnson, *Milwaukee Road Olympian*, 121.
2. Johnson, *Milwaukee Road Olympian*, 121; Lallas interview, Jun. 9, 2020.
3. Lallas interview, Jun. 9, 2020.
4. Stephen Fried, *Appetite for America: Fred Harvey and the Business of Civilizing the Wild West—One Meal at a Time* (New York: Bantam Books, 2010), 97.
5. Hand, "History of My Life," 11.

6. Hand, "History of My Life," 15–16.
7. Hand, "History of My Life," 12–14.
8. Hand, "History of My Life," 20; Roberts interview.
9. "Irene Hand Roberts: Lifelong Learner," *Helena Independent Record*, Dec. 2, 2012.
10. "A World for Perfect People," *Montana Public Radio*, Mar. 19, 2014, https://www.mtpr.org/post/world-perfect-people.
11. Hand, "History of My Life," 25.
12. Marga Lincoln, "Irene Roberts Shares Extraordinary Stories about Ordinary People," *Billings Gazette*, Nov. 24, 2016; Hand, "History of My Life," 23.
13. Roberts interview.
14. Roberts interview.
15. Roberts interview.
16. Roberts interview.
17. Lallas interview, Jun. 9, 2020.

Chapter 17

1. "Local Weather Report," *Billings Gazette*, Jun. 18, 1938, 2; U.S. Department of Commerce, Bureau of the Census, 1950; McCarter, *Guide to the Milwaukee Road in Montana.*
2. Haughian et al., *Wheels Across Montana's Prairie*, 199–201.
3. Meriwether Lewis, *The Journals of Lewis and Clark*, ed. Bernard DeVoto (Boston: Houghton Mifflin, 1953), 148.
4. *Terry Tribune*, Jun. 23, 1938, 1.
5. *Investigation Inv.-2278*, 3.
6. *Investigation Inv.-2278*, 12.
7. *Investigation Inv.-2278*, 12.
8. *Investigation Inv.-2278*, 12.
9. Helen Warner Grue, "June 18, 1938, Custer Creek Trainwreck," typewritten letter, Prairie County Museum, Terry.
10. Grue, "June 18, 1938, Custer Creek Trainwreck."
11. *Terry Tribune*, Jun. 23, 1938; *Investigation Inv.-2278*, 16–17.
12. Robert A. Howlett, National Oceanic and Atmospheric Administration, phone interview by author, Apr. 1, 2022.
13. Howlett interview.
14. "37 Bodies Recovered," *Minneapolis Star*, Jun. 20, 1938.
15. Milwaukee Road, Timetable and Train Schedule, Jun. 1938.

Chapter 18

1. *Investigation Inv.-2278*, 10.
2. *Milwaukee Road Employee Journal*, Dec. 1954, 28.
3. Christian Wolmar, *The Great Railroad Revolution: The History of Trains in America* (New York: PublicAffairs, 2012), 78.
4. Podas, "A Point in Time on the Milwaukee Road," 39.
5. Podas, "A Point in Time on the Milwaukee Road," 39; "Train Crash Takes Nearly 40 Lives," *Kalispell Daily Inter Lake*, Jun. 20, 1938.
6. *Investigation Inv.-2278*, 12.
7. *Investigation Inv.-2278*, 12.
8. *Investigation Inv.-2278*, 13.
9. Catherine Hahn Gregory, "Letter from a Survivor," *Montana Best Times*, Jul. 2004, 13.

10. Gregory, "Letter from a Survivor," 13.
11. Johnson, *Milwaukee Road Olympian*, 136.
12. *Investigation Inv.-2278*, 11.
13. Wilkerson, *Fifty Years of Olympians*, 40.

Chapter 19

1. *Investigation Inv.-2278*, 12.
2. *Investigation Inv.-2278*, 10.
3. Podas, "A Point in Time on the Milwaukee Road," 39.
4. *Investigation Inv.-2278*, 11.
5. *Investigation Inv.-2278*, 10.
6. "Porter Risked Life to Save Others," *Minneapolis Star*, Jun. 20, 1938.
7. Bugenstein, *Since the Days of the Buffalo*, 8.
8. *Terry Tribune*, Jul. 22, 1937.
9. Denise Harte, "A Tiny Montana Community Was the Scene of One of the Worst Train Disasters in American History," *Montana Best Times*, Jul. 2004, 12.
10. Hand, "History of My Life," 33.

Chapter 20

1. *Miles City Star*, Jun. 21, 1938.
2. "Chicago Train Plunges into Montana Creek," *Chicago Tribune*, Jun. 20, 1938.
3. "Train Crash Takes Nearly 40 Lives," *Kalispell Daily Inter Lake*, Jun. 20, 1938.
4. *Lincoln (NE) Star*, Jun. 20, 1938.
5. Podas, "A Point in Time on the Milwaukee Road," 49.
6. *Lincoln Star*, Jun. 20, 1938.
7. *Lincoln Star*, Jun. 20, 1938.
8. Lallas interview, Jun. 9, 2020.
9. "Dawson Men Aided 18 or 20 Other Victims," *Minneapolis Star*, Jun. 20, 1938.
10. Lallas interview, Jun. 9, 2020.
11. *Miles City Star*, Jun. 20, 1938.
12. *Miles City Star*, Jun. 21, 1938.
13. Gregory, "Letter from a Survivor," 14.
14. Podas, "A Point in Time on the Milwaukee Road," 45–46.
15. Gehrig interview.
16. "34 Dead or Missing in Train Disaster," *Great Falls Tribune*, Jun. 20, 1938.
17. Hand, "History of My Life," 33.
18. *Great Falls Tribune*, Jun. 21, 1938.
19. Hand, "History of My Life," 33; *Great Falls Tribune*, Jun. 21, 1938.
20. *Great Falls Tribune*, Jun. 21, 1938.
21. *Great Falls Tribune*, Jun. 21, 1938.
22. "Instructions to Porters, Attendants and Bus Boys."
23. "Estimate Twenty in Sleeping Car," *Edwardsville (IL) Intelligencer*, Jun. 21, 1938.
24. "Estimate Twenty in Sleeping Car," *Edwardsville Intelligencer*, Jun. 21, 1938.
25. "Terrific Jerk Awoke Those in Pullmans," *Great Falls Tribune*, Jun. 20, 1938; "60 Feared Dead in Rail Disaster," *Daily Herald* (Provo, UT), Jun. 20, 1938.
26. "Porter Hero Wins Cheers of Survivors," *Great Falls Tribune*, Jun. 20, 1938.
27. "Porter Hero Wins Cheers of Survivors," *Great Falls Tribune*, Jun. 20, 1938.
28. "Additional Bodies of Rail Wreck Victims Are Found," *Billings Gazette*, Jun. 21, 1938.
29. "Missoula Man on Ill-Fated Limited Train," *Great Falls Tribune*, Jun. 20, 1938.
30. Jones, "Wreck of the Milwaukee Road's Olympian," 8.

31. Jones, "Wreck of the Milwaukee Road's Olympian," 8.
32. *Great Falls Tribune*, Jun. 21, 1938.

Chapter 21

1. *Lincoln Star*, Jun. 20, 1938.
2. *Minneapolis Star*, Jun. 20, 1938.
3. *Lincoln Star*, Jun. 20, 1938.
4. Podas, "A Point in Time on the Milwaukee Road," 45.
5. *Minneapolis Star*, Jun. 21, 1938.
6. Podas, "A Point in Time on the Milwaukee Road," 46; Gehrig interview.
7. Lallas interview, Jun. 9, 2020.
8. "City Man's Story of Rail Wreck," *Minneapolis Star*, Jun. 21, 1938.
9. "Searchers Find More Bodies of Mishap Victims," *Billings Gazette*, Jun. 22, 1938.
10. "Searchers Find More Bodies of Mishap Victims," *Billings Gazette*, Jun. 22, 1938.
11. "Searchers Find More Bodies of Mishap Victims," *Billings Gazette*, Jun. 22, 1938.
12. "Terrific Jerk Awoke Those in Pullmans," *Great Falls Tribune*, Jun. 20, 1938.
13. Jones, "Wreck of the Milwaukee Road's Olympian," 8.
14. *Great Falls Tribune*, Jun. 20, 1938; Jones, "Wreck of the Milwaukee Road's Olympian," 17; *Miles City Star*, Jun. 20, 1938.
15. *Seattle Daily Times*, Jun. 21, 1938.

Chapter 22

1. *Miles City Star*, Jun. 21, 1938.
2. "Graphic Wreck Account Given," *Billings Gazette*, Jun. 20, 1938.
3. Hand, "History of My Life," 33.
4. Hand, "History of My Life," 33.
5. *Miles City Star*, Jun. 21, 1938.
6. "Missoula Man on Ill-Fated Limited Train," *Great Falls Tribune*, Jun. 20, 1938.
7. "City Man's Story of Rail Wreck," *Minneapolis Star*, Jun. 21, 1938.
8. "City Man's Story of Rail Wreck," *Minneapolis Star*, Jun. 21, 1938.
9. "27 Bodies Found After Train Plunges into Swollen Stream," *Pantagraph*, Jun. 20, 1938.
10. *Seattle Times*, Jun. 20, 1938; "Total Dead 49 Is Belief of Officials," *Great Falls Tribune*, Jun. 23, 1938.
11. George F. Flynn, "Disaster at Custer Creek," *Milwaukee Railroader*, No. 1 (2002): 34–39.
12. Judy Emerson, "Survivor: Accident Part of Life's Journey," *Rockford (IL) Register Star*, Oct. 12, 2003.
13. "Train Wreck Casualty Toll," *Billings Gazette*, Jun. 20, 1938.

Chapter 23

1. Haughian et al., *Wheels Across Montana's Prairie*, 213–14.
2. *Terry Tribune*, Jun. 23, 1938.
3. Jones, "Wreck of the Milwaukee Road's Olympian," 17.
4. Jones, "Wreck of the Milwaukee Road's Olympian," 17; "Train Wreck Casualty Toll," *Billings Gazette*, Jun. 20, 1938.
5. Roberts interview.
6. "Survivor Stories," *Miles City Star*, Jun. 20, 1938.
7. "A Survivor Photographs the Worst American Train Wreck Since 1887," *Life Magazine*, Jul. 4, 1938, 9–11.

8. Katie Boyce, interview by author, Bozeman, Sep. 2019.
9. Gregory, "Letter from a Survivor," 14.
10. Gregory, "Letter from a Survivor," 14; Gehrig interview.
11. Jones, "Wreck of the Milwaukee Road's Olympian," 18.
12. Jones, "Wreck of the Milwaukee Road's Olympian," 18
13. *Miles City Star*, Jun. 20, 1938.

Chapter 24

1. "34 Dead or Missing in Train Disaster," *Great Falls Tribune*, Jun. 20, 1938.
2. *Great Falls Tribune*, Jun. 21, 1938.
3. "Frank J. Newell, Publicity Director, Retires," *Milwaukee Road Magazine*, Sep.–Oct. 1958, 13.
4. Frank J. Newell correspondence, Jul. 9, 1938, "Custer Creek, Montana Disaster," Milwaukee Road Archives, http://www.milwaukeeroadarchives.com/CusterCreek/Custer%20Creek.htm.
5. Newell correspondence.
6. Newell correspondence.
7. Newell correspondence.
8. Derleth, *Milwaukee Road*, 248.
9. "Coroner Opens Inquest into State Rail," *Billings Gazette*, Jun. 22, 1938.
10. "Coroner Opens Inquest into State Rail," *Billings Gazette*, Jun. 22, 1938.
11. Jean Freese, "Wreck 50 Years Ago Went into Record," *Miles City Star*, Jun. 17, 1988.
12. *Miles City Star*, Jun. 20, 1938.
13. "Many Killed, Injured and Missing Sunday in Eastern Montana Railroad Disaster," *Billings Gazette*, Jun. 20, 1938.
14. Hand, "History of My Life," 34.
15. Roberts interview.
16. Roberts interview; Hand, "History of My Life," 34.
17. Florence Maguire letter to Bernard Maguire, Jun. 20, 1938, Maguire Family Collection, privately held.
18. Bernard Maguire letter to Florence Maguire, Jun. 21, 1938, Maguire Family Collection.
19. Western Union telegrams, Hand-Maguire Family, Jun. 19, 1938, Maguire Family Collection; Roberts interview.
20. *Great Falls Tribune*, Jun. 21, 1938.
21. H. R. Kester, "Scene of Disaster Described by First to See It from Air," *Great Falls Tribune*, Jun. 20, 1938, 1.
22. "Miles City Pastor Describes First Rescue Train's Arrival," *Great Falls Tribune*, Jun. 21, 1938.
23. "Many Killed, Injured and Missing Sunday in Eastern Montana Railroad Disaster," *Billings Gazette*, Jun. 20, 1938.
24. *Boston Globe*, Jun. 21, 1938.
25. *Boston Globe*, Jun. 21, 1938; Lucille Stumley, Certificate of Death, State of Montana, Jun. 19, 1938.

Chapter 25

1. "Miles City Pastor Describes First Rescue Train's Arrival," *Great Falls Tribune*, Jun. 21, 1938.
2. "Helena Resident Describes Scene of Desolation at Rail Tragedy in Eastern Montana," *Billings Gazette*, Jun. 22, 1938.

3. "Helena Resident Describes Scene of Desolation at Rail Tragedy in Eastern Montana," *Billings Gazette*, Jun. 22, 1938; "Tidbits," *Miles City Star*, Jun. 21, 1938.
4. "Helena Resident Describes Scene of Desolation at Rail Tragedy in Eastern Montana," *Billings Gazette*, Jun. 22, 1938.
5. "Helena Resident Describes Scene of Desolation at Rail Tragedy in Eastern Montana," *Billings Gazette*, Jun. 22, 1938.
6. Podas, "A Point in Time on the Milwaukee Road," 53.
7. *Miles City Star*, Jun. 21, 1938.
8. *Miles City Star*, Jun. 20, 1938.
9. "Many Killed, Injured and Missing Sunday in Eastern Montana Railroad Disaster," *Billings Gazette*, Jun. 20, 1938.
10. *Miles City Star*, Jun. 24, 1938; *Great Falls Tribune*, Jun. 21, 1938.
11. Clancy Family, email conversation via Ancestry.com, Jan. 29, 2019.
12. *Miles City Star*, Jun. 20, 1938.
13. *Miles City Star*, Jun. 20, 1938.
14. Jean Freese, "Wreck 50 Years Ago Went into Records," *Miles City Star*, Jun. 17, 1988.
15. *Miles City Star*, Jun. 22, 1938.
16. *Seattle Times*, Jun. 20, 1938.
17. Flynn, "Disaster at Custer Creek," 35–36; *Miles City Star*, Jun. 22, 1938; "Total Dead 49 Is Belief of Officials," *Great Falls Tribune*, Jun. 23, 1938; *Seattle Times*, Jun. 28, 1938.
18. *Miles City Star*, Jun. 20, 1938; Flynn, "Disaster at Custer Creek," 35–36.
19. "Crews Dig for Bodies Entombed in Car as 40 Die in Train Plunge," *Evening Star* (Washington, D.C.), Jun. 20, 1938.
20. "Total Dead 49 Is Belief of Officials," *Great Falls Tribune*, Jun. 23, 1938.
21. *Evening Star*, May 21 and Jun. 21, 1943. Both Perkins boys had attended the elite Landon School for Boys in Bethesda, Maryland. Active in the life of her boys and a fervent believer in Landon's mission, Theron Perkins found part-time work at the school. Looking to heal after George's death, Milo and Theron started a victory garden at Landon. Working his connections in the U.S. Department of Agriculture, Perkins secured hundreds of hybrid azaleas for the Landon garden. Today the Perkins Garden, as it is known, features one of the largest collections of azaleas in the country. Every spring, the Landon Azalea Festival celebrates the flower and the founding work of the Perkins family. "Perkins Garden Celebrates 70th Anniversary," Landon.net, 2014, https://www.landon.net/cf_news/view.cfm?newsid=1364.
22. Lallas interview, Jun. 9, 2020; *Miles City Star*, Jun. 20, 1938.
23. "Additional Bodies of Rail Wreck Victims Are Found," *Billings Gazette*, Jun. 21, 1938.
24. *Miles City Star*, Jun. 24, 1938.
25. *Miles City Star*, Jun. 24, 1938.
26. "Clancy Funerals to be Conducted Monday Morning," *Pantagraph*, Jun. 24, 1938.
27. Podas, "A Point in Time on the Milwaukee Road," 53; "Three Clancy Bodies on Way to Bloomington," *Pantagraph*, Jun. 26, 1938.
28. *Miles City Star*, Jun. 24, 1938; Merrifield Family Memorial Funeral Book, Jun. 1938, provided by Candi Knittel.
29. Merrifield biography; *Miles City Star*, Jun. 20, 1938.
30. *Miles City Star*, Jun. 24, 1938.
31. *Seattle Times*, Jun. 22, 1938.
32. "Total Dead 49 Is Belief of Officials," *Miles City Star*, Jun. 26, 1938.
33. "Tidbits," *Miles City Star*, Jun. 21, 1938; Emerson, "Survivor: Accident Part of Life's Journey," *Rockford Register Star*, Oct. 12, 2003.
34. Gregory, "Letter from a Survivor," 14; *Miles City Star*, Jun. 20, 1938.
35. *Miles City Star*, Jun. 20, 1938.

36. Flynn, "Disaster at Custer Creek," 34.
37. "Editorial," *Billings Gazette*, Jun. 22, 1938.
38. Flynn, "Disaster at Custer Creek," 34.

Chapter 26

1. Editorial, *Billings Gazette*, Jun. 22, 1938.
2. *Miles City Star*, Jun. 20, 1938.
3. *Kalispell Daily Inter Lake*, Jun. 22, 1938.
4. *Terry Tribune*, Jun. 23, 1938.
5. *Investigation Inv.-2278*, 12.
6. "Coroner Holds Rail Crash Inquest," *Billings Gazette*, Jun. 22, 1938.
7. "The Custer Creek Disaster," *Chicago Tribune*, Jun. 21, 1938; "Railroad Expected to Face $750,000 in Suits," *Minneapolis Star*, Jun. 20, 1938.
8. *Chicago Tribune*, Jun. 22, 1938.
9. H. A. Scandrett to all Milwaukee Road employees and officers, Jun. 20, 1938, "Custer Creek, Montana Disaster," Milwaukee Road Archives, http://www.milwaukeeroadarchives.com/CusterCreek/Custer%20Creek.htm.
10. *Miles City Star*, Jun. 26, 1938; Newell correspondence.
11. Milwaukee Road correspondence, "Custer Creek, Montana Disaster," Milwaukee Road Archives.
12. Milwaukee Road correspondence, "Custer Creek, Montana Disaster," Milwaukee Road Archives.
13. *Investigation Inv.-2278*, 12.
14. "The Passing Parade," *Miles City Star*, Jul. [n.d.] 1938.
15. "Railroad Expected to Face $750,000 in Suits," *Minneapolis Star*, Jun. 20, 1938.
16. *Investigation Inv.-2278*, 19.
17. Lallas interview, Jun. 9, 2020.
18. Podas, "A Point in Time on the Milwaukee Road," 54.
19. Podas, "A Point in Time on the Milwaukee Road," 54.
20. Podas, "A Point in Time on the Milwaukee Road," 54; Flynn, "Disaster at Custer Creek," 35.
21. Jones, *Custer County Area History*, 39.
22. H. Roger Grant, foreword to Derleth, *Milwaukee Road*, xxi, xxv; Jones, *Custer County Area History*, 39.
23. Grant, foreword to Derleth, *Milwaukee Road*, xxv.
24. Podas, "A Point in Time on the Milwaukee Road," 52–53.
25. "Top Trans-MO Conductor Retires," *Milwaukee Road Employee Journal*, Dec. 1954, 28; "Captains of the Yellow Cars," *Milwaukee Road Employee Journal*, Jan. 1916, 18.
26. "Operating Division," *Milwaukee Road Employee Journal*, Aug. 1952, 13, 25; "Frank J. Newell, Publicity Director, Retires," *Milwaukee Road Magazine*, Sep.–Oct. 1958, 13.

Epilogue

1. Merrifield biography, 3.
2. Merrifield biography, 7.
3. Merrifield biography, 10.
4. Merrifield biography, 14.
5. "Church Crowded at Rites of 3 Wreck Victims," *Pantagraph*, Jun. 28, 1938.
6. "Church Crowded at Rites of 3 Wreck Victims," *Pantagraph*, Jun. 28, 1938.
7. Clancy family member, author communication via Ancestry.com, Jan. 29, 2019.

8. Podas, "A Point in Time on the Milwaukee Road," 54.
9. Emerson, "Survivor: Accident Part of Life's Journey," *Rockford Register Star*, Oct. 12, 2003.
10. Jones, "Wreck of the Milwaukee Road's Olympian," 19.
11. Dean Veith Hanscom obituary, *Dartmouth Alumni Magazine*, Mar. 1964, 88.
12. Hanscom obituary.
13. Haughian et al., *Wheels Across Montana's Prairie*, 174.
14. Louis Goplen obituary, *Terry Tribune*, May 21, 1979.
15. Lallas interview, Jun. 9, 2020.
16. Lallas interview, Jun. 9, 2020.
17. Lallas interview, Jun. 9, 2020.
18. Tommy Rakus, email communications with author, Aug. 2020.
19. Lallas interview, Jun. 9, 2020.
20. Kathleen Maguire, phone interview with author, Oct. 22, 2020; "Woman Escaped from Submerged Coach by Climbing Out Window," *Billings Gazette*, Jun. 22, 1938.
21. "Rail Wreck Kills Over 30," *Billings Gazette*, Jun. 20, 1938.
22. *Cullman (AL) Banner*, Jun. 24, 1938; "Pullman Porter Who Saved 22 Lives When Train Was Wrecked," *Pittsburgh Courier*, Jul. 9, 1938.
23. "The Custer Creek Tragedy," *Billings Gazette*, Jun. 22, 1938.
24. "The Modest Porter," *Pantagraph*, Jun. 24, 1938.
25. Milwaukee Road letter to Mr. J. L. Simpson, Jun. 29, 1938, "Custer Creek, Montana Disaster," Milwaukee Road Archives, http://www.milwaukeeroadarchives.com/CusterCreek/Custer%20Creek.htm; Podas, "A Point in Time on the Milwaukee Road," 51.
26. U.S. Railroad Retirement Board, Employee Registration Card, May 9, 1955.
27. Roberts interview.
28. Roberts interview.
29. Maguire interview.
30. "Bodies of 29 Wreck Victims Are Recovered," *Great Falls Tribune*, Jun. 21, 1938.
31. Maguire interview.
32. Hand, "History of My Life," 35.
33. Hand, "History of My Life," 40; *Billings Gazette*, Jun. 13, 1961.
34. Hand, "History of My Life," 43.
35. Maguire interview.
36. Jones, "Wreck of the Milwaukee Road's Olympian," 18.
37. Haughian et al., *Wheels Across Montana's Prairie*, 200–201.
38. Kiley, "Montana's Red-Headed Legend," 64–65; Haughian et al., *Wheels Across Montana's Prairie*, 203.
39. Laqua, Tracy, "Haughian Family Shares History of Family Ranch," 2010, https://milescity.com/forums/posts/view/143083/1; Donna (Haughian) Faber, interview by author, Sep. 27, 2019.

Index

Numbers preceded by "P" refer to photo section.

Ian Campbell Wilson is a writer and historian who lives in Bozeman, Montana. He is the author of "Goddesses of the Sun: Tucson's Hacienda del Sol School for Girls," an article about the origins of an elite 1920s girls' school in Tucson, Arizona, published in 2017 in the *Journal of Arizona History*. Canadian by birth, Campbell Wilson holds undergraduate and graduate degrees from the University of New Hampshire. His website is iancampbellwilson.com.